" He

hoists a signal

for a distant nation.

He

whistles

them up from the ends of the earth;

and look, they come,

swiftly, promptly **"**

(Isaiah 5:26)

GOD'S WHISTLE

"I will whistle for them to gather them together, for I have redeemed them; and they will be as numerous as they were before." *(Zechariah 10:8)*

GOD'S WHISTLE

A CALL TO INNER HEALING AND

WHOLENESS IN CHRIST JESUS

A RECIPE FOR LIVING!

First published in Great Britain February 1999
Revised edition October 1999
Reprinted June 2005

Nihil Obstat: Michael Jackson, s.t.l., Censor Deputatus
Imprimatur: John Hull, Vicar General, Diocese of Arundel & Brighton
Cum Permissu Superiorum D.H.S.

A catalaogue record of this book is available from the British Museum

ISBN 0 9529159 6 0   Cased Edition

Typeset in Souvenir 11pt © Gerald Vann
Artwork © Gunvor Edwards
Cover © Gunvor & Peter Edwards and son, Per Edwards

This book is dedicated to

Jesus

our Saviour

who gave His life

that we might live

and through Him

come to Eternal Life.

The words found at the beginning of each chapter were given to me as an entirety by the Lord for this book as I travelled by train to Cornwall.

My prayer for you

I pray that as you use this book you may find through it a God who is a God of Love and Healing.

I pray that the Holy Spirit may empower you making you whole in body, mind and spirit.

I pray that the more you are aware of the Father's love for you, the more Jesus will become your friend for ever.

My prayer with you

O Holy Spirit, light of my life,
Flood my mind with your kindest thoughts.
Fill my heart with a burning, compassionate and tender love.
Enlighten the eyes of my soul
 that I may see as You see,
 that I may do what You want me to do,
 that I may go where You want me to go,
 that I may bless everyone who comes in my path,
As I humbly try to serve You, to Your glory, with honour and joy, in adoration of the Trinity. Amen.

Josephine Walsh D.H.S.

Olney, 25th March 2005

CONTENTS

FOREWORD

This delightful book will meet the needs of all who are on the journey of faith and who at many turns come across difficulties and obstacles.

One of the greatest obstacles we meet today is a general apathy about religious things, about the existence of God, and his presence in our world and indeed in our lives. To make the faith real and to help us sense that presence, Sr. Josephine has written this book and I warmly recommend it to you.

The gentle reminiscences drawn from childhood reveal to us the natural root of that peace which her work exudes. However, there is another and deeper root, which she has found within her own congregation, and its charism, devotion to the Holy Spirit.

This book is timely as we commemorate the year dedicated to the Holy Spirit and are looking for ways to deepen our appreciation of the influence of the Spirit in our lives.

Holy Scripture is a gift to us of the Holy Spirit, for the sacred authors wrote under the inspiration of the Holy Spirit. This book is replete with references to the Holy Scripture- indeed it is fully braced with a marvellous concatenation of Scriptural passages.

It is clear that Sister draws her own spirituality from Sacred Scripture, most particularly the words of Christ himself. Perhaps the following passage will not only demonstrate that, but also present the very purpose which has prompted her to write: 'If we want to know God, to become his close friends, we must learn to contemplate with the eyes of a child, with the simplicity and humility of heart'.

I hope that all who approach this book in this spirit will become closer friends of the God who has first loved us.

+mario

Bishop Mario Conti, Bishop of Aberdeen.
(Now Archbishop of Glasgow)
Feast of the Immaculate Conception, 8th December 1998.

INTRODUCTION

The idea of God's whistling intrigues me.

Our God is a God who can do everything. So why can't He whistle? We find three references in Scripture to God whistling. *(Isaiah 5:26, Isaiah 7:18, Zechariah 10:8)* Sometimes I have the picture of His calling out to us rather like the shepherd whistling and calling out to his sheepdog. He is the Good Shepherd, and we listen to His voice. "I am the Good Shepherd," Jesus says. "The Good Shepherd is the one who lays down His life for His sheep. I know My own and My own know Me." *(John 10:11,14)*

God's whistle comes in a variety of calls – and some of these 'calls' form the topics of chapters in this book – a Call to being what we are created to be; a Call to bless His Holy Name; a Call to Fullness of Life; a Call to Contemplate; a Call to Awareness; a Call to the Present Moment, and so on until the chapter where He Calls us Home.

Just as the sheepdog listens to the whistle of his master so we should be attentive to the call of our Master, answering His whistle "promptly and swiftly". *(Isaiah 5:26)*

"Your call, my God, as it comes to us, has innumerable different shades of meaning; each vocation is essentially different from all the rest." *('Hymn of the Universe', Teilhard de Chardin, p 137)*

So, I have written this book in response to a Call from many people who over many years have asked me to put on paper the thoughts from my 'inner-healing' weekends. I have found this enormously difficult to do, because every week-end is different and the Holy Spirit speaks in different ways for each week-end. I find I can never use my notes a second time, as the material given for each session comes in prayer for a particular group of people, just before or even during the weekend itself. I find also that during preparation, through my 'tongue' prayer for the weekend (or seminar, or preaching or whatever I'm asked to do) the Holy Spirit shows me the right approach and gives me the appropriate theme.

There are, as well, some favourite thoughts, poems, scriptures, prayers, that have helped me through life and on my journey towards God, and I share them with you, humbly and hesitantly. Prayer like these can be said on your own and at any time. If they are of help, use them, if not, then know that even by your setting out to read this book, I have prayed for you and yours, and God can make up what is wanting in my poor faltering words.

I meet many people who are longing for a better quality of spiritual life. Church doesn't satisfy them, and the sense of community and belonging unfortunately are sadly not very strong, in some parishes. Many people today, especially Christian people, are looking for 'more' in their lives. They are seeking a peace the world cannot give them. Some are suffering a great deal of stress at work and at home. There are many pressures and injustices around, causing insecurity and sometimes 'unnoticed' poverty. The added threat of redundancy hangs over people's heads, causing even greater pressure and unease. Redundancy has helped destroy stability in society. Some people have been forced into early retirement or worse still are jobless. They have little money, and too much time on their hands, not knowing how to use it constructively.

Others again seem unable to opt out of over-pressurised jobs while their family life is being gnawed away or even disintegrated, with no time for togetherness, sharing or relaxation. One wonders what life is all about as unjust and dishonest systems thrive at other people's expense!

The Holy Spirit, who hovered over the chaos at the beginning of creation, bringing order and beauty, still hovers over the world today. He is still speaking through all that is happening. Might it not be His way of giving many people more time for prayer, for getting to know God, for evangelisation and witness, for living simply, for helping and meeting one another? Is it giving us more time to be ourselves, more time to pray, more time to find God? Many have found their faith the only mainstay and they find week-ends away most helpful and encouraging. It is for these especially that this book is written and for those too who are looking for hope, for God, for forgiveness, for peace, for understanding sorrow and death, for fullness of life and for healing.

I believe God works powerfully with us when we give Him 'time out'. For most people a week-end away, looking at the things that matter most in life, is a treat, but when it is with lovely faith-committed Christian people, it is like a mini-holiday. One returns home refreshed and ready to start again. Everyone must have a need at some point to recharge their batteries and to get away from the hustle and bustle of life, (even if life is fairly 'normal' and happy) to a quiet place where one can 'be' rather than 'do'. It's a little bit of Heaven!

To share your faith, your love, your hopes, your dreams, your successes and failures, your vision for the Church and the World, with real vibrant Christians who love the Lord Jesus, must surely be one of the greatest privileges on Earth. Opportunity is provided to pray alone, or in a group or with laying on of hands (as mentioned in the Scriptures) for healing and wholeness, and especially for healing of memories. It is a wondrous thing to see the grace of God unfolding and to experience the Holy Spirit bringing new life, gentle healing and balm, through His gifts.

We know that all healing comes through Jesus Christ, and He has left us the legacy of the Holy Spirit to be our Comforter. Jesus alone is the answer to life's problems. He alone can unlock all doors and hearts. He alone paves the way for new life, promising a future full of hope. We meet all sorts of people along the way, some raring to go, while others would need a 'bomb' behind them to make them move. Others are trapped by their fixed ideas and attitudes or by their past sins or memories, and seem unable to move on, or to forgive the hurts that were allowed to fester and damage them as children or even later on as adults. Some go over and over hurts in their minds and live continually in the past, their lives never see the 'light of day'. One can hardly say they are 'alive'. Yet we find, the Holy Spirit can do all things, He can transform our lives, He can take people from where they're at and lead them on, enabling them to yield to His grace, and so they begin to experience a fuller life in Him. We witness many miracles. Others just need a little 'top up' from time to time; they live a simple and uncomplicated life, serving others and trying to put others' needs before their own, and so they experience a tranquillity of life that money cannot buy.

Each of us has a story, valuable to God and sacred to us. We must reverence our past, never deny it. We are the product of our upbringing, our environment, our education, our inheritance, our genetic make-up, and of course, of circumstances, often beyond our control, which have shaped our lives. If we really want to be healed of any destructive influences, past or present, we must choose to 'let go' and to come to Jesus, the healer. He may not blot out the hurtful memories, but He can anaesthetise the pain, and anoint with the healing balm of the Holy Spirit. He can cleanse us, give us peace and restore us.

Sometimes what has affected us may be only a minor incident, even of our own making, but which can take on enormous proportions. It may be an awkward personality trait that is hard to accept or change, or conquer, or it could be constant clash of personality with someone with whom we have to live or work.

No matter what it is, God can do something for us. Everything that has ever happened to us is registered in our unconscious or sub-conscious memory. If we keep 'pressing down' bad memories, even denying them, eventually, like my sister's ironing, packed into her cupboard, they will all tumble out one day (maybe when we least expect it) and make themselves felt. In the end, they will have to be dealt with or they will deal with us.

"Jesus Christ is the same yesterday, today and forever" *(Hebrews 13:8),* and so every memory can be healed in Him and is present to Him as if it is happening now. He has no problem healing at any time, if we allow Him. Time and space mean nothing to Him. He wants us to "give the past to Him to make a fresh start, and to look forward to what lies ahead". *(Philippians 3:13).* The Lord Jesus is the specialist in healing yesterday's wounds today! We find it hard to let go of memories which could ruin our lives if unhealed.

If the saints, like Paul, Peter, Augustine, Ignatius and others, kept dragging up their past, their sins, their bad experiences, where would they be today? But, with God's grace, they were able to let them go, and they believed in God's forgiveness and love for them. *The past event does not change,* but what can change, sometimes dramatically, is the way we recall it. We can see the past in a new light, so instead of recalling it with sadness or even bitterness, we can recall it, as an occasion to glorify God.

I want to tell people, that in spite of negative experiences, of sorrows, of setbacks, of brokenness, of failures, of sufferings, of illusions, of illness, of sin, it is possible to live again, and to grow and change, and to become the person God wants you to be. "I want you to be always happy, always happy in the Lord, what I want is your happiness" are St. Paul's words to the Philippians *(4:4)* and also to us. God does not create unhappiness, though he often gets blamed for it. I want to tell couples, especially young ones, that it is possible to overcome the problems that want to destroy them and their marriage, and divide their families.

I want to tell Religious Sisters or Brothers, that it is possible to live 'in love with Jesus' and be happy, even amidst adverse circumstances and misunderstandings, injustices and even absence of sisterly or brotherly love (as I sometimes hear).

I want to tell priests that it is worth 'hanging in' there, because we need you, even though you feel worn out and inadequate. Jesus called you and He is faithful. "Listen to me, faint hearts, you who feel far from victory, I bring victory near, already it is close, my salvation will not be late" *(Isaiah 46:12)*.

I want to tell the elderly and the lonely, that God will always be your strength and your shield, and He will never leave you alone. Stay close to Him in your old age. I was very struck by my grandmother's response when asked where she lived just before she died in hospital, "I live with God and myself in Charlotte Quay," was her response. I want to tell you lovely young people, so full of goodness and generosity, to give the Church a chance, and to let Jesus' love fill your life. He chooses to need you. Why not think of giving six months or a year to serve Him in the poor in a third world country? This is a very desirable and generous thing to do; rewarding for you too. The more you give, the more you receive. "Give and there will be gifts for you: a full measure, pressed down, shaken together, and running over, will be poured into your lap; because the amount you measure out is the amount you will be given back." *(Luke 6: 38)* This is so true and God is never outdone in generosity. Think about it.

God is asking us to let Him have control of our lives. He is always waiting for us to yield to the Lordship of His Son Jesus. He alone can transform our 'desert' yesterdays, into oases of new life 'todays', where 'flowers' will appear again. As Scripture says, "Let the desert bring forth flowers like the jonquil, and let it rejoice and sing for joy".

What we thought was wasteland, gives rise to streams of water, which gush forth. What we thought was scorched and burnt up, can become a lake, our weary hands and trembling knees can be straightened; and all faint hearts can become courageous at the coming of God. "Then the eyes of the blind shall be opened, and the ears of the deaf unsealed, then the lame shall leap like the deer, and the tongues of the dumb shall sing for joy, for the wilderness and dry land will exult, the wasteland will rejoice and bloom" *(Isaiah 35)*.

Perhaps you could even pause right now and take a look at your life. Ask yourself:
1) What are the areas you thought were scorched and burnt up? How are they now?
2) What are the 'New Flowers' appearing in your life right now?
3) What areas seemed to be 'Desert' areas and are now yielding to springs of life?
4) What healing are you experiencing in this life?
5) Are you changing?

St. Paul encourages us to give up our old way of life. "You must put aside your old self which gets corrupted by illusory desires, your mind must be renewed by a spiritual 'revolution' so that you can 'put on' the new self that has been created in God's way in the goodness and holiness of Truth." *(Ephesians 4:22-24)*

It would be good to be 'the water' in someone's desert today, not by looking for the opportunity itself but just by recognising it when it comes. Can we not each recall one way in which this wondrous thing has already happened for us? Can we not all quote times in our lives, when God used our brokenness to heal another? Can we not see that the worst thing that ever happened to us, can become the best, most freeing?

Most of us can witness to certain mini-miracles in our own lives. Up to this very day, I can honestly say that God has healed me and even more that He has used my weakness, even my sin, to the good, to help others, and to help me to understand. Nothing is lost with God. We are so undeserving of His goodness and love. We can never measure up to Him. St. Peter tells us in his second epistle: "If anything dominates you, you are a slave to it". *(2 Peter 2:19)* When people take these words to heart and start to live by them, they see changes. When they stand back and look at the dominating forces in their lives, it is often as if scales fall from their eyes and a new life begins. We are often unaware that we are allowing a particular influence, problem, situation, person, memory, to dominate our lives, and to gnaw away at our energies. The moment we discern what is dominating us, we can decide upon a new approach (where possible) and so begin to experience the freedom of the Holy Spirit of God. Some forces are harmful and destructive and need to be challenged and removed (if at all possible) . Living with certain problems, like, for instance, alcoholic problems, cannot be easy.

Unfortunately the problem is so great at times that it is difficult not to let it destroy relationships, the family peace and even family life itself. Facing the truth is the only way ahead for alcoholics and here the AA programme is of immense importance. Adhered to, it can save lives, and restore what was lost. Some people who live with alcoholic partners, have told me how they've tried this approach and it works, it helps them to keep going. Other problems (financial, sickness, terminal illness, divorce, redundancy etc.) can also take their toll and wear people down unless they have a very positive attitude to these evils.

Problems can sometimes be used so positively. Tensions can sometimes lead to growth. In fact I would say, a certain amount of tension is desirable for growth. It is good practice to invite Jesus into each situation and to yield the problem to Him. Why not pause and do it now? He sees everything that is happening to you. He, the Master Craftsman, is able to draw good out of every impossible situation. Like the Potter in Jeremiah chapter eighteen, who every time the pot he was making came out wrong, he would start afresh and work it into another vessel, and God says, "as the clay is in the potter's hand so are you in Mine". So, there are no mistakes – only opportunities for growth or indeed for sharing His Cross. *Remember God is always with you to help you but He will never interfere with anyone's free will.* He awaits permission at every turn. Life can make or mar us, depending on how we see it and react to it. "Two men looked out of prison bars, one saw mud, the other saw stars".

I have seen those on small income so content that they even give away what they have, generously and without count, like the widow whom Our Lord praised. I have seen those with plenty give so little and think, it was generous. I have seen saints like Don, crippled with arthritis and couldn't move a limb, as he lay on his hospital bed for years, never complain, but speak only of how he could help others. I have seen those imprisoned (even unjustly) take up the fight and start to live again. I have seen the pain of broken relationships mended. I have seen the pain and hardship of our friends in Bosnia's Refugee Camps, families living in railway carriages or squashed into prefab buildings, keep their hearts up through their faith and generous sharing of the little they have. What they share is pure gold to them, a glass of juice or a tiny cup of pure ground coffee. I have been truly humbled by what I have seen there. Their lovely eyes glisten with a certain serenity, though they have lost homes, possessions, even family members. Little do they realise how much they are teaching us when we visit them. What they give us could never be bought. Even with the little they have they teach us gratitude.

I believe God wants us to be happy and one way to happiness is certainly through gratitude and through cultivation of a 'grateful heart'. Jesus loved grateful hearts. Remember how He pointed out that, of the ten lepers cured, only one bothered to return to give God thanks. So don't be put out if the people you do most for seem ungrateful. That's the way life is sometimes. But for yourself, always be growing in gratitude, and take your standard from Jesus Himself who was continually thanking His Father in Heaven. "And for all these things, give thanks to God, because this is what God expects you to do in Christ Jesus". *(1 Thessalonians 4:18)* He Himself showed us how to give thanks. Just as I believe much unnecessary sorrow is brought upon ourselves through unforgiveness, so I believe much unhappiness in life comes through ingratitude to God and to each other. We need to adopt an 'attitude of gratitude' for everything. The choice is ours. We can become a people of thanksgiving. Grateful people are *happy* people!

Why don't we start today being grateful? In no time we will experience a change in our lives, and in other people's attitude to us. People say sometimes, "I wish he would say 'Thank You'." Don't let that be said of us. People sometimes say to me, "I wish I had a God like your God," and I say "Of course you can, He's the same God for me as for you and He has no favourites". "What's your secret?" they say. "You seem to be always happy." "Well, I don't know, but I think it may be linked with gratitude, knowing Jesus' love for me personally, together with the gift of joy and a sense of humour."

I thank God continually for His goodness to me. There's so much to thank Him for each day, from the breath that wakes me up, to the sleep that refreshes me at night. I'm a spoilt child and I know it. "Think of the love the Father has lavished on us by letting us be called God's children and that is what we are". *(1 John 3:1)* This is one of my favourite verses of scripture which I often recite to myself during the day no matter where I am or what I am doing. It brings me great peace, happiness and assurance. "His word is a lamp to my feet", so that there shines a light that never dies. Within our darkest night, there shines the light

of His word. "Hearing My word, receiving it, producing more fruit". *(Mark 4:20)*
"The word of God is alive and active, it cuts like any double-edged sword". *(Hebrews 4:12-13)*

Start today and let His word sink into your heart; let it make its home in you as Jesus Himself suggested. Repeat the words of scripture with faith and love and you will be surprised how they will become active within you.
Too often in life we tend to look the wrong way. Comfort is within but we seek it without. Give thanks continually.

St. Augustine writes:
"I found Thee not without, I sought Thee without in vain for Thou art within......
Seeing then, that the Bridegroom whom Thou lovest, is the treasure hidden in the field of thy soul, for which the wise merchant, gave all that he had, so thou, if thou wilt find Him, must forget all that is thine, withdraw from all created things and hide thyself in the secret retreat of the spirit, shutting the door upon thyself, that is, denying thy will in all things, and praying to the Father in secret, then thou, being hidden within Him will be conscious of His Presence in secret and wilt love Him, possess Him in secret, and delight Him in secret, in a way that no tongue or language can express".

"I am the Way, the Truth and the Life", Jesus said. *(John 4:6)* Why don't I take these words to heart? Jesus tells us to rise up in splendour and live in His light.
"Arise shine out for your light has come, the Glory of the Lord is rising upon you". *(Isaiah 60:1)* "Let the Lord always guide you, let Him give strength to your bones, and you

shall be like a watered garden, like a spring of water, whose water never runs dry". *(Isaiah 58:11)* Let His beauty shine out of you .

Inner Healing and healing of memories, makes people look more beautiful, as they become more healed; they also become more self-assured and more true to themselves. It is wonderful to behold. Every time I see Frank, our healed alcoholic and John (healed through AA) my heart gives a leap of joy and thanksgiving. They look younger, more handsome every time, their eyes sparkle with a new light, a new dawn of hope, a new found joy. "Your beauty now is all for the King's delight". *(Psalm 45:11)*

Each of us, has people God has placed in our path to bless us and likewise He has placed us in other people's paths, to bless them. Every relationship is a responsibility and a blessing. Whether the relationship 'went wrong' or not, the Lord can use everything that has ever happened in it for His Glory and ours. "Through His wounds we are healed." *(Isaiah 53:5)*, through our sufferings we too can become healed. We may think sometimes, we would have been better off, if we had not met 'so and so', but I think not. *What has happened has happened and God can bring good out of even the worst thing that could have happened to us.* "We know that by turning everything to their good, God co-operates with all those who love Him, with all those that He has called according to His purpose". *(Romans 8:28)*

In fact, if you look closely enough, there is good in everything, somewhere. God is in charge. We forget this sometimes. He is tuning us, He is actually fine-tuning us through suffering. If you are a musician or even musical, you will know what this means. Tagore puts it beautifully: "When all the strings of my life will be tuned, My Master, Your almighty touch will make the music of love resound".

There is a lovely story told of a woman visiting a sculpture exhibition. She passed a beautiful statue of an elephant. She gazed at it in rapture. "How is it so beautiful?" she said to the sculptor who was proudly standing beside it. "Oh, madam," he said, "I just kept chipping away everything that was not elephant." And so God prunes us until He chips away what is not of Him, until we become our true selves.

'Twas battered and scarred and the auctioneer
Thought it scarcely worth his while.
To waste much time on the old violin,
But held it up with a smile:
"What am I bidden, good folks," he cried,
"Who'll start the bidding for me?"
"A dollar, a dollar"; then "two!" "Only two?
Two dollars, and who'll make it three?
Three dollars, once; three dollars, twice;
Going for three – " But no,
From the room, far back, a grey-haired man
Came forward and picked up the bow.
Then wiping the dust from the old violin,
And tightening the loose strings,
He played a melody pure and sweet
As a carolling angel sings.

The music ceased, and the auctioneer,
With a voice that was quiet and low,
Said: "What am I bid for the old violin?"
And he held it up with the bow.
"A thousand dollars and who'll make it two?
Two thousand! And who'll make it three?
Three thousand, once, three thousand, twice,
And going, and gone," said he.
The people cheered, but some of them cried,
"We do not quite understand
What changed its worth?" Swift came the reply:
"The touch of a master's hand."

And many a man with life out of tune
And battered and scarred with sin,
Is auctioned cheap to the thoughtless crowd,
Much like the old violin.
A 'mess of pottage', a glass of wine;
A game – and he travels on.
He is 'going' once, and 'going' twice,
He's 'going' and almost 'gone'.
But the Master comes, and the foolish crowd
Never can quite understand
The worth of a soul and the change that's wrought
By the touch of the Master's hand.

('The Touch of the Master's Hand',
Myra Brooks Welch)

I have many people in my life to thank for pointing me in the right direction, even the people I would rather have done without. As a young sister, I was sent to study 'A' level science, chemistry, botany, zoology. My dream was to be a botanist. I was so intrigued by the exquisite formations and patterns in cutting sections of stems and studying them under the microscope. I found it enthralling, staining the sections and seeing their structure. What a God, I thought, to put such beauty into things we couldn't see!

However, my dream was shattered. A decision was made for me by the Provincial (who neither liked nor understood me), that my life was to be diverted away from science into music. I was really upset at the time, even though I come from a musically talented family. But now I have to thank her because as a result I've had a lovely life 'in music' and have met so many wonderful people, and been to places I might never have seen. Also, I've had many more blessings than I would have had if I had continued studying science and ended up in a school laboratory.

So without my knowing it, my life has been shaped for me. When I entered the convent I never gave a thought as to what I might 'do' in the religious life. All I wanted was to give my life to God as a nun. And that is, of course, how it should be. Religious are 'sent', and what is important is that they do what they are sent to do. But, in fact, I have enjoyed my music life very much and I am glad I didn't go down the road of science. So, unwittingly the Provincial did me a great favour! How mysterious are the ways of God.

I had an enriching five years working with the late Bishop Francis Thomas in his Diocesan Liturgical Commission. He inspired everyone with his 'hopeful' vision for the Church. Then in 1973, I met Br. Damian Lundy and other de la Salle brothers, who through their dynamism, leadership and friendship, developed in me a great love for the Mass and all things liturgical.

My whole life was dramatically changed in 1975, when a Retreat given by Fr. James Hawes of the Brentwood Diocese, brought me untold blessings and set me on a spiritual journey I would hate to have missed. Strangely enough, it was the first retreat Fr. James had ever given – and he hasn't given another retreat since. For me, it was the first Retreat for the rest of my life. I believe things happen for us 'at the right time'. If it is in someone else's time *for* us, it will not last. I firmly believe, that if God has to bring someone from the other ends of the earth for us, at a particular time in our lives, He will. His timing is perfect. As Ecclesiastes, chapter three says "There is a season for everything, a time for every occupation under Heaven."

Nuns usually live in community and, in every community I have been in, God has given me some wonderful companions. Without them the mission for the Church entrusted to me could not have happened.

He has also given me many wonderful friends, priests and lay people, who are enthusiastic about the same things as me, especially making Jesus known. This is our only desire, to work for Him in His vineyard, branches of the same vine. Their love and acceptance of me, have made me 'real', have helped me to become 'myself'. They have helped me to step forward into the 'Dance of Life', while holding firmly to the much-loved tradition of the Church and roots of our faith.

So you can see how my roots are very conservative, but my outlook is most forward looking.

My own congregation, the Daughters of the Holy Spirit, by their openness and support and attentiveness to the Holy Spirit (our patron) have also co-operated in the response to new calls of the Spirit and thus helped to 'light candles' in many different areas. What can I say but 'Thank You'? I feel I have become 'real'. What has happened for me can happen for you too, or indeed it may well have already happened, in which case I bless the Lord with you.

I would like to quote here an excerpt from the little book "The Velveteen Rabbit" by Margery Williams. It contains a conversation which takes place in the nursery between the Skin Horse and the Velveteen Rabbit. It is a child's classic, but has such depth of meaning, that I feel it could well be applied to the process of inner healing, which makes us 'real'. Wholeness does not happen all at once (in fact we shall need healing till we die) but once the process has begun it is possible to become more and more 'whole'. However it is also possible to go backwards bit by bit if we don't constantly co-operate with our healing. So just like the Rabbit, worn out by being 'loved to bits'!, becoming shabby and losing all its fur in the process, similarly being loved and healed by God brings you most comforting rewards.

"What is real?" asked the Rabbit one day, when they were lying side by side near the nursery fender, before Nana came to tidy the room. "Does it mean having things that buzz inside you and a stick-out handle?".
"Real isn't how you are made," said the Skin Horse.
"It's a thing that happens to you. When a child loves you for a long, long time, not just to play with, but really loves you, then you become real."

"Does it hurt?" asked the Rabbit.
"Sometimes," said the Skin Horse, for he was always truthful.
"When you are real you don't mind being hurt."

"Does it happen all at once, like being wound-up," he asked, "or bit by bit?". "It doesn't happen all at once," said the Skin Horse. "You become.
It takes a long time. That's why it doesn't often happen to people who break easily or have sharp edges, or who have to be carefully kept. Generally, by the time you are real, most of your hair has been loved off, and your eyes drop out and you get loose in the joints and very shabby. But, these things don't matter at all,

because once you are real you can't be ugly, except to people who don't understand."

"I suppose you are real?" said the Rabbit. And then he wished he had not said it, for he thought the Skin Horse might be sensitive. But, the Skin Horse only smiled.
"The boy's uncle made me real," he said. "That was a great many years ago; but, once you are real you can't become unreal again. It lasts for always."

Without Christ in my life, it would be so empty. I feel I need to be grafted into Him as He says Himself 'A branch of the Vine'. I can do nothing without Him. I am nothing without Him. I often wonder how atheists or agnostics cope, especially in the face of death. If death is the end, I cannot imagine what's next. Fortunately for us Christians, it is but a new beginning. I know God has prepared a place for us, as Jesus told us, a home where there are 'many mansions'. All He asks of us on earth is to have 'a heart full of love'; only His love can fill the earthenware vessel that can hold this treasure. "You must live your whole life according to the Christ you have received, Jesus the Lord. You must be rooted in Him and built on Him and held firm in the faith that you have been taught and full of thanksgiving". *(Colossians 2:6-7)*

How can I ever thank God for the grace of Renewal in my life which has taught me to see everything that happens to me as part of God's plan for me? With St. Paul I can say: "I forget the past and strain ahead for the prize to which God calls us upwards, to receive Jesus Christ Our Lord". *(Philippians 3:14)*

Life is never black and white, but out of its different hues, God is making a beautiful tapestry of our lives, integrating for us, all the different shades. As God begins to take over our lives, life becomes more simple, and prayer is of the essence. We will always need those very special intimate times with Him, our Beloved, like any lover thinking of his or her earthly beloved. "Set me as a seal on your heart, so that I have no love but yours", we read in the 'Song of Songs'. The Holy Spirit teaches us everything and leads us to all truth. This gift of the Holy Spirit was Jesus' dying gift to us. The Holy Spirit will complete the 'good work' begun in us, to the Glory of God the Father. I pray I will always remain one of His 'little' ones, resting on His lap. My mom used to say I was in God's pocket. Though I fail

Him many times, He will never fail me - even when I sin and let Him down badly: "For you, Lord, have cast all my sins behind your back". *(Isaiah 38:17)* Such love, how can I take it in? It will never change, it is everlasting, unconditional, total, faithful.

"I have loved you with an everlasting love so I am constant in my affection for you". *(Jeremiah 31:3)*
God's essence is love and so He can only love me.
"God is love". *(1 John 4:16)*
"We ourselves have known and put our faith in God's love towards ourselves." *(1 John 4:16)*
"Not our love for God but God's love for us when He sent His Son to be the sacrifice that takes sins away". *(1 John 4:10)*

Like the child with the Velveteen Rabbit, God just can't help loving me. I can always count on His love for me. If I could only lay hold of this fact and live by it daily, my life would be much happier. God's love, unlike human love, isn't just 'words only'. God is faithful. I feel the need to be 'reconditioned', as it were, every so often, to make sure my mind is set on true and correct thoughts about who I am in God's sight and what His love does for me.. "The road is narrow," Jesus says, "and few there are that find it". *(Matthew 7:14)*

Can there be such a thing as a full human being? How many truly alive Christians do you know? I hope I will always be one of those who finds the road, and if for any reason, I should step off it, I pray I will quickly return to it again. Are we Catholics not blessed with the sacraments, rivers of life? Try never to take them for granted and try to receive them as often as possible.

Life will bring us daily joys and sorrows, but never forget God is in everything. Just this week I found Him in the loss of a dear friend, with whom I spent a good deal of time as he lay dying. I call this a grace. He died as he lived. Years ago, he designed a shield for his school, the motto chosen being 'God's will be done'. Norman lived like this. His little wife said, "Every morning he used to say to God: 'What do you want me to do for you today, Lord?'" Cherished moments!

As we journey on together, may we continually help each other 'to become holy, as that is what God wants'. *(1 Thessalonians 4:3)* May we continue to "sing the words and tunes of the Psalms and hymns when we are together, and go on singing and chanting to the Lord in our hearts, so that always and everywhere, we are giving thanks to God, who is our Father, in the name of the Lord Jesus Christ." *(Ephesians 5:19-20)* And so let us, "Everyday, as long as today lasts, keep encouraging one another". *(Hebrews 3:13)* "Do everything without complaining or arguing, so that you may be innocent and pure, as God's perfect children, who live in a world of corrupt and sinful people. You must shine among them like stars, lighting up the sky, because you are offering it the word of life." *(Philippians 2:14-16)*

Do not be afraid when God calls you. He will not fail you.
Do not be afraid when He appears silent. He is listening.
Do not be afraid to 'let go' to Him.
Do not be afraid when He wants to prune you.
Do not be afraid to speak out for Him.
Do not be afraid to keep quiet.
Do not be afraid to tell of your healing.
Do not be afraid of His love for you.

Do not be afraid if He calls you to marriage.
Do not be afraid if He does not.
Do not be afraid if He calls you to Religious life/Priesthood.
Do not be afraid of 'the dark road ahead'.
Do not be afraid to live for Him.
Do not let Him down by sinning.
Do not be afraid of His compassion and mercy for you.
God is greater than His call. God is always calling.

Do not be afraid of your future.
Only believe and answer God's call.
"Here I am, Lord, send me...
... Help me never to be afraid of Your demands."

God's call will never fail you.

"I called you into being, and before you knew Me, I called you. Without Me you would not be here. You owe Me your very existence in My world. Know My concern for you, as you respond daily to My call."

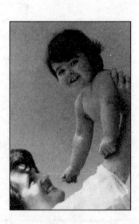

A CALL TO BEING

Our first call, is a call to being by God, our Heavenly Father. When God created the world He fashioned man out of the dust of the earth. He formed man in His own image:

"God created man in the image of Himself,
in the image of God He created him:
male and female He created them.
God blessed them; saying to them:
'Be fruitful, multiply and fill the earth and conquer it.
Be masters of the fish of the sea, the birds of Heaven and all living animals on the earth.'" *(Genesis 1:26-28)*

God called us before we were in our mother's womb. "Before I formed you in the womb, I knew you, and before you were born, I consecrated you". *(Jeremiah 1:5)*

Lord, I thank you for the wonder of my being, that I am fearfully, wonderfully made. I thank you that you are always watching over me and that you call me by my name. I thank You that You delight in me, and that You are always with me. I thank You that I am an original, that there is no other like me (many would say 'Thank God') and that there is only one thumb like mine in the whole world.

You show me how precious my name is to you, when you told the apostles and me to-day: "Do not rejoice that demons submit to you. Rejoice rather that your names are written in Heaven" *(Luke 10:20)*

Lord, I thank You for this. It gives me something to look forward to throughout my life. I thank You that I need never be afraid. I thank You that you tell me each day of my life not to be afraid. Scripture recounts three hundred and sixty six times this message for me. Your sensitivity omits nothing and there is even an extra one for a leap year. Only You could know this Lord, thank You. What a God!

You comfort me even when I am old.
"You who have been carried since birth,
Whom I have carried since the time you were born,
In your old age, I shall still be the same.
When your hair is grey, I shall still support you,
I have already done so, I have carried you,
I shall still support and deliver you." *(Isaiah 46:3-4)*

Can anyone compare with our God?"You are precious to me" God says "and I honour and love you." *(Isaiah 43:4)*

It takes daring, the unconscious daring of a young child, to believe all this, to launch out, to trust, to say 'Yes', to let go and live, to risk believing the scriptures, so full of wonderful hope and promise, and to allow the message to be absorbed into the very marrow of our bones. "Let the message in all its richness make its home in you." *(Colossians 3:16)*

It takes humility to stand before God believing you are precious to Him, especially since He has no need of us and could have made the universe without us, since we add nothing to Him. He is complete in Himself and has indeed no need even of our praise. However, He chooses to need us and He chose to create us. It takes greatness to know how small we are, how insignificant, how totally dependent upon Him. "Even the very hairs of your head are numbered by Him." *(Luke 12:7)* Our days too are numbered even before they began. The psalmist tells us: "My days listed and determined, even before the first of them occurred." *(Psalm 139:17)* If God took our breath away this minute, we would die. All is gift from the moment you awaken to the moment of sleeping.

"What is man that you should keep him in mind, mortal man that you care for him?
His days are like a breath, his life like a shadow.
Yet you have made him little less than a god, with glory and honour you crowned him." *(Psalm 8:3-4)*

Because God loves us, it makes us lovable. We must therefore love ourselves, it is a duty. Liking yourself and being 'at home' in your own skin is what God desires for you. We have a command to love our neighbour as we love ourselves. This is very difficult sometimes as our own self-image can be so poor, that our love for ourselves is non-existent. How therefore can we fulfil the commandment to love others as we love ourselves? To be a healthy, fully-alive Christian, you must cultivate a great love for yourself. This means giving yourself the essentials of a healthy life and most of all trying to accept yourself as you are and being grateful to God for creating you. Enjoy His gifts of music, art, drama, literature, science, technology, medecine, etc. To love oneself does not mean to be filled with vanity and to be so puffed up that every one will detest you! Humility is truth!

I've heard of a famous Jesuit, John Powell, who decided he was going to love himself and so when anyone gave him a compliment, he would write it in a book. He experienced a transformation in his own self-awareness, and attitude to life, as he began to react positively to himself and to words of praise. He decided to accept and acknowledge his gifts and qualities as part of God's blessing upon him. He made a list of every good thing about himself, from the colour of his eyes, to his love for music, to his sensitivity to others. He simply began to thank God for everything and gave God the glory for any praise he might receive. Whenever he was given another compliment, he would quickly add it to his long list which is kept in his bottom drawer. Currently there are three hundred good qualities.. In the event of his counselling people suffering from a poor self-image he would show them this list, (to their amazement), and he would then encourage them to keep their own list. There would be no problem in writing his obituary! The idea is not of course self-glorification (as might be at first thought) but acknowledgement of God, from whom all good gifts come.

Denying God's gifts in you is hardly humility. Remember what happened to the one who denied his one talent and hid it. Use your gifts, acknowledge them, develop them and thank God for them. Recognise the gift that you are before God and give Him thanks. Thank Him for all the people who have made you who you are today, especially those who have loved you into life. You were made for Jesus, "All things were made for Him not one thing had its being but through Him." *(John 1:3)* So it is "In Him we live and move and have our being." *(Acts 17:28)*

The more we believe the message of scripture, the more we believe that God loves us unconditionally, the more wholeness we will experience in ourselves. "Be beautiful inside your hearts, with the lasting charm of a gentle, quiet spirit, which is so beautiful to God." *(1 Peter 3:4)* Make your outward appearance to the best possible. "No one hates his own body but lovingly cares for it", *(Ephesians 5:29)* and look after yourself and keep yourself well. Let no one steal your beauty or push you down. Always remember the truth. I am God's child.
God is my Father, my Creator. From Him comes everything I am and have. I am His alone, His original, unique, well-loved child. There is no other who has been planned from all eternity like me. I have been created in love, held in love. 'I am the apple of my Father's eye'. *(Psalm 17:8)*

I belong to God's Family and so have many brothers and sisters. We have only one Father. I am never alone. I am somebody because I am loved by my Father. I am special because He desires me. My Baptism has made me an heir to His Kingdom. How then can I feel inferior? I am of value to God. His plan is special to me. He reminds me in Jeremiah that He has a plan for my life, a plan for peace and not disaster. *(Jeremiah 29:11)* I must be positive in my attitude to myself and believe in

His unconditional, faithful, perfect love for me, as that is what would give my Father the greatest pleasure.

I came across this delightful poem by Dr. Schuller, which beautifully sums up who I am:

"I may be young, I may be old
    But I am Somebody
For I am God's child.

I may be educated, I may be unlettered.
    But I am Somebody
For I am God's child.

I may be black, I may be white
    But I am Somebody
For I am God's child.

I may be rich, I may be poor
    But I am Somebody
For I am God's child.

I may be fat, I may be thin
    But I am Somebody
For I am God's child.

I may be married, I may be divorced
    But I am Somebody
For I am God's child.

I may be single, I may be widowed
    But I am Somebody
For I am God's child.

> I may be successful, I may be a failure
> > But I am Somebody
> For I am God's child.
>
> I may be a sinner, I may be a saint
> > But I am Somebody
> For I am God's child.
>
> For Jesus is my Saviour
> I am God's child."

('Healing of the Self-Image',
Betty Tapscott and Fr. Bob de Grandis, p 26)

Because I am Somebody, I can do more than I ever could. Someone once said, you're a nobody till somebody loves you. That's why it's so important for us to try to love others, and help them in whatever small way we can, to let them know they are loved.

Of course we want more than anything else for others to know that God loves them because when a person knows this, I think they know everything there is to know. *This is the best piece of knowledge you could ever acquire.* Human love certainly helps us to know divine love. When you see someone in love, you know they know. Love just changes everything.

Once we know we're loved, life changes. Life begins, and we can begin to grow to our full stature. There are far too many 'dwarfed' people around, people who will not believe in their Father's love for them.

Jesus came to bring us the fullness of life and in Him, to let us know who we are in relation to our Father. When we know we're loved, we begin to accept ourselves – just as we are, with all our faults and failings and past regrets. Acceptance of self helps us in turn to accept others, and to have a happier life. Once you decide to live in this way, others will see the change in you, and your family and friends will benefit. You will be a sign of hope to others.

Solo or Group Exercise

Close your eyes now and be still before your Heavenly Father. Think of a time when you felt deeply loved. How was that love shown to you? In gestures, looks, words, a letter, phone call etc. Stay with the scene as long as you can, as long as you feel something of the love that was yours when the event took place. Seek and find the presence of the Lord in this scene. Give thanks.

> "Lord, I thank you, from my heart
> Since you have heard what I say.
> In the presence of the Angels I sing to you
> And bow down towards your holy Temple."
> *(Psalm 138:1-2)*

> "Since you yourself have created my very being
> and put me together in my mother's womb
> In wonder I thank you for making me
> How mysterious, like everything you make.

You know me through and through
from having watched my bones take shape
When I was being assembled in secret
Stitched together in the darkness of my mother's
womb. " *(Psalm 139:13-15)*

I came across three lovely prayers of acceptance by Carmen Bernos de Gasztold in 'The One who listens'. *(Michael Hollings and Etta Gullick)*

"A little patience, O God, I am coming, one must take nature as she is. It was not I who made her. I

do not mean to criticise this house on my back. It has its points but You must admit Lord it is too heavy to carry. Still, let us hope that this double enclosure, my shell and my heart, will never be shut to You."

(Prayer of the Tortoise)

"It is I, the elephant, Your creature, who is talking to You. I am so embarrassed by my great self and truly, it is not my fault if I spoil Your jungle with
my big feet. Let me be
careful and behave wisely,
always keeping my dignity
and poise. Give me such
philosophic thoughts that I
can rejoice everywhere I go,
in the lovable oddity of
things."   *(Prayer of the Elephant)*

"See, Lord, my coat hangs in tatters, like homespun, old, threadbare. All that I had of zest, all strength, I have given in hard work, and kept nothing for myself.
Now my poor head swings. I offer up all the loneliness of my heart.
Dear God, stiff on my thickened legs, I stand here before You, Your unprofit-able servant. Oh, of Your goodness, give me a gentle death."

(Prayer of the Old Horse)

Lord, I ask you now to help me to accept myself. I ask you to pervade every area of my being with your Holy Spirit. Fill me from head to toe. I pray that those who see me may see You in me, so that they may give Glory to the Father who made me. I pray that Your love may protect my being, and that at the end of each day, I may be comforted by the thought of your love as I delight in the wonder of who I am. Amen.

> *Come in; let us bow and bend low;*
> *Let us kneel before the God who made us.*
> *For He is our God and we, the people who*
> *belong to His pasture, the flock led by His hand.*
> *(Psalm 95:6-7)*

O that today you would hear His voice, that you would accept His love, that you would not harden your heart, that you would believe the message of the Scriptures, and that you would be filled with thanksgiving and praise for the wonder of your being. Amen.

"I have formed you, I will not forget you."
(Isaiah 44:21)

"I call you to praise My name; for praise pleases My heart. There is nothing you can give Me but praise and thanks. When weak and discouraged, discover the power of praising Me. This will keep Satan at bay, and then you will keep your soul in tranquillity and peace."

A CALL TO A LOVE DUET OF NAMES

'Our Father. Hallowed be Your Name.' Jesus taught us to bless His Father's Name.
The psalmist, also, often cries out in praise of God's Name, and we, too, cry out with him in praising God's Name, now and for ever.

"Your name is the greatest in the whole world.
Your Majesty is higher than the Heavens.
Chanted even by children and babes in arms." *(Psalm 8:1)*

"Always I shall extol my King
I shall bless Your Name forever
Blessing You day after day
I shall praise Your Name forever.

He, Yawheh, is merciful, tenderhearted,
slow to anger, very loving and universally kind.
Yawheh's tenderness embraces all creatures.

Always true to His promises
Yawheh shows love in all He does
Only stumble and Yawheh at once supports you
If others bow you down, He will raise you up!

Righteous in all He does
Yawheh acts only out of love
Standing close to all who invoke Him
Close to all who invoke Yawheh faithfully.

Yawheh's praise be ever in my mouth.
And let every creature bless His Holy Name
for ever and ever. Amen."
(Psalm 145:1-2.8-9,13-14,17-18,21)

There is no doubt that God wants us to bless His Holy Name till we draw our last breath. "From farthest east to farthest west My name is great among the nations; and everywhere incense and a pure gift are offered to My name." *(Malachi 1:11)* Wouldn't it be a great grace, if, like our late Bishop Francis Thomas of Northampton, we were to die with His Name upon our lips? Our Bishop's last words as he died on Christmas Day were: "Thank You, Jesus".

Our lives need to be a constant daily praise, "Hallowed be Your Name." If we don't praise Him, Jesus says "even the very stones will cry out!" *(Luke 19:40)* God made us for praise; we can give Him nothing else. He has no need ever of our praise but it is for our own sakes we praise Him. It lifts our spirits to our Father in Heaven, as we love Him, like the psalmist who gathers everything into an enormous song of praise, we too can say: "Let everything that has breath, praise the Lord, Alleluia!" *(Psalm 150:5)*

We can learn to praise Him as we invent names for Him, or use some of the many names already mentioned in scripture: "My God, my Father, my Lord, my King, my Shepherd, my Rock, my Shield, my Fortress, my Counsellor, my Song, my Love, my Delight." In fact, if I see everything that I am and have as His gifts to me, I have to say, 'My Everything'.

Often during the day we can call upon His Name. When we were in the noviciate, we had to stop every time the clock chimed the quarter of an hour, and raise our hearts to God, blessing His Holy Name. This gave us a wonderful training in the practice of the presence of God. When the clock chimed, whoever was "on the bell" (as it was called), said aloud (nervously!) in French! "Let us raise our hearts to God", and everyone just prayed!

How endearing, in the Holy Land, to hear the children calling their father, 'Abba'! ('Daddy'!). Why not start calling Him often during the day, 'Abba', as Jesus did. As I read through the scriptures, I am made so aware of Jesus' own relationship to His Father, especially evident in John's Gospel. He is constantly calling on His Father, calling His Name, consulting Him, thanking Him, blessing Him. We too have every reason to call on Him as Scripture reminds us of the dignity He has bestowed upon us. "Think of the love the Father has lavished on us by letting us be called God's children and that is what we are." *(I John 3:1)* Living in this knowledge can surely put ourselves onto another plane of living, where nothing can steal our peace, or assurance that we are truly loved. I find this truth so consoling and encouraging. Try believing these words.

To have had an earthly father who doted on me is an immense advantage! Baptism is of course the first and great grace that puts us in this 'special' relationship with our Heavenly Father, and even if we thanked Him every day of our lives for the gift of faith bestowed then, it would never be sufficient to thank Him. No matter what happens to us, no matter what people say against us or for us, no matter what injustice or praise we experience, it matters little compared with the constant love God has for us as His children. Nothing can shake it. Let it sink into your consciousness. My own father used to cradle me to sleep as a baby; how much more will my Heavenly Father want to cradle me and caress me as He lovingly recites my name.

So "Let us boast about the Name of God and we shall stand firm." *(Psalm 20:7)* "The Name of Jesus is a strong tower, the just man runs to it, and is safe." *(Proverbs 18:10)* "Call upon God's Name and you will be saved" *(Romans 10:13)* "God save me by Your Name" *(Psalm 54:1)* "Rescue us for the sake of Your Name, blot out our sins" *(Psalm 79:9)* "God, in your temple, we reflect on Your love. God, Your praise, like Your Name, extends to the limits of the world" *(Psalm 48:9-10)*
"From the rising of the sun to the going down, the Name of the Lord is praised." *(Psalm 113:3)*

His Name is Wonderful, Counsellor, Mighty God, Prince of Peace, His Name is Saviour, His Name is Emmanuel, God with us, Jesus Christ the Anointed One. His Name is above all other names, His Name is Holy, His Name is Healing, His Name is Mercy, His Name is Hope, His Name is Strength, His Name is Love, His Name is Eternal, His Name is Comfort, His Name is Consolation, His Name is Wholeness, His Name is Power. St. Paul tells us that no one can say the Name of Jesus unless he is under the power of the Holy Spirit. He reminds us that constantly calling on the Name of Jesus with faith, brings His Presence and His saving power.

Remember that your body is the temple of the Holy Spirit and the anointing yourself with the Name of Jesus brings power against the enemy. As I drive along, I quite often anoint myself with the sign of the cross and call on the protection of the Name of Jesus. This is a powerful weapon against the enemy. If you feel tempted to sin, why not try using the name of Jesus. Saturate yourself with the Name of Jesus as you would your loved one's name. Saturate your family with the Name of Jesus. Saturate the area in which you live, with His Holy Name. Claim each family for Jesus; claim each street etc. Make reparation to Him for any abuse or disrespect for His Precious Name. Say it with love for those who use it blasphemously. Become so familiar with the Name of Jesus, that it will always be in your heart and on your lips. "My Beloved (Jesus) is mine and I am His. He pastures me among the lilies." *(Song of Songs 2:16)*

The 'Jesus Prayer', as it is called, is a wonderful means of fostering devotion to the Name of Jesus, and to praying constantly. "The interior and constant practice of the 'Jesus Prayer' involves a continuous uninterrupted invocation of the Name of Jesus with the lips, with the heart, and with the understanding, together with the awareness of His presence at all times and in all places, even during our sleep. ('I sleep but my heart is awake'). It is expressed in the words: "Lord Jesus Christ, have mercy on me a sinner!" This was the blind man's cry to Jesus as He passed by. Let's make it our own.

"Anyone who makes habitual use of this invocation experiences great consolation as a result, and feels the need to repeat it over and over again. After a while he cannot do without it, to such an extent, that he hears it repeated within him without his having spoken it with his lips … Say it softly without hurrying, this is how you will arrive at that uninterrupted activity of the heart! Try to drive all other thoughts away and repeat this experience frequently." *('In Search of the Beyond': Carlo Carretto, p70)*

The Staretz was the spiritual director of the Russian Pilgrim mentioned in the book 'In Search of Beyond' who gave him this advice about how to pray continually: "What heights of perfection, what ecstatic joy man can experience when the Lord wishes to reveal the secrets of prayer to him and purify his passions. It is an indescribable state, and the revelations of this mystery is like a foretaste of Heaven. This is the gift which they receive who seek the Lord with love and with singleness of heart."

"Here are some beads," the Staretz said, "with which you can begin to recite three thousand invocations a day. Standing or sitting, lying down or walking, keep repeating to yourself: 'Lord Jesus Christ, have mercy on me'. Say it softly, without hurrying. This is how you will arrive at that uninterrupted activity of the heart.

Joyfully I took in what the Staretz said, and made my way to my little hut. Exactly and faithfully, I began to put what I heard into practice. I had some further difficulty for a couple of days, then it all became so simple that when I was not repeating the prayer, I felt the need to start saying it again, and it ebbed and flowed within me easily and gently, with none of the tension of the first few days.

I told the Staretz about this and he commanded me to repeat it six thousand times each day adding 'Don't be anxious about it, try to be faithful to what I have recommended. God will have mercy on you.'
As I continued to pray in this way, I became light-hearted and happy . I was no longer poor. Invoking the Name of Jesus made my travelling a joyous affair, and everywhere I met with kindness. It seemed that everyone was predisposed to love me.

So here I am on the road once more, constantly reciting the Jesus Prayer, which is dearer and more precious to me than anything else. Often I cover more than seventy kilometres a day, and I have no idea where I am going. When the cold bites into me I recite the prayer more attentively, and immediately feel warmer.

If my hunger becomes too acute, I call on the Name of Jesus more frequently and forget that I am hungry.
If I feel ill, or if my leg or my back aches, I concentrate on the prayer and the pain passes.
If anyone offends me, I think of nothing but the sweet Jesus Prayer, and immediately the anger or hurt disappears, and I forget all about it. I have become a bit strange!
I no longer get anxious about anything. External realities have no hold on me, my only wish is to remain alone and pray continually. Then I am completely happy.
God knows what has taken place within me; I do not. I only know that I am happy, and that I now understand what the apostle meant when he said: Pray constantly."

('In Search of the Beyond', Carlo Carretto, p71)

The Russian Pilgrim found it easy at first but before long he experienced the powers of evil trying to prevent him from praying.

Satan tries to make things difficult for us and to give us a distaste for prayer suggesting to us that it is boring and there are far more important things we could be doing, instead of wasting time praying.

"The Lord is near to those who call upon His Name, those who are crushed in spirit, he saves." *(Psalm 34:18)*

In the Acts of the Apostles, we find the immense power of the Name of Jesus throughout and when the apostles worked miracles, it was always in the Name of Jesus. The power of His Name was so great that the authorities tried to silence the Apostles and prevent them from using His Name. "By what power and by whose name have you men done this?" they questioned. "It is the Name of Jesus, through our faith in it, which has brought back the strength of this crippled man whom you see here and who is well known to you. It is faith in that Name that has restored this man to health as you can all see." *(Acts 4:7,10)*

"The Name of Jesus Christ ... There is no other Name under Heaven, given to men, by which we must be saved." *(Acts 4:12)*

I could not do better now than to quote from Rev. John Woolley's book 'I Am With You', in which Jesus Himself revealed His message personally to him:–

"The almost instinctive speaking of My Name when life is dark and uncertain.

It is the cry of a child when reasoning ceases to function,

when human help is absent, when confidence in oneself is no longer there ...
The speaking of My Name brings into the foreground of your situation the one vital factor.
My Name can be said in helplessness ... but can be said in joy and thankfulness only seconds later!
The speaking of My Name ensures, at that very moment, the retreat of evil forces ... acknowledging that they are defeated in whatever they planned for your life.

My child, the whispering of My Name ... on waking ... on surrendering to sleep.
And very frequently during each day.
My child, call upon Me as soon as any hurtful or overwhelming situation arises, firstly, so that you may learn the lesson I have for you in it; secondly, so that I may break the pattern of events before it becomes too burdensome for you.
My child do not be afraid, at certain times to be 'invaded' ... seen in all your human weakness, but with a very definite trust in Me.
Do not feel that this vulnerability will deter others. Rather it will wonderfully speak of My power to uphold one human life ... yours."

We are told in scripture, that His Name is like ointment poured out. Allow His Name to rest on your tongue, whisper it: "Jesus, Jesus, Jesus, my love, my Lord, my God, I believe in You, I love Your Holy Name." As the priest elevates the host at Mass, speak to Jesus present on the altar. Believe He is close; call His Name Jesus, Saviour, thank Him for dying for you. Believe you are at His banqueting table and the banner over you is love *(Song of Songs 2:4)* His love. Only His love matters, receive it, let yourself be immersed in it. If and when you know the love of Jesus, then you have found the secret of life.

His Name is balm. My beloved Jesus lifts up His Voice, He says to me, "Come then, my love, my lovely one, come, for see, winter is past, the rains are over and gone. The flowers appear on the earth, the season of glad songs has come, the cooing of the turtle dove is heard in our land. Come then, my love, my lovely one, come. Show me your face, let me hear your voice, for your voice is sweet and your face is beautiful" *(Song of Songs 2:10-14)*

Dwell with Him, pronounce His Holy Name. Yield to His authority and Lordship. Our Father in Heaven, hallowed be Your Name, forever and ever. Amen.

"I call you to receive My Love, so precious that at times it will overwhelm you.
As you hear Me call your Name in the depths of your being, rejoice in Me."

There she stood, in the garden where Jesus had been buried, weeping inconsolably, absolutely heartbroken, wondering where He was. For a moment Mary Magdalene thought she had lost her love, her beloved Jesus. In panic, she searched everywhere for Him. "They have taken away my Lord", she said to the figures she didn't realise were angels sitting there where the body of Jesus had been, "and I don't know where they have put Him". As she was speaking, she saw another figure standing there whom she didn't recognize either! Jesus said to her, "Woman, why are you weeping, who are you looking for?" Supposing Him to be the gardener, she said, "Sir, if you have taken Him away, tell me where you have put Him, and I will go and remove Him." "Mary", Jesus said to her. The moment He spoke her name was the moment she knew who He was and she said to Him in Hebrew, "Rabbuni" which means "Master". *(John 20:11-16)*

Put yourself in Mary's place. What a moment for her! She must have been ecstatic, overjoyed, comforted, consoled, reassured, restored ... words could hardly describe her feelings. Here she encounters the Lord Jesus Himself, the Holy One of Israel, the Crucified Saviour, the Risen Lord of the Universe. No one else in the whole world mattered to her at that moment, as she heard Him lovingly pronounce her name: 'Mary'.

Imagine you are there in the garden as well and you, too, hear Jesus pronounce your name. As you hear Him whisper your name, your heart will glow with a new response of love and gratitude.

Just like Mary you will experience and believe in His deep personal love for you; your life will change and you will begin to become whole. Nothing else will matter to you except knowing His wonderful love. Everything will come together for you, the more you allow His love to penetrate your whole being. You will be changed.

Only love changes us. Only love restores, gives us a new chance, a new vision. Only love hopes in us again and allows us to live and blossom once more. Their two hearts met, so must ours, as they began to beat as one. We find it so hard sometimes, when we feel unloved, to listen to the loving words that God is saying to us. It is more than we can take, too good to be true. We are good at hearing Jesus condemn us (a thing, of course, He never does!). Only Satan condemns the brethren *(Revelation 12:10)*. Some of us have still to discover the God of love, as Mary did on that great day of Resurrection.

> "I will betroth you to Myself forever
> betroth you with integrity and justice
> with tenderness and love.
> I will betroth you to Myself with faithfulness.
> And you will come to know Yawheh...
> I will love the Unloved.
> I will say to 'No-People' of mine, you are 'My People'
> and they will answer 'You are my God'."
>
> *(Hosea 2:19-20:24)*

There would be no turning back for Mary now. She knew His love for her, so deep, so tender, so personal, so reassuring. How could she ever doubt Him again? She could rely on His faithfulness; she needed to know no more. It wouldn't matter now what life would bring, disappointment, opposition, rejection, etc ... She knew the one thing necessary. She would never need to look for Him again. He had found her.

Isn't it always the same with God? He gives us freedom to do what we like, go where we like, keep His commandments or break them. Like the father awaiting his prodigal son's return, God is always there. "I have branded you on the palm of my hand". *(Isaiah 49:16)*

God can never look at the palm of His hand without seeing your name.

This is the content of our faith: "Not our love for God, but God's Love for us when He sent His Son." *(1 John 4:10)* God is love, God loves me. Not only that but Jesus prayed the night before He died to the Father "that you love them as You loved Me.... so that Your love for Me may be in them". *(John17:23,26)* Incredible! How can we take it in? As she turned, Mary saw Jesus standing there, though, as I said, she did not recognize Him. *(John 20:15)*

Is there a message here for me? Is He not sometimes so close that I cannot see Him? Can I accept His faithful, unconditional love for me? Can I believe my name means so much to Him? Am I too busy seeking Him in every newfangled idea, every wonder-worker healer, that I forget He is within me? 'The kingdom of God is within you'.
Do I forget that He promised to be with me always? And even if I am too busy, I can still, "Place the tents far apart, and draw near with the heart."

So listen as He calls your name:– Jane - Anne - Helen - Maria - Frances -Laura - Andrea - Evelyn - Betty - Mary - Moira - Peter - Jim - Cyril - Thomas - Gerald - John - James - Michael, etc. etc. Let your preciousness to Him sink into you as He lovingly recites your name. Hear Him say your name like nobody else's. Even if your spouse or your best friend loves you and repeats your name, it could never contain so much love as if Jesus said it.
Let it ring in your ears.... listen again. 'O, that today you would listen to His voice ...' Believe in His appreciation of you, His total acceptance of you, just as you are, His

respect and recognition of you, His courtesy towards you. See how He delights in you. Remember His words to you every day in scripture, telling you who you are in Him. Just as you read over and over again your friend's or your lover's letter, read His words to you. "I am my beloved's and His desire is for me". *(Song of Songs 7:10)* As you feel Him close to your heart, hear Him say to you: "I shall give you the gift of my love" *(Song of Songs 7:14)* and your response could be: "Set me as a seal on your heart, so that I have no love but yours" *(Song of Songs 8:6).* Again "His love is strong as death, it's a love no flood can quench, no torrent drown". *(Song of Songs 8:7)* Let these words sink into your heart, as you imagine Jesus standing or sitting beside you.

Imagine you hear Him inventing names for you. What names does He invent? What do you feel when you hear Him call you by these names? Don't be anxious if, at first, you cannot hear Jesus saying your name lovingly. If your self-image is poor, you will find this exercise doubly difficult. If you are used to thinking negatively about yourself, you will find it hard to believe anything positive about yourself. You will not want to hear Jesus calling you love-names. Many of us still have a long way to go to realize that God's love makes us lovable and His Love is therefore healing. We are not used to unconditional love! The more we grow in wholeness in Him, the more we discover the truth of who we are before Him.

Our love-duet will be more in tune as we let Him love us, as we grow to believe in His Love; we will become more truly ourselves.

Go one step further and imagine you hear Jesus inventing exactly the same names for you as you invented for Him, all the names except those that directly express His divinity.... Do not be frightened ... expose yourself to the intensity of His love ... His indescribable love. It streams from Him like a never-ending spring. "He who believes in Me will never grow weary". *(John 6:35)* "Whoever comes to Me will never thirst ... From his breast will flow fountains of living water" *(John 7:38)* Jesus longs for us to experience His refreshing love. Only His love will refresh us spiritually. Stop worrying now about whether you deserve His love. Of course you don't. *You never can.* Stop trying to earn His love, you cannot. It is freely given. Simply rejoice in it and receive it. Let yourself be spoilt by it.

> "O come to the water, all who are thirsty
> though you have no money, come!
> Buy corn without money, buy and eat!
> and at no cost buy wine and milk.
> Why spend money on what is not bread;
> your wages on what fails to satisfy?
> Listen, listen to me.
> And you will have good things to eat
> and rich food to enjoy.
> Pay attention, come to me;
> Listen, and your soul will live.   *(Isaiah 55:1-3)*

In this passage above, God is talking about His everlasting love for us. Love is manifested as a free gift – unfailing, creative love. We cannot force God to love us. We can only receive His love. All that He does is done out of love, for His essence is love. Scripture tells us "God is love". *(I John 4:16)* What a revelation! How can we grasp it!

"My song is love unknown
My Saviour's love to me
Love to the loveless shown
That they might lovely be.
O, who am I, that for my sake
My love should take frail flesh and die?

Here might I stay and sing
No story so divine;
Never was love, dear King,
Never was grief like Thine.
This is my Friend, in whose sweet praise
I, all my days, could gladly spend."

(Samuel Crossman, 1624-1684)

Since I am a free person, I can choose to accept His love, or separate myself from His love. It's a good practice to just sit with Him for a few moments daily, to allow Him to love you. I find it a great help to do this before the Blessed Sacrament. I simply tell Him I've come to let Him love me for a while. I hear Him say, "Josephine, I love you". (You can do this even while you are waiting for the vegetables to cook!) I try to absorb His love, which sometimes overwhelms me.

I am part of a Love-Duet between God and myself. Though a duet would normally be two equal parts, the love we have for God and our response to Him could never equal His love for us. However, we can do our best and praise Him with our whole being and make our life a Song of Praise and so join in His Creation Song with more awareness and love, until creation is fulfilled.

Final Prayer

I love you Jesus, my love, above all things. I repent with
my whole heart for ever having offended you. Never let
me be separated from you. Grant that I may love you
always and daily do your will. Help me never to doubt
your love. Thank you for loving me. Let your love
transform me. Forgive me all my sins. Forgive the times
I forget that you still love me. Forgive the times I don't
believe in your love. Help me to be more *aware* now of
that love. Jesus, I love you. I bless your Holy Name.

Thank you for calling me by my name.

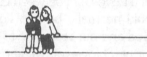

"I call you to fullness of life, which I came to bring you. In Me you'll know a fullness never known before. Thank Me for everything which contributes to this fullness."

A CALL TO FULLNESS OF LIFE

For me, fullness of life began in 1975.

Prior to that time, I thought I had a fairly full, contented life, having had a happy childhood at 5, John Street, Limerick, Ireland. As a child, I was immersed in the love of five sisters and two brothers, and of course beloved parents. They lived for their children, loved them dearly and always put them first. It is, therefore, to my parents that I first owe my love for life.

Dad was lively and talented, with a good sense of humour. He had a great love of everything good and wholesome; nature in all its seasons, art, music, poetry, carpentry and above all, life itself. One never knew what new creation would emerge from his skilled hands. He sang very well, loved painting, bird watching, kept birds and bred them, was a keen cyclist, swimmer, even fisherman at times, wrote poetry 'at the drop of a hat', and generally brought to the world a brightness and giftedness which were so much part of him, that they could easily be taken for granted.

He could have been a professional singer, or even a professor, had opportunity passed his way. His maxim was: 'make every post a winning post or take the ball on the hop'. This was a very apt saying for one who taught us how to live positively, by making the best of every opportunity. He passed on so much love, inspiration, goodness to us. As I prayed by his death-bed, he sat up, for the last time, said his last words clearly: "Everything is perfect", and he fell back and died. He certainly had left everything in perfect order. Mass was just about to be celebrated for him in his room as he died peacefully in the arms of the church on the 8th January 1981.

What a privilege to give him such a send off. In his poem, "The poet is dead", he sums up a little his motivation in life:

> "I tried to make the world bright
> and picture it with pride.
> I tried to rhyme the future
> By many a river-side".

Before my Father married he spent many a happy hour in his little hut beside the bank of the River Shannon in Plassey, Limerick. Here, in this peaceful spot, he experienced a deep sense of God's presence in Nature. This shows itself in his poetry, his prayer, his thankfulness to God for the joy of living and his love for the 'open air' life.

Thus, in a wonderful way, I would say, my father lived a fullness of life that few experience today. He was married at forty, had eight children, and was greatly blessed by God. He had a living faith in God, who would never let him down. His own father died when he was two years old, and having been deprived of a father's love and companionship as a boy, he did everything in his power to make sure we were not deprived in the same way. He was a great father.

I remember him lulling my little sister Anne to sleep as he fondly cradled her in his arms, singing, or humming sweet lullabies. We all had the same treatment. Each child in turn was consecrated to Our Lady of Lourdes at birth, (the picture hung over the mantelpiece) and through this dedication, a father's blessing and protection was claimed over each one of our lives from babyhood. The family rosary sometimes recited here or the Angelus regularly recited, brought everything to a standstill.

One moment of faith-testing for my parents must have been when my eldest sister, Mary and brother Jim, almost died of a fatal disease, contracted while visiting a sick uncle in hospital. Only the prayers of my family, the nuns at school, friends, doctors and nurses, brought the desired healing, giving glory to God who never fails to hear the cry of the poor and of those in distress.

Jesus says "Ask and you will receive" and he reminds us of the importunate friend in Luke chapter eleven, who called one night to a friend in great need. "I tell you" Jesus says, "if the man does not get up and give for friendship's sake, persistence will be enough to make him get up and give his friend all he wants".
Isaiah reminds us too "Long before they call me I will answer, before they stop speaking I shall have heard" *(Isaiah 65:24)*

The powerful prayer of everyone saw a truly great miracle in our family. As a thanksgiving, my father never allowed us to eat meat on St. Stephen's Day, offering a little "family" sacrifice to our Heavenly Father, in gratitude for sparing the lives of his two beloved children.

I still vividly recall the great day they returned from hospital. I must have been so small, but I remember the excitement, and the tears, the two kind nurses to tea, the enormous box of chocolates that appeared in thanksgiving, and even the sweet I couldn't wait to choose, as I had never seen such a big box of chocolates in my life. *Good memories always bring healing and new life, and it is important to return to them from time to time and even to enjoy them again.*

Home for me was about love, security, cosiness, good parents, acceptance, fun and laughter together, singing as a family, hurts and forgiveness, simplicity of life, success and celebration, outings in the country, mushroom, cowslip and primrose picking, bike rides, love and healing. I had a truly blest childhood.

My mother was the heart of the home, always serving and self-sacrificing, cheerful with a good sense of humour. She loved a good laugh, and we used to sometimes find her sitting by the fire, engrossed in a good story, laughing away to herself. She was a loving, watchful, presence. Her quiet strength reminds me of Mary, our heavenly mother, "who pondered all these things in her heart". She was a great support to my father in every way and allowed him to blossom into the person he became.

Irish mothers in those days were saintly, (some still are), often humble and self-effacing, with little or no thought for themselves. Their role was in the home. We would be devastated when we arrived home from school to find our mother out. Our greatest joy was to arrive home to the smell of apple or rhubarb tart, and it wasn't long before most of them were devoured by hungry children. A treat!

In her own way my mother was a natural psychologist, who understood the needs of each child. She knew how to humour or reprimand. She gave encouragement and hope to many people around and I still hear her words ringing in my ears, "You'll see, everything will be alright, trust in Almighty God, He knows best". It was like a refrain that so often came from her lips that sometimes I thought we'd never reach the town, as she talked to so many people on the way! The week before she died, she revealed her secret to me. I was in her room, alone with her, and I said to her "Mom, isn't it strange how I'm the only one who became a nun", and she let out her secret. Had my dad known! She told me that she prayed every day that one of her six girls would become a nun. God heard her prayer.

Many Irish mothers realised the great privilege of having a son or daughter specially consecrated to God and they prayed that one child might be a priest or a nun. I wish it were the same today, for "the harvest is rich but the labourers are few". *(Matthew 9:37)* God needs many more labourers from generous homes. My mother died peacefully on 25th March 1981, with the family gathered round her saying the rosary. My sister and I, who had often spent night and day with her, for six weeks before she died, had just left the room. This is often how it happens in the end for those who are very close. Indeed a sacrifice!

My mother's greatest sacrifice when she was dying was that, having spent her last years looking after dad, she was too ill herself to be there the day he actually died.

My brother, Jim, beautifully sums up my parents' life in the following two poems, written by him after their death in 1981.

To My Mother, Josie

My mother is the very throb of love,
The sheer embodiment of all my good,
The softness of the woodland dove,
The heart and soul of every gentle mood.

She is the refuge where life's sorrows fade,
The place of peace where all is still and calm,
The quietness of the primrose-speckled glade,
The troubled spirit's healing, easeful balm.

No thought of self her mind can ever fill,
She gives to others all she has and more,
Like mountain stream or meadow's rippling rill
Her bounty fills my life for evermore.

Her strength lies hidden 'neath her gentle cloak,
Her inner core a courage to amaze,
As deeply-rooted as the forest oak,
Wellspring of hope for others all her days.

Her work is done and she has gone away,
Her life's last lessons into us instilled,
To join her spouse on sunny uplands gay,
Until they greet us there, by God's sweet will.

Ode to Plassey Falls
- On The Death of a Poet -

Thy Falls are gentle now, their thunder stilled,
The roaring waters gone for evermore,
To light our homes and towns and drive our mills,
From quiet dams, so far from Plassey's shore.

The salmon, giants of yesteryear, are dead,
Their race diminished by the shrunken flow,
And little islands claim the river's bed,
Where once the rushing waters tumbled o'er.

Thy Poet, too, is dead, the bell has tolled.
His agile pen no more thy praise shall sing,
His body in the clay lies chill and cold,
His spirit waits the Judgement's joyful ring.

The Poet, the Salmon and the Falls in glory,
Have given of themselves that we might be,
To live in pride of them and tell their story,
To generations they shall never see.

His splendid spirit knew not Earth's restraints,
Untrammelled, free, his destined way he trod,
His inward eye did guide his joyful plaints,
And made him one with Nature and with God.

He and his chosen love gave all their seed,
The rich beginnings that they never had,
And nurtured, fostered, cared for every need,
That all our childhood memories should be glad.

He gave us strength and courage for the fight,
And school room weapons suited to our times,
That poverty our days should never blight,
Our lives secure in gentler, easier climes.

He is at peace now, and his spirit free,
To roam the sunny uplands of his dreams,
To mark the finches on the rowan tree,
And cast a fly on heavenly Plassey streams.

At the early age of ten, I felt the call to become a nun. I had no idea what this meant, except that I knew I wanted 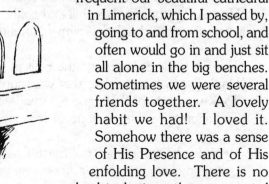 to give my life to God. I used to frequent our beautiful cathedral in Limerick, which I passed by, going to and from school, and often would go in and just sit all alone in the big benches. Sometimes we were several friends together. A lovely habit we had! I loved it. Somehow there was a sense of His Presence and of His enfolding love. There is no doubt during these *special* moments that the seed of a vocation to priesthood or religious life was sown. Sometimes I would walk around the cathedral and look up at the various statues. At the statue of St. Thérèse of Lisieux, I would ask her if I would become a nun, and nearly always she would nod her head in the affirmative. Strangely enough, if you look at a statue long enough, it will almost speak!

When I told my parents of my intention to become a nun, they tried to dissuade me, as I was only ten years old. I kept coming back to the idea for the next few years, pestering my parents especially my mother, to allow me to go away to school. So, at thirteen, having talked with my nun headmistress and my friend who came with me, arrangements were made for us to go to central Ireland, to learn 'how to become nuns'. God's ways are his own and his plan for our lives must be fulfilled, and so, he diverted our course to the Daughters of the Holy Ghost Juniorate in Monaghan, since my friend's sister, who was a Daughter of the Holy Ghost, told my mother to let us come with her order instead, as we would then get home on holidays and my parents would see us again. My poor Dad cried for three weeks after I left, as I split up the happy home and family, which, I believe was never the same again. The sacrifice for them was great, not only would they miss me, but they would also miss the savings needed for my outfit for the Juniorate. The very same day my sister, Mary, emigrated to South Africa, to be with her future husband.

After Dad's death in 1981 we found, still intact in his cabinet, a letter written to the Sister in charge of the Juniorate in Monaghan and her reply:-

5 John Street, Limerick.
August 23rd 1953.

Dear Sister,

With a feeling of profound sorrow I received your letter and I might inform you that each and every one of my children, (God blest her mother and myself with eight lovely souls) I have a sincere love for, and it is with deepest regret I part with my lovely child Josephine, 'welcome be the will of God.'

I have learned of her decision and she's had this calling for some time now, ever since she was ten or twelve years old. I would not interfere in my love's future. She has made this steadfast choice and never wavered, even when she was disappointed in other arrangements that were being made for her.

She was prepared to go alone, when the opportunity offered and now, she is about to leave her happy home for the Vineyard of Him, who gave us life. I give my blessing and prayers that God in His goodness will give her the reward she deserves when her services in His regard in this life, draw to a close.

In conclusion, I invoke the Mother of God to give her grace and patience, strength and courage, in her young age, to carry out the duties which she has to perform in the coming years, and may the Holy Ghost, her spouse, grant her every consolation, when parting with her father, and mother, brothers and sisters, in those lonely days, that are coming fast now, with her departure.

Sincerely yours,

J. E. Walsh

Caritas !   Holy Ghost Convent,
                                                                   Monaghan,
                                                                   25.8.53

Dear Mr. & Mrs. Walsh,
I received dear Josephine's letter and yours this morning
and am delighted you are willing to allow your child to
give herself to God. You will never regret it. It is such an
honour and blessing to have one of your children specially
picked out by God, for His work in this world. It will bring
great favours on you and your children and whatever sacrifices
you make for the child, will return to you, in blessings
innumerable.

Our fee for a whole year's board and tuition is £40. Those
who can give it, do so, but those who cannot come up to
that amount, try to give the half and never miss it, as God
is never outdone in generosity. I leave it to you to send
what in all justice you can afford.

We would like Josephine to come on the 12th Sept.
If you have no one to bring her, sister will meet her at
Amien Street Station at 2.30 p.m. at the latest - She will
take charge of her there and bring her safely here.
With all good wishes and asking God, to bless you with
your family.

Sincerely yours in Spiritu Sancto,

Sr. Genevieve of the S.H.

Sister Genevieve of the Sacred Heart, (D.H.G.)

I stayed in Monaghan, Ireland, for two years and then went on to school in Pontypool for another two years, after which time I entered Religious life. I was seventeen, and was professed at nineteen. I remember Profession day well. The weather was beautiful and the service was out of this world. My parents were there with my eldest brother and his girlfriend. One of the most moving events of the day was receiving the blessing from our own father in silence, just before Mass. All that day I felt I was in Heaven, walking on air. We were told that if we died that day we would go straight up.. Not sure if that was what I wanted. 'Safer on earth', I thought!

I found being a Religious a great blessing. It freed me in many ways to devote myself to God and His work. Nothing mattered to me only Him, and though I felt quite incapable of being a student teacher (the task assigned me), I knew I would overcome anything with God's help. His presence overwhelmed me and that was all that mattered. I remember trying to do my best in everything, with only one thought to please Him. There were jobs I was given that I wasn't prepared for but in some miraculous way God rescued me and brought me through everything.

As the years passed, community life was reasonably happy, though there were some challenges! I qualified as a musician. My dream was to ensure equality of opportunity in music for Catholic children in state schools, and so I volunteered to leave the convent school, and work in St. Gregory's R.C. School in Bedford. It was hard pioneering work as the school had nothing but a broken drum. However, on appealing to the headmaster and music adviser for Bedford, my demands were met and I was treated like a spoilt child. I was given books, instruments, instrumental teachers, a music room, in fact every encouragement to fulfil my dream. I was very happy. It was not long before the fruits of my labours were evident, and we soon had a choir and an orchestra, which improved weekly. The good seed sown is still bearing fruit in this school today! I loved music, I felt I was winning and we had great joy in working together. I ate, slept and drank music. At the same time, my spiritual life was getting along reasonably, I thought. Prayer was a bit boring and meditation, morning and evening, was an excuse often for an extra half hour sleep! I felt small talk was a waste of time especially when I could be doing music, and so was slow to encourage coffee after Mass or any meetings where I might have to speak.

As already mentioned a retreat changed my life. Fr. James Hawes spoke about God's love, Salvation, New Life etc., and I began to feel different. Later on, of course, I realised that he was giving us a Life in the Spirit Seminar without our knowing!

God is very wise, He knows how we tick and He alone knows how to get through our barriers. He knows that I am a spontaneous person, and if something did not happen for me immediately I would have nothing more to do with it.

Fr. James was a superb speaker and he had a great gift of encouragement to get us to praise God every evening for about an extra hour. Since I played the guitar, I went along, and even enjoyed the evenings. On the fifth day, he invited anyone who wanted to be prayed with, to come forward for individual prayer. I was rather nervous about this and wondered what on earth I would ask prayer for. I decided to ask for prayer so that I would give my life to God more. I thought I couldn't go wrong in asking for this! I was very shy in those days, wouldn't even read at Mass, so the idea of asking a priest to pray over me was almost beyond my capabilities. I knocked at his door, "Come in sister" he said, "Do you want to sit or kneel?" "Oh, I'll kneel please Father," I said. I thought that would be safer!

I know he prayed in a funny language over me, as he placed his hands on my head, for about two minutes. I got up, thanked him and came out to find everything looking different. It was as if scales had fallen from my eyes. Everything looked more beautiful – the trees, shrubs, flowers, atmosphere, even the Community had a new glow and I felt I could like people better, even those I hadn't previously liked too well! "Earth is crammed with Heaven and every common bush afire with God, but only he who sees, takes off his shoes." *(Elizabeth Barrett Browning)* I shall never forget that moment.

My desire for spiritual things grew, and He led me more and more to streams of living water. It was the beginning of something wonderful, of a new way of life. The whole orientation of energy in my life was channelled to new pastures and I began to experience an amazing new life style, more joyful, more invigorating, more spirit-filled than ever before. I felt I was coming alive as a 'whole person'.

One day, about a month after Fr. James' prayer over me, I was praising God for the beautiful horse chestnut trees down our drive, on my way to school, when suddenly my praise went off into 'tongue' prayer. Suddenly I realised that I had been speaking in tongues. This delighted and amused me! I never wanted the gift of tongues but God chose to give it to me to transform my prayer life and to help with 'words of knowledge' when praying with people for inner healing. Sometimes through this 'tongue' prayer God will give you a helpful word or picture for the person with whom you are praying. This greatly speeds up and facilitates the prayer for healing. Often deep emotional hurts are healed in this way. I believe the gift of tongues is beautifully summed up by St. Paul:

"The Spirit, too, comes to help us in our weakness. For when we cannot choose words in order to pray properly, the Spirit himself expresses our plea in a way that could never be put into words and God, who knows everything in our hearts, knows perfectly well what He means, and that the pleas of the saints expressed by the Spirit, are according to the mind of God". (Romans 8:26-27)

It was Jesus Himself who first mentioned the gift of tongues. In Mark's Gospel we read: "These are the signs associated with believers; in My Name, they will cast out devils; they will have the gift of tongues." *(Mark 16:17-18)*

Then people began to say, "What's happened to Josephine? She's on drugs." And sure enough, it was the drug of the Holy Spirit. It must have been like a Tabor experience, the happiness of which I had never experienced before. God had filled me with joy, he had released me to become myself, freely and out of love for me. I was overwhelmed. I glowed all over. It was as if I was taken up on to another plane of living. I used to be critical before this experience but I just felt I couldn't criticise after that. I began to like myself better. People's opinions of me have never bothered me since that day! If they think I'm good or wonderful, it doesn't make me so, and if they think the contrary that I'm not so good, it doesn't make me bad either. If they don't like me it's their loss, not mine.

But I knew I was beloved of the Father, and in the depths of my being I experienced the deep personal love of Jesus for me like never before, so nothing else mattered to me. My prayer life changed and I changed from being someone who watched the clock to being someone with a living relationship with God. Jesus came alive for me in a most wonderful way. I wanted to sit with Him all the time. Scripture came alive, and I wanted to actually talk about Jesus and my faith for the first time in my life. It came quite easily.

I was given a gift for speaking out boldly for the Lord, and for evangelising. Mother Teresa once said "Evangelisation is this: I have Jesus in my heart, and I want to put Him in yours." This became my dream. It still is. Jesus Himself assures us "If anyone openly declares himself for Me in the presence of men the Son of Man will declare Himself for him in the presence of God's angels." *(Luke 12:8)*

My faith seemed to have taken on a new 'leap', so I began to expect much more from God when I prayed, and things began to happen. I began to see God's Providence working in extraordinary ways, especially for the poor and needy. He provided me with a café for the homeless for one year, plus everything we needed for the running of it, including food, fridge, etc. We fed many people during that year, not only physically, but spiritually too. A very kind and generous benefactor allowed us to use his premises for nothing.

The horizons of God's poor quickly opened wider and wider as God put me in touch with the needy. On one of my visits to the shrine of Our Lady at Medjugorje our guide invited us to visit refugees living in railway carriages in a siding ten miles away. We found over a hundred families in appalling conditions. It was just after the war. They had no sanitation, very poor food and little clothing. The carriages were stifflingly hot in summer and extremely cold in winter with only parafin heaters. We were so overwhelmed at their poverty that we gave them all we had. We just had to get back to help them. How to find a way of doing so? The task seemed impossible.

I went to the prayer meeting at Milton Keynes and I asked God to find a way. Gerard Pomfret, a member of the prayer group, gave me a Newsletter through which, after a number of phone calls, I was eventually led to Sheila Brunt. She was God's answer to our prayers!

Unknown to me for the past five years she had been taking aid to refugees in Bosnia, Albania, Ukraine, and Romania. She holds an H.G.V. licence and drives big articulated lorries. She kindly agreed to transport our aid for us to the railway carriages in Capljina. It was God who put us in touch in an amazing way, just when we needed someone to help us get aid out to the refugees.

Then recently, out of the blue, Pat and James, a couple whom I had never met, phoned offering to pay for me to go with them to Capljina, in view of their helping the refugees.

Sheila Brunt came with us, and on our way back we felt

that the refugees greatest need at the moment was for money, one of the reasons being that the Canadian Government was offering a new life in Canada to these refugees if they could get a visa and a medical.

Since they are so poor, we decided we must get some money out to them quickly. There are fifty train carriages in all, and if we gave one hundred pounds to every family living in the train carriages, we would need at least five thousand pounds. I didn't think this would be a problem to God. When Jesus needed money to pay his taxes He sent Peter to find a shekel in the fish's mouth! *(Matthew 17:27)* We thanked God in advance there and then for hearing our prayer, and for giving us the £5,000.

The very next day, I had to go to Falmouth in Cornwall to lead a week-end on prayer. On arrival in London Paddington I had time for a cup of coffee. A gentleman approached the very small table where I was sitting. "May I sit here?" he asked. "Certainly," I said, "you're welcome." I told him that I had just come back from Bosnia, and was very upset about the plight of the refugees, and that I had never before seen their morale so low. "It's amazing," I said. "I don't find them bitter, although they have lost everything. I have some photos here of them if you would like to see them." He had hardly seen them when he took out his cheque book and wrote me a cheque for one thousand pounds for the refugees. It was all done in such haste that he forgot to sign it!

I thank God for this generous good samaritan's wife who later signed and returned the cheque, and for her husband's spontaneous response to the cry of God's poor. May he be blessed always in what he does, and may those to whom he gives be blessed also. There's nothing better than someone giving from the heart.

God seemed to hear our prayer immediately, since after his generous start, money simply flowed in. Within five days God gave us the £5,000, which Sheila Brunt took out and distributed to the very grateful families.

And then on my return from Cornwall my heart was so touched by a letter I received from a young unmarried mother who gave all she had:

Dear Sister Josephine,

God must be working through you for these families. I've not felt able to give to charity, being a single parent with a six year old.

Then it made me think, all I have comes from God, and I have more than them. Money I hadn't expected came to me and I am able to share my good fortune.
Bless you in your work,

Margaret and Jennifer.

P.S. I enclose £50.00 for your poor.

And so the miracles continue! I share this Good News with you because I believe we do not share the good news enough. Nobody wants to come to your door to share good news, yet they will come and share bad news. One of our neighbours was so overjoyed the other day, because she had become a grandmother. Sr. Helen suggested she called the neighbours together to celebrate, and why not?

We don't celebrate life enough. Jesus tells us in the Gospel about the woman who lost something, found it, and called the neighbours together to celebrate. I must admit, that since the Lord changed me, I now know how to celebrate life, and I try to help others to do the same. This does not mean that you will never feel pain. You may actually feel more pain than ever before, because you are more in touch with people's pain and happiness. Try not to let life pass you by, and do your best for everyone whenever and wherever you are. In this small way, you and I will then help to change the world, and make it a more beautiful place to live in.

We shall only pass by once, so whatever kindness we can do today, let us try to do it, knowing that it is to Him! It is much easier and nicer to be kind rather than to be harsh and miserable. What are we waiting for? Make someone happy today. Brighten someone's life with a smile, a gift, a kindness, overlook a fault and be more positive. Stop being negative and saying negative things. Look up. See Christ in each other. He longs to shine forth in our lives.

After God had blessed me during this retreat, I had a burning desire to start a prayer group. Before this I thought that my prayer life was my own personal possession, and not to be shared with anyone else. I ran a mile from prayer meetings, and I certainly didn't think much of people jumping up and down praising Jesus. This wasn't for me!

However, the Master Plan is always in operation, whether we know it or not. God arranged that I was late for lunch one day and there was no place to sit in our quite full dining-room, except opposite a visiting priest. I was full of this retreat I had just made, and was longing to start a prayer group but had no idea how to do it. I started to talk to him about this possibility. Enough said! God had already arranged it. This priest was similarly interested. So, at his invitation, a group of us, with large 'L' plates on, launched out into this awesome way of praying and the group that started in 1975 is still in existence and from it several other groups have been kindled around the country. This group continues today under the leadership of Marcel and Sylvia Grech-Marguerat. The Lord lit a flame that has grown into a fire, that no one can put out.

Everything spoke to me of Him – the stars, each called by name, the moon, the sun, the wind blowing through my hair, the frost, cold, thunder, lightning. His touch was in everything, all around me. Teilhard de Chardin's writings came alive for me and I love the Hymn of the Universe and the 'Milieu Divin' to this day.

The sacrifice of the Mass came alive in a new way, and I began to understand the Communion of Saints more clearly, and the power of offering joys, sufferings, work, prayers to God in union with each Mass offered throughout the world to save souls. Isn't it wonderful to know that every minute of the day somewhere in some country around the world the Holy Mass is being offered?
So we can make the Mass our daily offering, whether we can physically attend or not. Mass is everything. I learnt that, wherever I went, He was there too.

"Wither shall I go from Your Spirit?
Or whither shall I go from Your Presence?
If I ascend to Heaven You are there,
If I make my bed in Sheol You are there!
If I take the wings of the morning
And dwell in the uttermost parts of the sea,
even there Your hand would hold me,
Your right hand hold me fast" *(Psalm 139:7-10)*

At the 1978 International Charismatic Conference in Dublin, we were enthralled at the harmony and beauty of the tongue prayer of at least twenty thousand people, gathered together by the Holy Spirit from eighty different countries in the world. In the early days of renewal we learnt much very quickly, and in no time, the Holy Spirit showered His gifts upon us for ministry. He never let us down. He gave us specific gifts like discernment of spirits when dealing with a deliverance ministry. We have seen many wonderful healings before our very eyes. The Lord Himself led me step by step through the type of training He wanted for me, sometimes within my own Catholic family, sometimes with our fellow Christians.

A useful training was a three year course in pastoral counselling which included a psychotherapy group which taught me much about 'projection'. This knowledge serves me well in helping people towards inner healing, and in understanding how we project our own hurts onto others.

Requests to give week-ends in liturgy, days of renewal, and inner healing seminars in the Holy Spirit started to come, as well as other specific work with teenagers and young adults. So, the pasture land changed to shepherding the sheep and feeding the lambs in a more spiritual way. Charismatic Renewal, I believe, is one of the greatest sources of life and healing within the Catholic church. It is sad that it is misunderstood by many Christians (even bishops and priests). It is a tool of the Holy Spirit to renew the church.

Baptism in the Holy Spirit, (a special anointing and dedication of one's life to Jesus as Lord), is among the greatest of graces for any individual Christian. It is a very personal commitment to Jesus Christ as Lord of your life. Only you can make this commitment and only Jesus baptises in the Holy Spirit. The people who might pray with you, are only instruments. This grace however can be given by God at any time, I have a friend, David Lloyd, who received it while standing at his kitchen stove cooking porridge. Even now, he still calls it his 'gas stove experience'.
Others receive it while praying alone, or even while out walking appreciating God's world, others again experience it while resting in bed. Others, still, receive Baptism in the Spirit in their darkest moments like St. Ignatius, who tormented himself over his past sins, though he had confessed them. He had no peace of mind.

Rahner explains: "Like a man threading beads on a string, Inigo (Ignatius) reflected on sin after sin from his past. No confessor was of any avail. All taste for spiritual things vanished. The whole effort of conversion suddenly appeared absurd. Then he would try to force the return of grace through an eight day fast. In vain! Soon he was on the brink of desperation and suicide. Like a cry from the very depths rose his appeal to the God who had deserted him: 'Hasten, Lord, to my aid, for I find no salvation in man and creatures. If there were a dog I might run after to secure help, I should do it.' God gave him the answer. Slowly there came into his tortured soul, the comfort of grace. Suddenly it was 'as though a cloak had been taken from his shoulders'. Fearful yet enraptured, he questioned himself: 'What is this new life, which I am now commencing?' The grace of the Spirit streamed now over his soul.

It was on the steps of the Dominican church, as the evening Angelus was pealing, that his spirit began to be raised aloft and in the imagined harmony of three wonderful organ keys, he contemplated the mystery of the Trinity. Tears of joy ran down his cheeks; from now on until his life's close, Inigo's eyes were to remain inflamed by this weeping before God. He beheld as from afar, the humanity of Our Lord, the manner of His Presence in the Blessed Sacrament, His Holy Mother.

And all this so clearly with such sweet simplicity, so unspoilt by man's clumsy understanding, that Inigo could describe the new manner of knowledge only in these terms: 'At Manresa, God treated me as a child and I should dishonour the very majesty of God were I to doubt that God had indeed treated me thus.'

Another time, Ignatius had an experience on the bank of the River Cordoner, where the eyes of his spirit began to open and he understood spiritual things beyond him. Were he to put together all the experiences of his life time they would not have been as great as this great grace received on one single occasion. His spirit was illuminated. He threw himself down on his knees before the Crucifix which stood nearby, to express his gratitude to God. Such was God's grace as he sang with the psalmist:

'The Lord's unfailing love and mercy still continue fresh as the morning, as sure as the sunrise. The Lord is all I have and so I put my hope in Him.' These precious moments changed Ignatius' life forever." *('St. Ignatius Loyola', Leonard von Matt and Hugo Rahner, S.J., pp 33-34)*

Besides the gift of Tongues, the gift of Tears is sometimes given with the Baptism in the Holy Spirit, as is often the gift of deep peace, joy or even laughter. These are surely signs of the Holy Spirit. God comes in all ways and at all times. "The wind blows where it will, you hear its sound, but you cannot tell where it comes from or where it is going. That is how it is with those who are born of the Spirit" *(John 3:8)*

"A breeze passes in the night. When did it spring up? Whence does it come? Whither is it going? No man knows. No one can compel the spirit, the gaze or the light of God to descend upon him. On some given day, a man suddenly becomes conscious that he is alive to a particular perception of the divine, spread everywhere about him. Question him: When did this state begin for him? He cannot tell. All he knows is that a new spirit has crossed his life."

('Le Milieu Divin', Teilhard de Chardin, pp 128-9)

Some people are very frightened by anything to do with the Holy Spirit or His gifts or charisms, and imagine they will lose control of their lives. They forget that 'self control' is one of the fruits of the Holy Spirit. "That's not for me", they will say, "my faith is fine. I go to Mass, that's enough." Well, is it? God is surely never outdone in generosity and He longs for His children to love Him more and more and, more importantly, for His children to know His unconditional, eternal love for them. We must never set limits to what He wants for us.

I didn't want to change. I thought I was fine as I was, quite comfortable in my faith and life generally. I disliked intensely what I thought was Renewal, especially Charismatic Renewal, almost making fun of people who praised God and jumped about waving their hands. I saw no sense to this, thought it was mere exuberance and notice-seeking! I also thought that if I got involved in that sort of thing I might lose my faith altogether and end up Pentecostal or something else! How wrong I was. Easy to misjudge when you don't know! Satan cunningly traps us into thinking 'This way is not for me. I don't like it'. So, we are fearful of what we don't know, and critical of what we think is not for us. What a big mistake!

God calls each and every one of us in 'His own way' to Himself. He never forces. Just as there are many mansions prepared for those who love Him, so too, there are many ways to Him, and He can use everything in our lives to draw us to closer union with Him. My dear old dad at eighty eight years, loved to see people holding their Rosary beads during Mass, and he was quite upset after Vatican II, when he thought no one prayed at Mass any more, simply because they stopped using their Rosaries. We tend to love the familiar and think it is the only way. And so I would say, judging by my own experience and that of several others, that Charismatic Renewal, that wonderful tool of the Holy Spirit, is greatly misunderstood and misjudged in the church today. I'm convinced it's worth going for it!

I was delighted to hear a Catholic priest in London say from the altar only two weeks ago, that the reason why his congregation has grown and keeps on growing is that he offers them continually Life in the Spirit Seminars. I believe this must be true. I don't know any better way to renew a parish and bring it to life spiritually.

St. Paul tells us: "Earnestly desire the spiritual gifts", *(I Corinthians. 14:1)* and for him these gifts or charisms are essential to the existence and life of the church. The renewed flowering of these gifts today, is a sign of the church's recovery of her strength and health. All these charisms were evident in the early church but as time passed, they somehow became dormant. Where the Holy Spirit is very active in the church, we will see the spiritual gifts mentioned by St. Paul manifested again. These gifts are wisdom, knowledge, expectant faith, prophecy, interpretation, tongues, healings, miracles and discernment of spirits.

"All these gifts are manifestations of the same Holy Spirit and given to each person for a good purpose."

(I Corinthians 12)

Unfortunately many of us grew up with very limited thoughts of the Holy Spirit from our earliest teaching. I remember thinking He only had seven gifts, which I learnt by heart for Confirmation, wisdom, understanding, counsel, fortitude, knowledge, piety and the fear of the Lord. I know differently now! His greatest gift of course is love, and who could improve on that wonderful chapter in I Corinthians 13, or who could live it to the full? "Over all these things", St. Paul says, "Put on love". Love is the only thing that never hurts our neighbour or indeed ourselves. Only love will remain; faith and hope will pass away. We shall be judged on love. After Baptism in the Holy Spirit, one finds one has more love; and a greater capacity to give love and receive it. The grace of many new friends is yet another bonus from the Lord, and the desire to build community always follows.

The church today needs these spiritual gifts more than ever before, and if we could experience the wonder of the Holy Spirit, with Vatican II lived out in every parish, our churches would become alive and vibrant. Then perhaps our thousands of 'lost' young people would return 'home'.

Love speaks! Many of our young people I find are dedicated to good causes, and it was so impressive to see some of them, at their own expense, give time freely in Bosnia to the refugees. They love God but for some reason they seem unable to love the institutional Church. Are they speaking prophetic words to us by their absence? Is the Church today failing them?

"O Divine Spirit, sent by the Father in the name of Jesus, give aid and infallible guide to your church. Renew in our own days your miracles as of a second Pentecost". *(Pope John XXIII)*

We must become the Charismatic Church, the Church of the Poor, the Church of the Holy Spirit.

Pope Paul VI writing to a Charismatic gathering said:
"Nothing is more necessary to this more and more secularized world than the witness of this Spiritual Renewal that we see the Holy Spirit evoking in the most diverse regions and milieux. How then could this 'Spiritual Renewal' not be a 'chance' for the church and for the world? And how, in this case, could one not take all the means to ensure that it remains so?

We are immediately alert, immediately happy to welcome the coming of the Holy Spirit; more than that, we invite Him, we pray to Him, we desire nothing more than that Christians, believing people, should experience an awareness, a worship, a greater joy, through the Spirit of God among us. Have we forgotten the Holy Spirit? Certainly not. We want Him. We honour Him and we love Him and invoke Him. And you, with your devotion and fervour, wishing to live in the Spirit, this should be where your second name comes in – 'a Renewal'. It ought to rejuvenate the world, give it back a spirituality, a soul. It ought to reopen its closed lips to prayer and open its mouth to song, to joy, to hymns and witnessing. It will be very fortuitous for our times, for our generation of young people, who shout out to the world the glory and the greatness of the God of Pentecost.
And we will say only this: Today, either one lives one's faith with devotion, depth, energy and joy or that faith will die out". *(Quote from 'New Covenant' Vol.5 No.1, July 1975.)*

And so, in concluding this chapter, I would like to thank my parents for the life they showed me and for bringing me to the Altar of God for Baptism, the beginning of life in the Holy Spirit. I would like to thank Fr. James Hawes, whom God chose to give the retreat that changed my life and set me on a new way towards fullness of life. And so from now on I can say: "My joy lies in being close to God." *(Psalm 73:28),* and knowing His personal Love for me.

Above all, I would like to sing the praises of my God forever, who called me 'out of darkness into His glorious light, there to praise Him forever and ever, Amen'.

"I have come so that they may have life and have it to the full." *(John 10:10)*

"I call you to contemplate the face of My Father in Heaven, so that you will learn His enhancing influence upon every area of your life. Each day respond, like Mary, with an ever more fervent 'Fiat'. My Father is glorified by your bearing much fruit."

A CALL TO CONTEMPLATE

Laura asked me a searching question.

My little niece was seven or eight years old and we were walking along the country lanes of Drogheda in Ireland. "Auntie Josephine," she asked, quite out of the blue. "Do you know about your Heart Room?"

I was taken aback. "My heart room?" I said. "What do you mean by a heart room?" "Well," she said, "your heart room is the place right inside you where you go and meet Jesus. You can talk to God there. Not everybody knows that they have a heart room. Do you want me to tell you a little bit about it?" I encouraged her to go on: "Oh, yes!" I said, "I'd love to know more about that room. Please tell me a little bit more."

"Well," she began, "it was Sister Columba who told us about our Heart Room, and I love it. I love going into my Heart Room. Lots of adults don't know about it, but I wish they did, because it makes you feel better. You can go into your heart room at any time, whether you're happy or sad, and you'll meet Jesus there.

First, you find a place where you are comfortable. Next, you close your eyes. You say to Jesus "Good morning, Good afternoon or Good evening." Then Jesus will say

"Hello" to you. If you're sad, ask Jesus to make you happy. One day, I was very sad because someone stole one of my favourite things, so that night I went into my Heart Room before I went to sleep, and I told Jesus I was very sad, and I asked Him to find me what I had lost. The next day I was given it back, so I was very happy again."

She continued talking about her heart room, telling me that her favourite Heart Room prayer was the sun prayer. "How do you do the sun prayer?" I asked.

"Well, you see, Auntie Josephine," she said, "the sun cannot thank God for being the sun, but I can thank God in its place. You look up at the sky and you raise your hands towards the sun; then you wrap your hands around the sun, and you place it in your heart (she did the actions as she spoke). As you put the sun into your heart, you take a deep breath. This makes an empty space for the sun, and it begins to warm your heart.

Next, you go into your Heart Room, while you keep your hands clasped over your heart. Then you move close to Jesus. He is waiting for you in there. You become very quiet, so that you can feel Jesus very near to you. Now, ask Jesus to look into your heart, and He sees the beautiful sun there. Then you thank Him for the sun and all the wonderful things the sun does for us. Next you talk to Jesus about the sun, and tell Him about the different ways you love the sun. Thank Him for it. Spend a little time just enjoying it. Then you ask Jesus to help all the sick people. When you are ready, Auntie Josephine, raise your hands again and put the sun back into the sky. Say good-bye to Jesus. You kiss Jesus goodbye, but He is always with you - so it's not really 'goodbye'!

Come out of your Heart Room, slowly. Next time you see the sun, you will remember this prayer, and you will love the sun more as it shines on your face, warms the flowers and makes them open, and cheers everybody. It even makes you feel warm when you pray like this! "

I was humbled and grateful to my little niece who taught me so much without ever realizing it. "Out of the mouth of babes, comes the sound of praise" *(Psalm 8:2)* In 'The King and I' it says so rightly, "If you become a teacher, by your children you'll be taught."

We had thought, as children, that contemplative prayer belonged to enclosed nuns and monks. So, here I was, learning again to pray, having had a wonderful simple lesson in contemplative prayer from a child.
 Now, we realize that contemplative prayer is accessible to all God's children and He wants us all to live a 'contemplative' life. Through the grace of Charismatic Renewal we are all learning to become contemplatives, and what a joy this is.

Before evening was out, my little niece had stapled together a little book with the main points so that I could take it back to England and teach my children.

Andrea and Laura

I have, in fact, used the idea with several groups since, as I tell her story and lead people to experience the power of contemplative prayer in groups or alone, with various themes. The Holy Spirit touches hearts in the most simple, lovely way. He never lets us down. St. Thérèse of Lisieux has much to tell us about the Little Way of Spiritual Childhood and the principles on which she herself built her own prayer life. We can hear Jesus say: "If anyone is simple as a child, then let him come to Me." Again we have Jesus Himself praying: "I bless You Father, Lord of Heaven and earth, for hiding these things from the learned and the clever and revealing them to mere children (such as Laura!) Yes, Father, for that is what it pleases You to do." Then turning to His disciples, He spoke to them in private "Happy the eyes that see what you see, for I tell you that many prophets and kings wanted to see what you see and never saw it, to hear what you hear and never heard it." *(Luke 10:21-24)*

And this is the first thing we adults must learn as we enter the school of Prayer. The Father reveals Himself to the little ones, and hides Himself from the learned and proud *(cf Matthew 11:25).* This is serious! If we want to know God, to become His close friends, we must learn to contemplate with the eyes of a child, with simplicity and humility of heart. "Like a weaned child on its mother's breast, even so is my soul." *(Psalm 131:2)*

To sit in His presence and to be aware of and to receive His love is to contemplate; to be passive rather than be active in prayer; listening rather than speaking; waiting rather than being busy doing, adoring and receiving rather than giving. "Pause a while and know that I am God." *(Psalm 46:10)* The great contemplative St. Teresa of Avila used to say, "The important thing is not to think much but to love much." So she suggests doing a lot of loving (close to our 'Heart Room') if we want God to guide us through the darkness.

St. Teresa also suggests another way; that of allowing ourselves to be watched. To allow ourselves to be watched by God is to contemplate.

Imagine you see Jesus looking at you now, just notice Him looking at you.... That's all. It's so simple! Saint Teresa adds two very important adverbs: "Notice Him looking at you, lovingly, humbly. Try," she suggests, "to feel both attitudes as he looks at you. See Jesus look at you with love. See Jesus look at you with humility."

To communicate with God in this way is basic, like communication between the foetus and the womb of the mother. For any growing relationship with God, this type of prayer is essential. Saint Augustine once said that the closest thing to God is man himself. So the more I feel myself watched by God, allowing Him to touch me through the light which surrounds me and the stars that are above me, through the moon that guides me and the sun that caresses me, through the water that wets and refreshes me and the hunger that stimulates me and energizes me, through the friend that loves me and touches me, through the heart that beats for me and with me, the more I become aware, the more I become contemplative. He is never far from me. There is a sense in which He *awaits* me at every moment.

One of Saint Teresa's sisters who experienced great dryness in prayer practised this method of Contemplative Prayer for hours at a time. When asked what she did during her prayer, she said, "I just allow myself to be loved." I myself find this way of great benefit.

Some of us find it so hard to receive human love and so to imagine Jesus looking at us lovingly seems almost impossible. We sometimes imagine God to be harsh, to be an exacting judge, to be, as it were, a spy, waiting to trip us up. We even see illness, misfortune, untimely death as punishment for past sins. We see God as a serious kill-joy; or even worse, we see Him as an impersonal force, but not a Person capable and yearning for a personal love relationship with each one of us.

The second attitude we find even more difficult is to imagine:– Jesus looking at us humbly.

"His state was Divine
yet He did not cling to His equality with God
but emptied Himself, to assume the condition of a slave,
and became as men are, and being as all men are,
He became humbler yet, even to accepting death,
death on a cross."   *(Philippians 2:6-8)*

And again in John *(13:14,15)* we read,
"If I then, the Lord and Master
have washed your feet, you should
wash each other's feet. I have given you an
example. So that you, too, may copy what I
have done to you."

Jesus came to serve not to be served.
"At this time, the disciples came to Jesus and said: 'Who is the greatest in the Kingdom of Heaven?' So Jesus called a little child to Him and set the child in front of them. Then He said, 'I tell you solemnly, unless you change, and become like this little child, you will never enter the Kingdom of Heaven. And so, the one who makes himself as little as this little child, is the greatest in the Kingdom of Heaven'." *(Matthew 18:1-4)*

To become like a child is not easy. We become so respectable and grown up in our approach to God, so intellectual, sometimes even arrogant and proud, and so awkward in our attitude to God, that our prayer is more about us than about Him! "Only the children know what they are looking for," said the Little Prince to the railway switchman. "They waste their time over a rag doll, and it becomes very important to them; and if anyone takes it from them they cry ..." *('The Little Prince', Antoine de Saint-Exupéry, p 71)* We fail to experience His touch. We become impatient with God, with ourselves and with others. A child in the womb can only wait to be born. The Kingdom of God grows silently, imperceptibly. Stillness and silence are of the essence for true contemplative prayer – to wait on God is essential.

We do not know the mystery of God's working in a soul. How to accept that God brings it about without our knowing it, is a hard lesson to learn. What a joy when we begin to learn! To *know* that God is always working for our good no matter what circumstances prevail is happiness indeed! To know and believe and trust that God is in our work is peace indeed. We can contemplate God in everything!

I see His Blood upon the rose,
And in the stars the glory of His eyes,
His body gleams amid eternal snows;
His tears fall from the skies.

I see His face in every flower;
The thunder and the singing of the birds
Are but His voice, and carven by His Power.
Rocks are His written words.

All pathways by His feet are worn;
His strong heart stirs the ever-beating sea,
His crown of thorns is twined with every thorn,
His Cross is every tree.

Joseph Mary Plunkett, (1887 - 1916)

Let us ask for a contemplative heart, like Mary, so that we learn to see Him everywhere in everything. She must have been aware of Jesus all the time and before the Holy Spirit overshadowed her at the time of the Annunciation, her soul was already orientated towards her God. In all she did she was a contemplative. In all her work she must have found Him. As Jesus grew up, she must have delighted in living in union with the Trinity, as she went about her daily tasks with a heart filled with love. So too, we can find Him in our work as well as in our prayer, in our recreation, and in our study.

Listen to Teilhard de Chardin:
"God does not deflect our gaze prematurely from the work He Himself has given us. Since He presents Himself to us as attainable through that very work. Nor

does He blot out, in His intense light, the detail of our earthly aims, since the closeness of our union with Him is, in fact, determined by the exact fulfilment of the least of our tasks. We ought to accustom ourselves to this basic truth, till we are steeped in it, until it becomes as familiar to us as the perception of shape or the reading of words.

Try, with God's help, to perceive the connection, even physical and natural, which binds your labour with the building of the Kingdom of Heaven: try to realize that Heaven itself smiles upon you, and through your works, draws you to itself. By virtue of the Creation and still more of the Incarnation, nothing here below is profane for those who know how to see.

Then as you leave church for the noisy streets, you will remain with only one feeling, that of continuing to immerse yourself in God. If your work is dull or exhausting, take refuge in the inexhaustible and becalming interest of progressing in the Divine Life. If your work enthrals you, then allow the spiritual impulse which matter communicates to you to enter into your taste for God, who knows you better and desires more under the veil of His works. Never, at any time, whether eating or drinking, consent to do anything without first of all realizing its significance and constructive value in Christ Jesus, and pursuing it with all your might. This is not simply a commonplace precept for salvation; it is the very path of sanctity for each person according to one's state and calling. For what is holiness in a creature if not to adhere to God, with the maximum of His strength; and what does the maximum adherence to

God mean, if not the fulfilment - in the world organised around the church - of the exact function, be it lowly or eminent, to which that creature is destined both by natural endowment and supernatural gift?"

('Le Milieu Divin', Teilhard de Chardin, pp 64 & 66)

O come let us adore Him, Christ the Lord, in everything. When we have eyes to see, our whole life becomes contemplative with adoration and reverence, as we find the presence of God everywhere, in everything.

One of my favourite writers, Carlo Carretto, puts it so beautifully:–

"There is no longer any creature, star, flower, meadow or hill, storm wind or fine weather, ocean or bird, which does not speak to me of Him, which is not a message and a symbol, a word and a warning from Him. I feel I am in Him, like a bee in its hive, like a bride in her home or better still, like a child in it's mother's womb. This last comparison is the most faithful because it says in a very real way, that union with God is not something that has to be found, because it already 'is'. Just as the union between the mother and her infant already 'is'. At the most it is a question of becoming aware of it; of fostering it through our adherence to Him, of responding to His incessant calls, because in God 'We live and move and have our being'. (Acts 17:28)
However, though the relationship of babe and mother is unequal, our relationship to God is even more unequal. Our blindness is greater than that of a foetus! In Him we can do everything, for He alone is our strength. The child in the Womb of God, means peace

in the midst of the storm, security amid the trials of life, light in the darkness, hope in the face of death. What matters is that we should 'let go', live by faith, and trust our God."

('The Desert in the City', Carlo Carretto)

To trust like a child is the grace of contemplation. In order to enter and understand, we need to have the heart of a child. We must ask for it. Intelligence alone will not attain this gift for us. It is grace poured out in love. "It is only with the heart that one can see rightly," said the fox to the Little Prince, "what is essential is invisible to the eye." *('The Little Prince', Antoine de Saint-Exupéry, p 68)*

Let your whole life be steeped in Him, your Lord and Saviour, your Creator and Lover. Let Him embrace you through all the circumstances of your life, as you sense His presence in the wind blowing back your hair or His caress through the first rays of the morning sun, or His peace through the serenity and majesty of the setting sun. Experience Him everywhere. "Were not our hearts burning within us as He spoke to us on the way?" the disciples thought on the road to Emmaus.

And so, too, with us, as we journey on our way towards our Homeland, pilgrims together in a forward movement of love and hope until we meet Him face to face, the veil removed forever. 'O come let us adore Him, Christ the Lord.'

O worship the Lord in the beauty of holiness
Fall down before Him: His glory proclaim.
With gold of obedience and incense of lowliness
Kneel and adore Him- the Lord is His Name.

Low at His feet lay thy burden of carefulness
High on His heart He will bear it for thee
Comfort thy sorrows and answer thy prayerfulness
Guiding thy steps as shall best for thee be.

Fear not to enter His courts in the slenderness
Of the poor wealth thou would'st reckon as thine
Truth in its beauty and love in its tenderness
These are the offerings to lay at His shrine.

These, though we bring them in trembling and
fearfulness,
He will accept for the Name that is dear
Mornings of joy give for evenings of tearfulness.
Trust for our trembling and hope for our fear.
(J.B.S. Monsell, Anglican hymn- writer)

Contemplation is an end in itself. It is not a means to an end, but an end so rich and full of life that, in fact, it is inevitably expressed in action, as the vision of the Artist or Lover is expressed in stone or paint, in word or gesture.

God calls us to be holy, to be saints. We shall never be saints if we ignore our responsibility to the world, forget the law of love, close the bowels of mercy against our brother and try to build for ourselves a private beatitude. "By this alone shall men know that you are my disciples, if you have love for one another." And so, contemplation, love, action, reverence, adoration, – all combine in order that Christ may be born in us today. "Whoever does not receive the Kingdom of God as a little child will not enter into it". *(Mark 10:15)*

**"Lord, please give us the heart of a child;
give us eyes of faith to see You everywhere."**

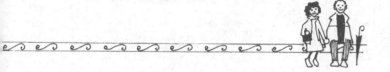

"I call you to an awareness of My presence everywhere and in all things. Through Me everything has come to be. Live in Me. Develop a deep sense of adoration and reverence for all that I have given you. We will come and make Our abode with you."

A CALL TO AWARENESS

L awrence Lowry paints loneliness.

An Englishman from the industrial north *(1887-1976)*, he is one of my favourite artists. I find him so full of understanding of human nature, so full of inspiration and childlike simplicity, so aware of the loneliness and the pain of mankind. It fascinates me that all his figures show loneliness and movement. Nobody is ever still in his pictures, there is always a sense of going somewhere, evident even in his landscape paintings (e.g. seascapes and lakes.)

"You know," Lowry says, "I've never been able to get used to the fact that I'm alive! The whole thing frightens me. It's been like that from my earliest days. It's too big, you know, I mean Life. It's like Rembrandt; he's too big, isn't he? That's why I can't stand him, he's like Life, you can't grasp him. I detest Rembrandt for that reason. O yes! the whole thing frightens me. It's all too big."

There is an innocence, directness about Lowry. It springs from the longing to know what will happen in the end to the sum of one's love and devotion. Lowry observes the lonely isolation of the human soul, as well as being aware of the fundamental characteristic of childlikeness in each person. We are fundamentally children - children who may return to paradise only when they have realised and accepted that this is their true state of grace.

Many of the saints have given us a wonderful vision of childhood, especially St. Thérèse of Lisieux. She looks on the supernatural in the same way as a child looks on the natural world. Her way is not childish but childlike. As sensitive as a child, she compares herself to a flower, an ordinary flower - her way being a humble way of spiritual childhood. She also compares herself to a little feeble bird. "I have eagles' eyes and heart," she used to say, "and I dare to look at the Son of Divine Love. I am so happy to be a fledgeling and frail." All artists use many brushes but she saw herself as the little brush that paints in the detail. It is to the little ones that the secrets of the Father are revealed.

As he wandered the streets of Manchester, he became so aware of the inconsolable loneliness and poverty of people that he portrays them in most of his pictures, especially in his portraits. "They're real people, sad people," he used to say. "I am attracted to sadness and there are some very sad things. I feel like them."

Lowry writes: "All those people in my pictures, they are all alone, you know. They have all got their private sorrows, their own absorption." His pictures show that we are alone, and that we cannot contact one another. We are isolated and cut off. "All my people are lonely," he said. "Crowds are the most lonely things of all. Everyone is a stranger to everyone else. You have only got to see them to see that.

I did. If I had more than suspected the fact before, I was doubly sure now. Each human creature is an island, quietly adrift in a vast sea, teeming with other solitary islands, that can never meet."

A Street Scene - St. Simon's Church, 1928

As you look at this picture, you will see, interestingly, how he sees the church as an isolated island, avoided by a crowd who pass by seeing it as irrelevant and out of touch - no wonder the church is in darkness! Is he prophetic or are we about to enter a new age when churches draw huge crowds to them? I hope in this regard he is wrong in his pessimism and that our churches become beacons of light.

The poet, John Donne *(1572-1631)*, on the other hand, writes that "No man is an island entire of himself." He emphasises how we need each other – a more Christian viewpoint, and one with which I agree. I do believe that there is often a loneliness, or maybe, more correctly, an 'aloneness' in every human heart, a space apart that can only be satisfied by God. Not even the deepest human love can make up for man's fundamental need for God. In each heart is the road to Zion. St. Augustine reminds us of the restlessness in man until he finds God: "Our hearts are restless until they rest in Thee."

John Donne's vision of our not being isolated from each other fits in much better with the Christian teaching on the Mystical Body of Christ, where each member is seen, not as a lone individual, but as, all of us together, forming one body, with Christ the Head. "You together are Christ's Body; but each of you is a different part of it. If one part is hurt, all parts are hurt with it. If one part is given special honour, all parts enjoy it." *(1 Corinthians 12:27&26)*

"People just don't use their eyes you know," Lowry often said. Now take his painting of the cripples. "My friends are always arguing that I just couldn't have seen as many cripples as that. Well, of course, I didn't see them all at once, but I have seen them all from time to time and here in this picture I have simply brought them all together." "Nonsense" said one of my friends, "there just aren't as many types of cripples in the whole of Manchester and Salford put together."

"All right," I said, "I'll prove there are!" So off we started on a ramble through the city and before very long, we passed a man with one leg, and a little later a woman with one arm. "What about those?" I said. "Oh! well," said my companion, "that's only an odd two!" But you know, after we'd wandered for some time and taken a bus ride out to Salford and back into Manchester again by taxi, we'd seen lots and lots of cripples and my friend was forced to agree, that he just hadn't bothered to keep his eyes open or to use them before."

The Cripples, 1949

We can learn much from Lowry about awareness of people and their pain. Socrates says, "The unaware life is not worth living." I myself often wander round the streets, the underground, big stores, and just pray for the sad or hardened faces I see as I go by. I wonder what pain people carry in their hearts and I give it to Jesus for them.

Lowry said: "My whole happiness and unhappiness were that my view was like no one else's. Had it been like, I should not have been lonely, but had I not been lonely, I should not have seen what I did see." Through his own suffering he found an empathy with mankind which he depicts in his pictures. Feeling 'different' can cause loneliness.

His painting of the 'Woman with the Beard' shows his observance of the eccentric and the different. He was once on a train journey from Cardiff to Paddington, at Newport a bearded woman got into his carriage and sat right opposite him. "She had a very nice face, and quite a big beard." He felt fascinated and sorry for her because of her beard but he couldn't let the opportunity pass, so, almost at once, he began to make a little drawing of her on a piece of paper. "After a while she asked rather nervously what I was doing. I blushed like a Dublin Bay prawn and showed her my sketch – the one from which I later made my painting of her. At first she was greatly troubled, but we talked, and by the time the train had reached Paddington we were the best of friends. We even shook hands on the platform."

People say, "Oh, but you couldn't have seen a woman with a beard like that!" But Lowry actually did see one and the bearded woman gave Lowry the material for a remarkable study of the isolation of the afflicted.
We never know the impact we have on somebody else's life. A similar experience of being touched by a fellow traveller is expressed by Sister Joan, one of the artistically gifted sisters of my own religious congregation who wrote much poetry and who died on 20th July 1998.

We sat in the compartment
Of a half empty train,
Silent for a while:
And then she spoke
And I replied 'Yes'
To what she said.

"Do you like the countryside?"
She broached.
"O, yes, I do," I said,
"Especially the hills,"
Thinking of my beloved Wales.

And then we fell to talking
Of topical things:
Of hopes and present fears
Which somehow led
To deeper things.
And, unawares, God crept in.

Many years have passed since then,
Yet a link was forged,
Though we never met
In person again.

And when I shall see
The tapestry of me,
She'll be there –
A tiny streak in it –
Stitched in by God
To complete the whole of it.

(Sister Joan Findlay, Daughter of the Holy Spirit)

Lowry, like many of us, disliked change. "I can't stand change," he said. "I get used even to the things I dislike, and I want them to go on and on... because I like monotony." None of us likes change; for its own sake it's useless, but for growth and movement it is vital. The great Cardinal Newman writes, "To live is to change; to change often is to grow."

Healthy attitudes to change help us to live a fuller life. The Good News is that our attitudes can be changed. "The greatest discovery in our generation is that human beings, by changing the inner attitudes of their minds, can change all the outer aspects of their lives," wrote Dr. James, the psychologist. "Happiness depends not so much on what happens to us, as on what happens in us: when we meet life and its circumstances positively and triumphantly, then no matter what comes, we will have learnt the secret of living. The way we see, interpret, and react, to whatever happens to us, is the important thing. Sometimes the very worst thing that may happen *to* us, can bring about the best thing that could ever happen *in* us. And we must assume this responsibility for our attitudes. Only if we accept this responsibility can we grow through the various circumstances of life". *(Dr. William James)*

Doctors often find that by helping patients to change their attitudes, their suffering can be relieved, more than by treating the symptoms, illness can even disappear. "It is to be noted that in so focusing the attention on the attitudes and away from the symptoms, attention is directed to the future rather than to the past. The implication is that whatever the conditions have been in the past which caused the symptoms, the important factor is not so much the uncovering of an underlying conflict responsible for the symptoms, as in the adoption of an attitude which makes possible a handling of the symptom." *(Dr. Robert Lesley)*

Jesus Himself tells us "If your *eye* is sound, your whole body will be filled with light, for the lamp of the body is the eye." *(Matthew 6:22)*

We are exhorted in scripture to renew our minds and put on the mind of Christ. Rather than imitate Christ, it is much more effective to try to *become* Christ.

"You know, sometimes people want to imitate Christ, but when a monkey plays a saxophone, that doesn't make him a musician. You can't imitate Christ by imitating His external behaviour. You've got to *be* Christ. Then you'll know exactly what to do in a particular situation, given your temperament, your character, and the character and temperament of the person you're dealing with. No one has to tell you. But to do that, you must *be* what Christ was. An external imitation will get you nowhere." *('Awareness', de Mello, p 96)*

Lowry had a great sense of wonder, especially in little things. He was remarkably childlike. Though his mind is complex and subtle, his sense of delight and wonder is pure and innocent.

> "If only we knew how to look at life
> All life would become a sign
> All life would become a prayer"
>> *(Michel Quoist)*

"The best
and most beautiful things
in the world,
cannot be seen or even touched.
They must be felt
with the heart."

(Helen Keller. (Blind, deaf, dumb)

From Lowry's paintings we can see that he also had a shrewdness which equipped him well to paint the human race. "Be wise as serpents," Jesus tells us, "but be simple as doves."

Lowry's childlike love gave him great respect for things, especially clocks. His home was vibrant with the ticking of fourteen clocks. "Wonderful companions clocks, real friends," he used to say. "They all have their own life you know, and, by the way, if you pick up an old clock which doesn't go properly, never take it to an ordinary clock repairer.

They will only disturb its works. It doesn't matter whether it keeps time or not, let it tick away as it wishes but don't disturb its works, I never know the time because, I don't know which clock, if any, is right!"

One of the ingredients fading from life today is respect for the individual and reverence for life in general. The more we restore these two virtues, the happier life will become. Lowry's thought regarding the repairing of clocks reminds me of Jesus' own words, "New wine must be put into new wine skins. No one tears a piece from a new cloak, to put it on an old cloak; if he does, not only will he have torn the new one, but the piece taken from the new will not match the old." *(Luke 5:37-39)*

Being aware that plastering over problems and difficulties never produces a lasting solution. Ezekiel *(13:10-12)* reminds us that surface patching up is of little use and won't last. "Instead of my people rebuilding the wall, these men come and slap on plaster... Tell these plasterers, it will rain hard, it will hail, it will blow a gale, and down will come the wall. They have misled my people by saying 'Peace', when there is no peace."

So if, for example, you are looking for peace a mere pretence of peace will never be successful. Papering over the cracks is of no lasting use. True peace gets to the root of the problem, it demands repentance, conversion of heart, courage, truth, reconciliation. It comes from a heart seeking God in all things.
"What matters is for him to become an altogether new creation." *(Galatians 6:15)*.
"And for anyone who is in Christ there is a new creation, the old creation has gone, and the new one is here. It is all God's work." *(2 Corinthians 5:17)*

The famous Lowry picture 'Good Friday: Daisy Nook' *(1946)* I find sad but fascinating. The setting is a fairground. It is teeming with people of all shapes and sizes moving around, looking bewildered. The loneliness of the non-Christians, trying to fill their 'day off', hurrying, searching for some sort of transitory joy, and being part of some community, shows the need to 'belong', even for seconds, to 'family'. Could the events of this tragic, though victorious, Good Friday have spoken to his heart? What a world of difference between the secular and the religious! Might he have, secretly, found an answer to the loneliness depicted in his pictures? The people are roaming around like sheep without a shepherd. Jesus is the Good Shepherd. This picture makes me think of the need to pray for labourers, for the harvest of souls is great, but the labourers are few.

A Beggar, c.1965

"When I look at this picture of the Beggar with his little clenched hand I find it so moving – he tries so hard, struggles so helplessly, tries to stand up for his dignity. He's not abject. Yet his hand is like a child's, such a small part of his dark, bent figure. Unable to look at his 'benefactor', he is nearly self-contained, but is saved by his pleading hand. I am glad that his other hand is open. This painting, to me, is about how we are, helpless but with a tension which surely is a prayer straight to God who made us." *(Gunvor Edwards, artist)*

While Lowry did not know (but knows now in death) Christians firmly believe that one day our old beggarly, crippled bodies will disappear, the wounds of sin and shame will be transfigured into newly created bodies, transparent and divine. "God will transfigure these wretched bodies of ours into copies of His glorious body." *(Philippians 3:21)*

Lowry's Paintings are full of potential transfiguration and the figures are always on the move, goodness knows where. They are moving and waiting for what they do not know. Waiting is, in fact, what the whole of life is about. The beggar is waiting. Waiting is what history is about, it is what my prayer, suffering, hope is about. God our Father waited for Mary until the moment was right for the Annunciation. He waits for us, too.

"The world is charged with the grandeur of God.
It will flame out, like shining from shook foil;
It gathers to a greatness, like the ooze of oil
Crushed. Why do men then now not reck His rod?
Generations have trod, have trod, have trod;
And all is seared with trade; bleared, smeared with toil;
And wears man's smudge and shares man's smell; the soil
Is bare now, nor can foot feel, being shod.

And for all this, nature is never spent;
There lives the dearest freshness deep down things;
And though the last lights off the black West went
Oh, morning, at the brown brink eastward, springs –
Because the Holy Ghost over the bent
World broods with warm breast and ah! with bright wings."
('God's Grandeur', Gerard Manley Hopkins, 'Selected Poems' p 18)

Lowry observed what many would miss. The freshness of his outlook, his gentle acceptance of the terms of reference into which the individual is born, his sweet belief that all will be well in the end reminds me of the wonderful hope of Julian of Norwich. "All shall be well, and all shall be well, and all manner of things shall be well." A useful mantra when things are going wrong!

Lowry's great sense of wonder and fun, were coupled with a beautiful, though alarming, personality. Alarming, because one is suddenly aware how far one is from the Kingdom of Heaven, which he, in his purity and humility, has so often beheld. "I think the party concerned will see us all right in the end," he used to reflect.

Only the arrogant would try to define 'the party concerned'. What a trusting phrase, containing the destiny of all those sad, curious, clumsy, toy-like figures which populate his wonderful canvasses. They wait, as we must wait, in our struggles and loneliness, our joys and happiness, until 'the party concerned' shall gather us up at the last, like corn, into the arms of His all-embracing Love.

"He painted Salford's smokey tops
on cardboard boxes from the shops.
Parts of Ancoats where I used to play.
I'm sure he once walked down our street
'cos he painted kids who had nowt on their feet.
The clothes they wore had all seen better days.

He said his works of art were dull,
'No room, old lad, the walls are full.'
But Lowry didn't care much, anyway.
They said he just paints cats and dogs

And match-stalk men in boots and clogs,
And Lowry said that's just the way they'll stay.

And he painted match-stalk men and match-stalk cats and dogs.
He painted kids on the corner of the street that were sparking
clogs.
Now he takes his brush and he waits
Outside them factory gates
To paint his match-stalk men and match-stalk cats and
dogs.

Now canvas and brushes were wearing thin,
When London started calling him
To come on down and wear the old flat cap.
They said, 'Tell us about your ways
And all about them Salford days.
Is it true you're just an ordinary chap?'

Now, Lowrys hang upon the wall
Beside the greatest of them all.
Even the Mona Lisa takes a bow.
This tired old man with hair like snow
Told northern folk it's time to go
The fever came and the good Lord mopped his brow.

And he left us match-stalk men and match-stalk cats and dogs.
He left us kids on the corner of the street that were sparking clogs.
Now he takes his brush and he waits
Outside them pearly gates
To paint his match-stalk men and match-stalk cats and dogs.

*(from 'Match-stalk men and match-stalk cats and dogs', words
and music by Michael Coleman and Brian Burke)*

I thank God for the joy which Lowry's paintings give to me. I also thank God for the gift that Lowry has been to mankind and for the wonderful way his pictures have awakened in me a greater awareness of suffering in mankind. I pray that he now knows the joy of communion with God. As I walk the streets, or take a bus or train ride, my eyes are opened to the peculiarities and pains of fellow passengers and pilgrims, wending their way Heavenward, though unknowingly and unobtrusively, and so my heart enlarges and fills with love and compassion for the sin and brokenness of the world and my prayer increases as I beg the Almighty Father to restore His creation and lead us all home to our eternal home, where loneliness will be banished for ever and there will be only glory, wholeness, fulfilment in Him.

**"Everything speaks of God
if only we had eyes to see"**

"I call you to an awareness of My Presence everywhere and in everything. Through Me everything has come to be. Live in Me. Invite Me into every moment and We will come to you and make our abode within you. Nothing is profane in My Presence. Cherish each moment of grace I give you each day. Keep close to My heart and you will know the value of the time I give you."

A CALL TO THE PRESENT MOMENT

God never calls us yesterday or tomorrow

He knocks on your door today, this very moment. His call is always for the present moment. "Come and see," always in the present tense.

All the Beatitudes are in the present tense. So Jesus says: "Do not worry about tomorrow, tomorrow will take care of itself. Each day has enough trouble of its own," *(Matthew 6:34)* "So, for all your worrying," Jesus says, "can any one of you add one single cubit to his span of life?" *(Matthew 6:27)* And the answer of course has to be 'No'.

God is in charge of every moment of our lives including the most important final moment of death. Jesus goes on to teach us: "Look at the birds of the air," He says, "they do not sow or reap, or gather into barns, yet your Heavenly Father feeds them. Are you not worth much more than they?" *(Matthew 6:26)* He warns us to be on our guard about His coming to call us home, for He does not want to catch us unawares! "Be on your guard," He says, "because you never know when the master of the house is coming – evening, midnight, cock crow, or dawn. If He comes unexpectedly He must not find you asleep; and what I say to you is 'stay awake!'" *(Mark 13:33-37)*

"Of two men in the fields, one is taken, the other left. Of two women at the millstone, one is taken, the other left. So stay awake, you do not know the day when the master is coming." *(Matthew 24:41-42)* In the twinkling of an eye life is changed, not ended!

And so the man in scripture who made bigger barns for his surplus goods was indeed very foolish, for Jesus said: "You fool, this night your soul shall be required of you and this hoard of yours, whose will it be then?" He did not call this man a fool merely because he possessed wealth. He never made a sweeping indictment against wealth. Rather, he condemned the misuse of wealth and over-attachment to it. "He who loves money never has enough. He who loves wealth never has enough profit." *(Ecclesiastes 5:9)*

Money, like any other force, such as electricity, is amoral and can be used for good or evil. Nothing in wealth is inherently bad, just as nothing in poverty is inherently virtuous! There is always a danger that we will let the means by which we live replace the ends for which we live.

"Watch out," Jesus said, "and be on your guard against avarice of any kind, for a man's life is not made secure by what he owns, even when he has more than he needs." *(Luke 12:15)* "What then will a man gain if he wins the whole world and ruins his life? Or what has a man to offer in exchange for his life?" *(Matthew 16:26)*

The rich man was a fool because he failed to differentiate between means and ends. The richer he became materially, the poorer he became spiritually. "So it is," Jesus says, "when a man stores up treasure for himself in place of making himself rich in the sight of God." *(Luke 12:21)* Sometimes, as people grow wealthier they contribute much to worthy causes and become a great blessing to everyone they help. But the man in the Gospel, on the other hand, thought he could live and grow in this little self-centred world he had created for himself, devoid of dependence on God and others. He was dead spiritually, even if he could have lived physically, for his heart was closed against his brother. True wealth is the inner treasure of spirit, which no thief can steal and no moth corrupt.

As John says: "If a rich man saw that one of his brothers was in need but closed his heart to him, how could the love of God be living in him?" *(1 John 3:17)*. Real love must be addressed to the need of the moment. It must show itself in action not in mere talk. We can take nothing with us when we die. If we are worried about storing our abundance until it overflows, then it is time already to consider 'letting go', to consider a worthy cause, or the millions of poverty-stricken people including refugees throughout the world. "In so far as you did this to one of the least of these brothers of Mine you did it to Me," Jesus said. *(Matthew 25:40)*

Sometimes we find it easier to help causes at a distance but forget that there are needy on our doorsteps and we are reminded of Jesus' own words "You have the poor with you always and you can be kind to them whenever you wish." *(Mark 14:7)* Charity begins at home!

It breaks my heart sometimes to see people struggling financially, without 'bread' for the moment! Thursday comes and there is little left in the kitty for food. What a wonderful privilege to be able to discreetly help someone in need like this, even more so when it is your own kith and kin! But do not let your right hand know what your left hand is doing. Jesus said: "Your Father sees what is done in secret and He will reward you." *(Matthew 6:18)* Do not forget that a moment of generosity might save someone's life! We are so often unaware of poverty on our doorsteps. Everyone has their pride and they keep their secret! It hurts so much, sometimes, to know how people are suffering!

The answer is simple. Poverty can be eliminated if we use the vast resources of the earth for the common good, sharing without greed and selfishness. Often the poor are the most generous; that is the paradox! They will give like the poor widow of the Gospel who gave her all in her 'mite', while the rich gave in a calculating manner. Life is so short. Moments fly by and are so precious. They will never return! "Make us know the shortness of life, that we may gain wisdom of heart." *(Psalm 90:12)*. In the twinkling of an eye man is gone! Like the grass of the field, gone forever! "Our life is over like a sigh." *(Psalm 90:9)*. God respects the fact that all we 'own' is the present moment – that which we can consciously bless and be aware of. We cannot 'really' own moments for they are God's gift to us. The past is gone into His mercy, the future is totally in His hands and known only to Him; the present we *can* do something about. Let's start now.

Let's not waste moments. St. Augustine writes: "One day, your radiance shone upon me, put my blindness to flight… you touched me and I became inflamed with desire for your love." What a moment of grace for him! Can you recall a similar moment of grace in your own life? We may imagine our life as a succession of present moments. Each successive moment will be an eternal act either of worship, gratitude and love or selfishness and blindness. God is beside us at every one of them, constantly calling us to live closer to Himself. His desire is always for us. "Lord, you have been our refuge age after age. Before the mountains were born, before the earth or the world came to birth, you were God from all eternity and for ever... To you, a thousand years are a single day, a yesterday now over, an hour of the night." *(Psalm 90:1-4).*

One moment is so small. Why should we want to drag our restlessness into it by continually living in the past? Or why should we want to be so busy that we live several moments 'at the same time'? A failing many of us have! Every moment is given by Him and precious to Him and also to us. Fill each moment to the full, as it is infinitely important in weaving the seamless tapestry of your life.

The Divine Weaver

My life is but a weaving
Between my Lord and me;
I cannot choose the colours
He worketh steadily

Oftimes He weaveth sorrow
And I, in foolish pride
Forget that He seeth the upper
And I the under side.

Not till the loom is silent
And the shuttles cease to fly
Shall God unroll the canvas
And explain the reason why

The dark threads are as needful
In the weaver's skilful hand
As the threads of gold and silver
In the pattern He has planned.

(Anonymous)

Close your eyes and be aware of the 'dark threads'. Be aware of the times the threads were knotted together and needed unravelling. Perhaps you have been overwhelmed at the death of a loved one, a failure, a fear, a heartache … Return to the scene – relive the event, seek the presence of Jesus in it. Dwell with it … Be aware of His healing presence. Speak to Him. Ask Him the meaning of what was happening to you. Listen to His reply. Do this frequently. When you are no longer upset by negative feelings coming from the event, then I believe you have "let go" and become healed and at peace.

I pray that the Holy Spirit will reveal something of the divine pattern in God's plan for you. I pray that nothing may ever be wasted or lost, for where there's a shadow there's a light.

I pray you will be patient with yourself, and with God, and that you will allow things to happen for you in His time. I pray that all shall be well for you. Amen.

"God, in all that is living and incarnate in Him, is not far away from us, altogether apart from the world we see, touch, hear, smell, and taste about us. Rather, He awaits us every instant in our action, in the work of the moment. There is a sense in which He is at the tip of my pen, my spade, my brush, my needle - of my heart and of my thoughts. By pressing the stroke, the line, or the stitch, on which I am engaged, to its ultimate natural finish, I shall lay hold of that last end towards which my innermost will tends." ('Le Milieu Divin', Teilhard de Chardin, p 64)

God enters our life through the present moment and through us to the world. That's why this moment, as you read this, is important. Much can be achieved in one moment. The signing of an agreement that can change the lives of millions of people can happen in one moment; likewise the opposite can happen, too. We can make or mar life by the event of one moment! De Mello says somewhere: "Problems are only solved through awareness, not effort. In fact," he says, "where there is awareness, problems do not exist." Why not stand still and be aware of the moment. Close your eyes and own the moment. Find one of the many faces of God in it. Give thanks.

So we have an amazing succession of moments making up our life: the moment of conception, of birth, moments of joy and happiness, of love and creation, of new life and renewal, of wholeness and healing, of success and acceptance, of unity and togetherness, of laughter and relaxation, of sport and exercise, of lightness and refreshment, of repentance and forgiveness, of relief and thankfulness, of prayer and holiness, of peace and serenity, of decision and faithfulness, of beauty and growth, of health, of food and feasting, of nourishment and truthfulness, of enlightenment and vision. Brother Roger of Taizé wrote, "My first book was 'Living today for God'. Now that I am old, I would say instead, 'Living the moment with God'."

There are moments we never want to forget, and indeed the poster says 'We remember moments' and 'good' moments are vital for our wholeness and well-being. It is helpful and life-giving to dwell with these moments from time to time.

Think of some of your favourite moments. Some of my favourite moments are the atmosphere after a storm, the freshness of the garden after heavy rain showers, the appearance of the rainbow, the double rainbow in Scotland, a beautiful sunset, the feel of the tiny hands of a newborn baby.

Remember some of the greatest moments of *your* life, like the moment of Baptism or Confirmation and what a gift to us all is the moment at Mass when the bread and wine are changed into the Body and Blood of Christ – surely the greatest moment on Earth!

Thank you Lord, that we're always waiting on moments, waiting for a baby to be born, waiting at the moment of death, waiting on God every day, on His will.

Close your eyes, even now, and allow the goodness and love of any one moment to surface. Invite Jesus into it and recreate the scene, with the people who were present at the time. Stay with the moment as long as it is life-giving. Thank Jesus for it.

"How long does the present last? A minute, a second? Much less, much more," said de Mello. "Less, because if you ever get into it, you will stumble upon the Timeless and will know what Eternity is." *('One Minute Nonsense', p 388)*

Other moments we would rather forget and wish they hadn't happened. Moments of rejection and unlove, of fear and unkindness, of injustice and unforgiveness, of loss and loneliness, of jealousy and bitterness, of unrepentance and unfaithfulness, of spite and hatred, of anger and insult, of revenge, of regret, of failure, of omission and indifference, of insensitivity and boredom, of denial and despair, of deceit and ugliness, of abuse and bad example. There is the dreadful moment of abortion, of euthanasia, of a life-support machine being switched off. A moment of 'impossible' decision, of the death of a relationship.

In God's mercy there is no unredeemable moment, except a moment of sin against the Holy Spirit. *(1 John 4:3)*. "Whoever blasphemes against the Holy Spirit never has forgiveness, but is guilty of an eternal sin." *(Mark 3:29, Matthew 12:32, Luke 12:10)*

"There are no limits to the mercy of God, but, anyone who deliberately refuses to accept His mercy, by not repenting, rejects the forgiveness of his sins and the salvation offered by the Holy Spirit. Such hardness of heart can lead to final impenitence and eternal loss." *(John Paul II, Catechism of the Catholic Church, p 411 art. 1864)*

Otherwise, with God there are no 'bad' moments, for repentance of heart leads to 'good' being brought out of 'evil'. What we think of as a 'bad' moment, God can turn to good by his love, which makes all things possible. Bad moments can become moments of grace, for God turns everything to good for those who love Him: moments of being troubled or worried or persecuted, of famine or fullness, of threat or attack. He can turn even a dreaded moment of truth, like being told you have cancer or some other disease that is terminal, into a moment of life, of faith and hope and challenge.

"For I am certain of this; that neither death nor life, no angel or prince, nothing that exists, nothing still to come, nor any power nor height nor depth, nor any created thing can ever come between us and the love of God, made visible in Christ Jesus Our Lord." *(Romans 8:38-39)*.

It is very healing to pray through these unhappy moments oneself. Just be still; take one moment at a time, and let the incident surface as the Lord gives it. Invite Jesus into it as you imagine the scene, the people, the feelings. Forgive if you must. Keep commuting between the moment and Jesus on the Cross. Give him your suffering, your fears, and let the moment go to Him. Thank Him for it. Pray for all concerned in it. Pray in the same way with happy moments. This is psychologically very sound!

"When I reach that painful moment, at which I suddenly realise that I am a sick man or that I am growing old, above all, at that final moment, when I feel I am losing hold on myself and becoming wholly passive in the hands of those great unknown forces which first formed me, at all these sombre moments, grant me Lord, to understand that it is You, providing my faith is strong enough, who are painfully separating the fibres of my being, so as to

penetrate to the very marrow of my substance and draw me into Yourself...." "Teach me to make a communion of death itself ..."
('Hymn of the Universe', Teilhard de Chardin, p 94)

Buddha was once asked, "Who is the holy man?" He replied, "Every hour is divided into a certain number of seconds and every second is divided into a certain number of fractions. He who is able to be totally present in each fraction of a second is indeed a holy man."

The Buddha explains how a Japanese warrior was arrested by his enemies and thrown into a prison cell. At night, he could not sleep, for he was convinced that he would be cruelly tortured the next day. Then the words of his Zen master came to his mind: 'Tomorrow is not real. The only reality is the present.'
So he came to the present and fell asleep. The man over whom the future has lost its grip resembles the birds of the air and the lilies of the field. No anxieties for tomorrow! Totally in the present! The Holy Man!

Another great master was visited by someone who said to him: "My suffering is unbearable", and the master answered: *"The present moment is never unbearable. It is what you think is coming in the next five minutes or the next few days, that drives you to despair. Stop living in the future!"* Sometimes we think we can see ahead of us to a future of happiness, joy, love, communion with God. Or it could be the opposite - and we see a future of sadness, loneliness, poverty or sickness. Either way it is a mirage. We forget God is right beside us *now*. No point in spending our life chasing after the 'shadow of God' when our faith tells us that He is already right here beside us. To give our attention to the present moment is the only way to make a success of our lives. It is to give the best that is in us to the framework of the present moment by personally responding to God's love for us, here and now.

Otherwise we can remain on the periphery of life and life can pass us by so easily in useless wandering, daydreams, or over-activity. You have to, you say, look out for the future, you have exams, work, family commitments, etc...... Then you have your children, your children's children, then your retirement, your pension, your house, etc., etc. These things must not spoil the life we have to live today. The tragedy is that one day there will be no tomorrow, and we won't have even started to live.

Lord forgive what I've been, bless what is to come and help me to live this present moment, as if it were my last. Make me aware of Your presence within me, of Your immense love for me. Make me know the joy of Your presence in this moment, with all its delicacy and fragility. Help me to direct this present moment, pregnant with possibility, to Your abiding care. Help me to abandon myself in it.

'Journalling', which means looking at moments or events in your life and writing about them, can be very helpful. You may like to talk about these moments with a trusted friend, alive or dead. Then write about how the friend sees the same event or moment. Lastly, write down how Jesus sees the same event or moment.

I wrote the following poem recently after one such moment:

'Moments'

Moments are for loving
And not for causing pain.
Used wisely, they will bless you
And glorify His name.
Chances missed may not return.
So remember every day
to live each present moment
In God's own delightful way.

We can't predict the future
Nor can we change the past.
Enough to live the 'moment'
And treat it as your last.
Befriend the poor and friendless,
Make charity your aim.
Then love, respect, compassion
Will grace each person's name.

The unkindest thing I do or say
May never be undone.
And friendships that I fail to win
May never more be won.
Thank God, then, for His mercies great,
On bended knee just pray,
And thank Him with a loving heart
For giving you this day.

(J. Walsh, February 1998)

God sometimes uses the moment to prune us in order that we produce more fruit. "My son, when the Lord corrects you, do not treat it lightly; but do not get

discouraged when He reprimands you. For the Lord trains the ones that He loves, and He punishes all those that He acknowledges as His sons. Suffering is a part of your training. God is treating you as His son. Has there ever been any son whose father did not train him?" *(Hebrews 12:5-6)*

One day, as a young novice, I was shown how to prune a vine. It upset me so much to snip away, with small scissors, several little grapes. I thought it was such a waste! But I did not then understand. When the harvest appeared I knew immediately the point of these 'painful moments', for the bunches of grapes were absolutely wonderful!

I look at all the treasured moments of Your own life that You share so generously with me.
The wonderful moment of Your Incarnation and of Your Mother's Fiat. The moment when Elizabeth and Your Mother met and John the baptist, Your cousin, leapt in his mother's womb, for the joy of meeting You.
The moment when John pointed You out to Your future disciples as 'the Lamb of God, who takes away the sin of the world'. The moment of their becoming Your followers.
The moment in the Temple when Anna the prophetess (84 years old) came by and praised God for You, the Hope and Deliverer of Israel.

The moment when Your Mother's heart was pierced by the sword, as the secret thoughts of many were laid bare, the painful moment for Mary at this prophetic word. The moment of Glory at Your Transfiguration on Mount Tabor with Peter, James, and John, when Your Father acknowledged You as His Beloved Son, in whom He was well pleased. The moment of Your first miracle (turning water to wine at Your Mother's request) and the moments of subsequent miracles – healing, deliverances, to follow.

The moment of Your death on the Cross in fulfilment of the prophetic word that Your Hour, made up of so many moments, had come. "It is consummated! Thy Will be Done!" The moment of Redemption for the whole human race. Thank You Jesus! What Precious Moments!
Thank You for the moments that have changed my life…

Thank you, Lord, for all the moments You have given me. Thank you for all the good moments and all the bad moments. Thank you, Lord, for each and every moment until the 'moment' fades into eternity. I cannot count them but they are all Your gift to me. Thank You...... Thank You...... Thank You...... Lord. Amen

Stilling Exercises of Awareness of the Present Moment

1.   Quieten your spirit by being aware of this moment. Make it yours. Breathe in God's love for you. Breathe out anxiety, fear, ugliness, unlove. Repeat a few times until you are calm.

2.   Believe in Jesus' Risen Power. He is with you this very moment, though you may not recognise Him.
Dwell with Him now.
Imagine Jesus either on the Cross or in His agony in the garden. Console Him... Minister to Him.

3.   Imagine Jesus, risen from the dead, popping into 'your boat'. "O you of little faith, why are you afraid?"

4.   Imagine Jesus on the sea shore cooking your breakfast. "Peace," He says to you, "I am with you." (If you do this before you go to work, then your mind is 'set' for a good day)

5.   Imagine Him in the garden of your heart, as He walks among the lovely flowers there, kind thoughts, love for others, gratitude for who you are, love for Him.

6.   Imagine you are a branch of the vine and your Father is pruning you to help you produce better fruit.
Pruning is painful, Lord. Please prune me to make me produce more and better fruit for You. Make me strong enough to withstand any painful pruning. Help me to produce some 'exquisite' blooms, rare and priceless. Father, may the moments of pruning bear lasting results, and may the fruit give You the Glory. Amen.

7.   Imagine God as a brilliant sun, giving warmth and light to every part of your body, sending rays out from the centre of your heart to the whole world. See the flames catching fire, feel the warmth of his love spreading from you to those who need your love.

Each one of these images could serve as a whole 'fantasy' contemplation in itself. St. Teresa of Avila, who scaled the heights of perfection and union with God, highly recommended this type of prayer. She suffered greatly from distractions in prayer, so she gathered all her distractions with her, learning to pray with her heart as well as with her head, while using her imagination to conjure up scenes filled with the presence of God. This is truly a delightful practice, but it's one that needs a certain amount of silence, stillness, and discipline in order to train oneself in the art of contemplation and stillness before God. It is, I believe, what our busy lives need today more than ever.

**"Each morning He wakens me to hear,
to listen like a disciple"**

(Isaiah 50:4)

"I call you to seek Me daily. Those who seek Me always find Me. Make Me the centre point of your being, then you will experience the fullness of life I came to bring you."

A CALL TO SEEK GOD

God is the happiness mankind is seeking.

God is also the love mankind is seeking, and Jesus Christ is the personal God for which mankind longs. No one is indifferent to God; either people love Him or don't want to know and, perhaps, get angry at the very mention of His Name.

Everyone reacts to God in one way or another, some would die for Him, as did the martyrs; while others deny Him and want nothing to do with Him. Others again show interest and enquire but they find it difficult to accept and respond. They keep 'putting off' the day when they might respond with a 'yes' to Him, preferring to muddle along, as they are, thinking they have all the answers themselves, and that they can 'go it alone'. They imagine life to be 'too good to be true' for believers, who can cast 'all their cares and worries' upon God. Sounds too simple for them! Then there are those who deter people from seeking God because they foolishly try to push 'religion' down people's throats convinced that Heaven must be made up of 'bleeding hearts', and 'holy pictures'! God is bigger than religion.

Each person has his or her own journey to God, and what switches one on, can so easily switch another off! Respect and sensitivity are crucial to any form of evangelisation! God is the Master of each one's search!

"God our Saviour wants everyone to be saved, and reach the full knowledge of the truth, For there is only one God and there is only one Mediator between God and mankind, Himself a man: Jesus Christ who sacrificed Himself as a ransom for all." *(l Timothy 2:4-6)*

Jesus Himself came to seek out and to save that which was lost. "I was sent," He said, "only to the lost sheep of the House of Israel." *(Matthew 15:25)* He was a friend of tax collectors and sinners. He drew the most unlikely people to Himself, like, for instance, Mary Magdalene, (prostitute and sinner) who received such love and healing from Him, that she lived for Him alone after her conversion.

"What she has done." Jesus said, "will be told throughout the world, wherever the Good News is proclaimed, in remembrance of her." *(Mark 14:9)* She did all in her power to show her sorrow for her sins. Mary anointed His head with oil, covered His feet with kisses, anointing them with ointment (forecast of His burial anointing, though she did not know it), washing them with her tears of sorrow, and drying them with her hair. Jesus said, "Her sins, her many sins, must have been forgiven her, or she would not have shown such great love." *(Luke 7:47)*

What a privilege Jesus allowed her! She must have been quite unaware of what other people thought of her; she saw 'only Jesus', that was enough! It was granted to her to announce the Resurrection of Jesus to the Apostles after His death. Moved by love, she hurried to the tomb, very early in the morning, of what was to become the most sacred Sabbath Day ever – Easter Day. She found the linen clothes and shroud lying there in the empty tomb. Jesus had gone. She was the first to see Him risen from the dead and to speak to Him. Jesus made her equal to the Apostles by making her the 'first-hand' witness to His Resurrection. Rejoice! Christ my Hope is Risen! Behold, this day, Death has been overcome, Jesus has risen by His own power. Alleluia!

Two other apostles were talking about the events in Jerusalem surrounding Jesus' death and His disappearance from the tomb. Jesus Himself came up and walked by their side but they did not recognise Him. Something prevented them from recognising Him. "You foolish men," Jesus said to them, "so slow to believe the full message of the Prophets. Was it not ordained that Christ should suffer and so enter into His glory? Then starting with Moses and going through all the prophets, he explained to them the passages throughout the Scriptures that were about Himself." *(Luke 24: 25-27).*

As evening drew on, they pressed Him to stay with them and He did. "Now while He was at table with them, He took bread and said the Blessing; then He broke the bread and handed it to them. And their eyes were opened and they recognised Him in the breaking of bread (symbol of hospitality and friendship), but He had vanished from their sight. Then they said to each other, 'Did not our hearts burn within us as He talked to us on the road, and explained the Scriptures to us?'." *(Luke 24:30)*

He appeared to them several times bequeathing His Peace. He told them: "This is what I meant when I said while I was still with you, that everything written about Me in the Law of Moses, in the Prophets, in the Psalms, has to be fulfilled." He opened their minds to understand the Scriptures, and He said to them: "So you see how it was written that the Christ would suffer and on the third day rise from the dead, and that, in His Name, repentance for the forgiveness of sins would be preached to all the nations, beginning from Jerusalem. You are witnesses to this. And now I am sending down to you what the Father has promised, stay in the city until you are clothed with Power from on High." *(Luke 24:44-49)*

Jesus was a sign of contradiction and always will be. He challenged the law, the people, the chief priests and the pharisees. In fact He challenges anyone who comes in contact with Him. He pointed out what was false and futile, while at the same time he drew others to Himself, to follow Him. 'Come follow Me!' was His simple invitation. Some, like the apostles, simple fishermen, just couldn't resist Him, and left all their possessions to follow Him, thus becoming His 'special' friends. They knew His love for them personally, individually. The extraordinary and wonderful thing is that He trained them, from the very beginning, to help others find Him and follow Him. Later on, through them, He actually 'set up' His Church which still exists today, namely the Universal Church.

To Peter He said: "You are Peter, and on this Rock (the name 'Peter' meaning 'Rock') I will build My Church. And the gates of the Underworld can never hold out against it. I will give to you the Keys of the Kingdom of Heaven. Whatever you bind on earth will be bound in Heaven,

whatever you loose on earth will be loosed in Heaven"
(Matthew 16:17-20).

He sent His followers out to proclaim the Kingdom of
God, and to heal. He said to them: "Take nothing for the
journey: neither staff nor haversack, nor bread, nor money;
and let none of you take a spare tunic. Whatever house
you enter, stay there; and when you leave, let it be from
there. As for those who do not welcome you, when you
leave their town, shake the dust from your feet as a sign to
them. So they set out and went from village to village,
proclaiming the 'Good News', and healing everywhere."
(Luke 9:1-6)

Jesus promised to be with them until the end, "Behold I
am with you always, even to the end of the world" *(Matthew
28:20)* We find that God's call to us is always answered
with a promise. He will never fail those whom He calls.

Jesus especially challenged the Jews who were waiting for
a military Messiah of Miracles, teaching them that His
Kingdom was not one of power, but one of faith and service
and entry to it is only by believing in Him.

The Jews professed belief in God, believing that God
brought their ancestors out of Egypt, that He fed them
with manna in the desert and with water from the rock,
and that He made a covenant with them to make them
His people. He gave them the Ten Commandments to
live by, He spoke to them through the prophets and
patriarchs, like Abraham, Isaac, Jacob, David, Moses and
others. They blessed God and sometimes lived with a
holy fear of Him, as they worshipped Him.

Sometimes, too, they turned their backs on Him, and even worshipped idols (false gods). He constantly pursued them, always calling them back to Himself, their Leader and Shepherd. In the end, after repeated infidelities, He made a covenant with them, writing His law in their hearts. Later on of course, we know He made the final covenant with His people through the Blood of the Lamb, His only Son, Jesus.

"When 'the hour' came, Jesus took His place at table, and the apostles with Him. And He said to them, 'I have longed to eat this Passover with you before I suffer, because I tell you, I shall not eat it again until it is fulfilled in the Kingdom of God.' Then taking the cup, He gave thanks and said 'Take this and share it among you, because from now on, I tell you, I shall not drink wine until the Kingdom of God comes'. Then He took some bread, and when He had given thanks, broke it, and gave it to them saying, 'This is My Body which will be given for you; Do this as a memorial of Me'. He did the same with the cup after supper, and said, 'This cup is the new covenant in My Blood which will be poured out for you." *(Luke 22: 14-20)*

And so the covenant God made with man is sealed with the Blood of Jesus. The sacrifice of the Mass comes to life. Jesus said, "Do this in Remembrance of Me." And so the Mass continues the sacrifice of Calvary.

We can pray with our ancestors, the following wonderful prayers from the Old Testament. These prayers would often have been used by the Jews to praise God, their Father and ours, "who made all things in creation, in Heaven and Earth, things seen and unseen." *(Hebrews 11: 3)*

"Blessed are you O Lord, God of Israel our Father,
Forever and ever,
Yours O Lord is the greatness and the power
And the glory and the Victory and the Majesty
For all that is in the Heavens and the Earth is yours
Yours is the Kingdom O Lord
And You are exalted as Head above all
Both riches and honour come from You
And You rule over all
In Your hand it is to make great
And to give strength to all
And now we thank You our God
And praise your glorious Name."
(1 Chronicles 29:11-14)

One who goes out in the days of Nissan (spring time) and sees fruit trees flowering should say: "Blessed be He who has left nothing lacking in His world and has created in it goodly creatures and goodly trees for people's enjoyment."
(Babylonian Talmud, Brakhot, 43b)

The Jews found it hard to believe in Jesus, Son of God, born of the Virgin Mary, Lord of Heaven and Earth. "Your Fathers ate manna in the desert and died." Jesus said to them, "but I am offering you the Bread of Life, come down from Heaven. I *am* the Bread of Life. If you eat this Bread, you will live for ever." *(John 6:35,58)*
But they were not equal to the challenge, and reacted angrily: "Who does He think He is, and who does He think we are? Don't we know His mother?" "This is intolerable language. How could anyone accept it?" *(John 6:60)* So they walked away, unable to accept Him or His message.

It is still the same today. Jesus turns sadly to His disappointed Apostles, "Do you want to go away too ?." Good old Peter comes up trumps: "To whom shall we go Lord; You have the message of Eternal life? You are the Christ the Son of the living God." This happened at Caesarea Philippi where Jesus made Peter head of the Church. "Flesh and blood has not revealed this to you, Peter," Jesus said, "but My Father who is in Heaven." *(Matthew 16:16)*

Jesus loves the Father, and He wants everyone to know Him. "The world must be brought to know that I love the Father." He said "and that I am doing exactly what the Father told Me." *(John 14:31)* Jesus constantly communed with His Father while He was on earth.

"Father in Heaven," Jesus prayed, "Hallowed be Your Name, Your Kingdom come, Your will be done ..." Jesus begins with His Father, His Father's interest, His Father's work, His Father's will, His Father's hour for Him. His whole life is Father-centred. "The Father and I are one." He said. He was never alone!

One can only know God 'from above', and as Christians we can come to know God only through Jesus. It is not a 'natural' knowledge. It cannot be attained through understanding, intelligence, science, technology, space probes or any other means. It is purely God's gift to the individual. It is a supernatural knowledge, the same knowledge that we will have when this veil of faith is torn aside and we will see God face to face. Only God Himself can give this knowledge, only God alone can reveal to us who He really is. Jesus Himself gave us His Holy Spirit, to lead us to all truth and to complete the work He Himself has begun in us and in the Church. We know from the depths of this sublime knowledge where the word of God and human wisdom meet that "whoever sees Me sees the one who sent Me". *(John 12:45)*

"By this you know the Spirit of God. Every spirit which confesses that Jesus Christ has come in the flesh, is of God." *(1 John 4:2-3)*
"He was manifested in the flesh, attested by the Spirit, seen by angels, proclaimed to the pagans, believed in by the world, taken up in glory." *(1 Timothy 3:16)*

It is God's will, that His Kingdom should come and that all men should confess the Lordship of Jesus Christ. "Whoever believes in Me." Jesus says "Believes not in Me, but in the one who sent Me." *(John 12: 44)* God wants *every* human being, without exception, to know Him. Jesus died for all. We know from Scripture also that "no one can say 'Jesus is Lord' except by the Holy Spirit." *(1 Corinthians 12:3)* It is a Trinitarian work in us.

To seek God is to live, to seek God is man's purpose in life. To know God, to love God, to serve God in this world and to be happy with Him forever in the next, is why God made man. There are so many people today who do not know God – some through deliberate choice of not wanting to know Him; others haven't yet had the chance to know Him. Just as Jesus wept over Jerusalem, longing to gather a people together, so He must still weep over our 'pagan' world today, which is becoming more and more 'secular'.

Mankind has always been seeking God, perhaps even

without realising it. Man has always been searching for something bigger than himself to solve the problem of pain, and suffering, but never with complete success. The search for a solution has often been through medicine, science or technology, and also through philosophy, Buddhism, Yoga, transcendental meditation etc.

The mystery remains, and the solution for many is incomplete. "The heart of man is restless and troubled. Man conquered space but is unsure of himself. He is confused about the direction in which he is heading. It is tragic that our technological mastery is greater than our wisdom about ourselves." *(Pope John Paul II, Wembley, 1982)*

It is evident that the world is in the power of darkness. People are in spiritual bondage, under the oppression of evil *(Ephesians 2: 1-3)* and the only answer is Jesus Christ, the Light of the World. This is not an optional extra, for Jesus Himself says "Cut off from Me, you can do nothing." *(John 15:5)* One of the biggest sadnesses in today's world is atheism. Not knowing God must surely be the worst thing on earth, a terrible poverty – much worse, I think, than any material poverty. I pray that all peoples will come to know Him. Will you join me in that prayer?

Recently, I was saddened as I spoke to a group of sixth formers, who professed to be either "nothing at all" or "atheist" or "agnostic." They weren't quite sure, but most of them said they wished they could believe in something or someone. They were like sheep without a shepherd, deprived of even the basic knowledge of God, that we took for granted as children. There was however 'a love' in them and a desire to serve. Though saddened at their lack of a personal knowledge of God, I know that through their charity (love), God will point the way ahead towards Himself. "Where love is, there God is". *(Hymn 'Ubi Caritas' based on 1 John 4:16)*

It is love which gives life meaning and value and if we go further, we find it was love and love alone that led Jesus to the Cross, to give His life for others including us. All goodness flows from Him for only God is good and only in Him can we find the fullness of life. *(John 10:10)*

How grateful I am to God for my Catholic upbringing in Ireland, where the faith has always been loved and cherished and where knowledge of God has been 'a way of life'. The old Irish people, like our grandparents, had an amazing sense of God. They talked to Him about everything. Their lives were totally God-centred. It is a joy to study 'Celtic' spirituality where we find the treasured 'roots' of our faith history, with strong awareness and love for God in all things and events and circumstances. It is worth studying a great Irish woman called Peg Sayers, who was 'illiterate' in worldly wisdom but a 'giant' when it came to trusting in God, and knowledge of spiritual things! These older Irish people lived 'with God'. "The secret of the Kingdom of God is given to you." *(Mark 4:11)*

I pray for these young people today and for all non-believers. As Abraham *(cf. Exodus 18)* pleaded with God to spare the city of Sodom, if He should find only five just men in it, so I beg God to spare these young people, and have mercy on them, and on all who seek to believe or who refuse to believe in Him. We must be careful not to 'play God' in our judgements for these are God's people and we do not know how He is working in each one, like a seed, hidden in the field, growing imperceptibly while we sleep; so too is God's grace at work in souls. Our job is to scatter as many seeds as we can for God. He alone can make the seed grow.

Jesus said that the Kingdom of Heaven is like this:

"A man throws seed on the land. Night and day, while he sleeps, when he is awake, the seed is sprouting and growing, how he does not know. Of its own accord, the land produces first the shoot, then the ear, then the full grain in the ear. And when the crop is ready, he loses no time, he starts to reap because the harvest has come." (Mark 4:26-29)

This parable is told only in the Gospel of St. Mark. It talks about God's Kingdom which is the Reign of God. It makes one feel so humble, for God is trying to tell us here, that even the farmer does not know how the seed grows and that he himself cannot make it grow. Life and growth is within the seed itself, tiny as it is, and only the seed has the 'secret of life'. Man cannot create life just as man cannot know God of himself. Philosophers, scientists, physicists, can discover things, can rearrange things, develop things, but never create things. We can frustrate God's plan, but we cannot usurp God's power or God's prerogative. He works imperceptibly, constantly, like the seed growing while the farmer sleeps.

If the seed in the ground does not die, it cannot produce the shoot. "Unless the grain of wheat falls into the ground and die," Jesus said, "it remains only a single grain, but if it dies, it yields a rich harvest."
(John 12;24)

Today I thank God for the seed of the 'Alpha' evangelisation programme, which began with Nicky Gumble and four other people (small beginnings!) at the Anglican Church of Holy Trinity, Brompton, London. It is now spreading like 'wild fire' across the land and beyond. It incorporates many cultures, languages and nationalities. It is sowing seeds of God's word everywhere, leading people in their search for God and satisfying, in a refreshing way, those who have found Him but thirst for more. Alpha always includes a meal together.

Alpha is fulfilling the secret longing of many hearts, for Jesus Himself is the focus. A personal relationship with Him is the outcome. God is drawing thousands of souls to seek Himself. It is God who gives life, and only God can give the increase.
We can help sow seeds with Him, and it is very humbling to know that God uses us in this way. In fact God uses all of us in some small way to spread knowledge of Him, while the mystery of growth remains His. Faith is said to be 'caught' rather than 'taught', though once we've been

'hooked' by Jesus' fishing rod, we need 'nurturing' in order to grow to full stature. It is exciting!

The Rite of Christian Initiation of Adults (R.C.I.A. Programme) is also worth mentioning here. It is bringing new life to the Catholic Church to all those who are seeking a journey in faith. The development of the lay apostolate is a wonderful sign of the active presence of the Holy Spirit in our Church today.

A living faith in the home helps enormously! Example speaks louder than words. For faith to take root and grow, it is essential that we be in touch with a living vibrant faith community.
Young people today are sadly deprived of opportunity for experiencing and sharing faith (though their hearts are generous). Schools which should offer 'sound' instruction and an act of worship each day (according to the 1944 Education Act) are tragically failing pupils. Assemblies are anything but an act of worship! The young are seeking truth, some unfortunately are 'side-tracked', (temporarily we hope), into false religions – New Age, Astrology, Occult, Spiritualism and the several 'weird' cults that 'pop up' overnight (like the one in America, where thirty nine young people died in a suicide pact, having made a video for their friends the night before!) They are misguided in their search for happiness through the misuse of drugs, sex, alcohol, as they try to lose themselves in a world of unreality, seeking happiness in everything other than God, who is, of course, the source of happiness.

Many people today do not know the Ten Commandments of God any more. They are like lost sheep seeking orientation and purpose in life. Others are following the 'call to serve', finding satisfaction and help in working voluntarily with refugees, the sick and handicapped, and those in need generally. Here 'in service' to others they find God – like Carol, who went to Bosnia as a volunteer, was a professed 'Atheist' and returned home a 'baptised' Catholic, 'in love' with Jesus, having found a husband, and is now married with a lovely baby. "Blessed is He who gives...."

There are still others who go about their daily routine, simply living a life of love and service, bothering no one, but just trying to live every day as it comes, as best as they can. I call them the 'salt of the earth' people, who seek God in their own 'quiet' unpretentious way and find Him! Let us not forget that it is always God who seeks us first, and who continues to seek us daily. He tells us in scripture to seek in order to find. "God rewards those who try to find Him." *(Hebrews 11:6)*

It may be difficult to respond to Him at first, but each effort is rewarding, as we try to 'set the sails' for Him, our knowledge will increase, and so our love for Him will grow like a tiny mustard seed. He awaits our personal response.

"To those who did receive Him, He gave power to become sons of God, to all those who believe in the name of Him, who was born, not of human stock or the urge of the flesh, or the will of man but of God Himself." *(John 12:13)*

Revelation is a two way process – God's doing initially and our response. St. Augustine writes: "Without God we cannot, without us God will not." Some atheists and agnostics say they envy me my faith, and wish they could believe in God as I do, while others try to joke about it! Some are apparently very 'good' people, kindly, loving, but don't know what they are missing! Others will tell you that they've never felt the need for God. "I've managed all these years without Him", they'll say, "and I'm fine. Religion is a 'cop out', for weaklings, fairies-at-the-bottom-of-the-garden stuff! Religion does nothing but cause wars." To them 'religion' and God are synonymous - a big mistake!

Ghandi said once, that if he could meet a fully alive committed Christian who lived the Gospel, he might convert. It was unfortunately never his experience, and yet he was such a 'good' man and believed in God!
Sheila Cassidy explains: "Ironically, it is often the non-believer who seems closest to following Jesus". ('Good Friday People', p. 23) Where there is love, there is God.
Many deny outright the very existence of God, rejecting the intimate and vital bond between man and God.

So often the Bible, the Book of Life, which marries Earth and Heaven, lies unopened or else it is used in a misguided search. We know that "All scripture is inspired by God and can profitably be used for teaching, for refuting error, for guiding people's lives and teaching them to be holy. This is how the man who is dedicated to God becomes fully equipped and ready for any good work." (2 Timothy 3:16-17)

It is instructive to distinguish between Atheism and Agnosticism, in case you are unsure (as I was) of the difference between them both.
"Atheistic Humanism considers man to be an end in himself, and the sole maker with supreme control of his

own history." *(Catechism of the Catholic Church, Art. 2124)*
"Atheism is based on a false concept of human autonomy, exaggerated to the point of refusing any dependence on God" *(Catechism of the Catholic Church, Art. 2126)*

Agnosticism, on the other hand, does not deny God but believes that there is a transcendent being incapable of revealing itself and that it is, therefore, impossible to prove its existence. Agnostics are sometimes searching for God but cannot accept a personal God. *(Catechism of the Catholic Church, Art. 2128)*

I would like to quote to you a passage of Scripture referring to 'God-lessness'. It may seem harsh, but it is God's Word.

> *"Yes, naturally stupid are all men who have not known God and who, from the good things that are seen, have not been able to discover Him Who Is, or by studying the works, have failed to recognise the Artificer.*
>
> *Fire, however, or wind, or the swift air, the sphere of the stars, impetuous water, heaven's lamps, are what they have held to be, the gods who govern the world.*
>
> *If, charmed by their beauty, they have taken things for gods, let them know how much the Lord of these excels them, since the very Author of beauty has created them. And if they have been impressed by their power and energy, let them deduce from these how much mightier is He that has formed them, since*

through the grandeur and beauty of the creatures, we may, by analogy, contemplate the Author.

Small blame, however attaches to these men, for perhaps, they only go astray in their search for God and their eagerness to find Him, living among His works, they strive to comprehend them and fall victim to appearances, seeing so much beauty.

Even so, they are not to be excused. If they are capable of acquiring enough knowledge to be able to investigate the world, how have they been so slow to find its Maker?"

(Wisdom 13:1-9)

"Many feel that leaving Me out of life is avoiding mystery and silence, and enjoying life's certainties. Those who are content to live without Me fail to see that although I cannot be superficially discerned, I am wonderfully met in that silence, and that apparent 'non activity'." *('I Am With You', John Woolley)*

"You refuse to come to Me to find true life". *(John 5:40)*
"The fool says in his heart 'There is no God!'...
God is looking down from Heaven at the sons of men
To see if a single one is wise,
If a single one is seeking God." *(Psalm 53:1-2)*

St. Irenaeus tells us that the "Glory of God is man fully alive." In no way does belief in God oppose the dignity of man. Rather it ennobles it. Was it not God who made man, at the beginning of creation, "male and female, in His own image and likeness" *(Genesis 1: 27)*? Do we not read in scripture that; "Your body, you know, is the temple of the Holy Spirit, Who is in you since you received Him from God? You are not your own property, you have been bought and paid for; that is why you should use your body for the glory of God." *(1 Corinthians 6:19-20)*

Worth quoting here too is that marvellous passage from Ecclesiasticus telling us how the Lord God made man in His own image: and of the dignity He bestowed on him from the beginning:

"The Lord fashioned man from the earth, to consign him back to it.

He gave them so many days' determined time, He gave them authority over everything on earth. He clothed them with strength like His own, and made them in His own image.

He filled living things with dread of man, making him master over beasts and birds. He shaped for them a mouth and tongue, eyes and ears, and gave them a heart to think with. He filled them with knowledge and understanding and revealed to them good and evil.

He put His own light in their hearts, to show them the magnificence of His works. They will praise His Holy Name, as they tell of His

*magnificent works. He set knowledge before
them. He endowed them with the law of life.
He established an eternal covenant with them,
and revealed His judgements to them.
Their eyes saw His glorious majesty, and their
ears heard the glory of His voice.
He said to them: "Beware of all wrong doing";
He gave them a commandment concerning his
neighbour.
Their ways are always under His eye;
They cannot be hidden from His sight."*

(Ecclesiasticus 17:1-15)

Someone once prayed: "My God, if You exist help me to know You." This prayer recalls the prayer of the epileptic boy "If you can do anything, have pity on us and help us!" "*If* you can.".. retorted Jesus, "everything is possible for anyone who has faith." Immediately the father of the boy cried out "I do have faith. Help my little faith!." *(Matthew 9: 22-24)*

This nascent faith and humble confession gained the man his son's cure. One can't look for faith as one looks for rational certainty; one can't reach faith by reason or argument, it is pure gift of God; it comes from above.

Everything that exists, exists in God alone. We know that God keeps all that He has made. In a revelation to St. Julian of Norwich, (mystic, anchorite 12th century) God showed her a little thing, the size of a hazelnut, in the palm of her hand, and it was as round as a ball. She looked at it with her mind's eye and thought, 'what can this be?'.

And the answer came, 'It is all that is made'. She marvelled that it could last, for she thought it might crumble to nothing, it was so small, and the answer came into her mind: "It lasts, and ever shall, because God loves it, and all things through the love of God." In this little thing, Julian of Norwich saw three truths: The first is that God made it, the second is that God loves it, and the third is that God looks after it." *('Revelations of Divine Love')*

"And I will lead the blind
In a way they do not know;
In paths that they have not known
I will guide them.
I will turn their darkness into light before them.
The rough places into level ground." *(Isaiah 42:16)*

As for religions other than Christian, the Catholic Church acknowledges "the search among shadows and images, for the God who is unknown yet near, since He gives life and breath to all things and wants all men saved. Thus the Church considers all goodness and truth found in these religions, as a preparation for the gospel of Jesus Christ and given by Him who enlightens all men, that they may at length have life." *(Catechism of the Catholic Church, Art. 843)*

St. Paul gives us advice on how to treat our non-Christian friends: "Be tactful with those who are not Christians, and be sure you make the best use of your time with them. Talk to them agreeably and with a flavour of wit, and try to fit your answers to the needs of each one." *(Colossians 4:5-6)*

Sadly, I find 'lapsed' Catholics are among those who sometimes deny their faith, and deny God most blatantly.

Some speak as if they are quite unsure as to whether there is a God or not. Is it a longing for truth, or for what's been lost or is it guilt or hurt that, for some reason, they often bring 'God' into their conversation? Is it a certain coldness and indifference that's been allowed to develop? It is amazing how hurts cause them to deny the 'truth' and often through projection of a hurt, the innocent (in this case God) gets the blame! Hurts caused at a particularly vulnerable time in their life, can lead to misunderstanding.

God, of course, understands all situations, and He sees why human nature struggles so much and why we have to blame someone for our grievances. His love never changes. Our arrogance, stupidity, pride, self-righteousness, are so pathetic at times, that one would wonder how God has patience with us. God's great desire is always for us. He is the Prodigal Father, waiting for us to return. He daily awaits us. It's not for us to judge the lapsed: we should be particularly gentle and compassionate to them. After all, they didn't leave our Church for nothing! They would have left for some good reason known only to themselves and to God. Does anyone ever know another fully?

Some lapse from the Catholic Church because they yearn for a 'renewed church', a 'post-Vatican II church', where they can find the Holy Spirit alive and active. They seek to worship God in other churches, which does allow them greater freedom of spirit.

Others never enter the Church at all as they find the idea of accepting a God of Love too much to take. They feel they should *earn* His love; and that they do not deserve His gratuity. They think they are not good enough. True!

In seeking God, we must humbly come to Jesus, the Saviour, who is always knocking at our door. "I sleep, but my heart is awake. I hear my Beloved knocking." *(Song of Songs 5:2)*

In Scripture God sometimes describes Himself as the one who knocks: "Behold I stand at the door and knock. If anyone hears me calling and opens the door, I will come in to share his meal, side by side with him." *(Revelation 3:20-21)*

Once His call is sounded, the way to go should become quite clear, even though it may entail sacrifice. C.S. Lewis was travelling in a bus up the hill in Oxford when God's call to become a Catholic came to him clearly. He obeyed.

The famous poem 'The Hound of Heaven' by Francis Thompson sums up beautifully man's attempt to run away from God, and God's pursuit of him:

"I fled Him down the nights and down the days;
I fled Him through the arches of the years;
I fled Him down the labyrinthine ways
Of my own mind, and in the midst of tears
I hid from Him ... from those strong Feet that followed,
followed after ...
But, with unhurrying chase and unperturbed pace
Deliberate speed, majestic instancy
They beat ... and a Voice beat more instant than the Feet
'All things betray thee who betrays Me ...'
'Naught shelters thee who will not shelter Me ...'
'Lo, naught contents thee who contents not Me ...'
I am He Whom thou seekest!
... Thou drawest love from thee who drawest Me!"

A further word from the Song of Songs *(1:4)* shares similar thoughts:

> "Draw me in your footsteps, let us run!
> The King has brought me into his rooms;
> You will be our joy and our gladness.
> We shall praise your love above wine;
> How right it is to love You."

God never gives up on us, fortunately, and He never gives up the search for us. "He sleeps not nor slumbers Israel's guide." Some sheep He finds lost in the brambles, others

in the pit, others up to their neck in trouble, others He finds have wandered off to other folds, but when He finds one, He puts it on His shoulder and He comes home rejoicing. "There is more joy in Heaven" Jesus says, "over one lost sheep that is found, than over ninety nine sheep that don't go astray." *(Luke 15:7)*
"I shall look for the lost one, bring back the stray, bandage the wounded and make the weak strong. I shall watch over the fat and healthy; I shall keep them in view; I shall rescue them from wherever they have been scattered during the mist and darkness. I shall feed them in good pasturage. I shall be a true Shepherd to them. *(Ezekiel 34:12,16)*

"How I grieve to see so many of My children led, in various paths, away from safety... away from Me. Because there is real freedom of will, I cannot always enforce a return to safety, but I do pursue... I never tire of making it possible for a choice to be made to return home. I pursue in far wanderings from My way. I also pursue when one of My children, (as yourself), wanders even slightly into danger. This is why you feel the uneasiness, the loss of peace, which accompanies the straying from My way."
('I Am With You', John Woolley p 226)

Whenever we wander, there is no escape from Him. He can always find us.

> "O Lord, You search me and You know me,
> You know my resting and my rising
> You discern my purpose from afar
> You mark when I walk or lie down
> All my ways lie open to You
> Behind and before You besiege me
> Too wonderful for me this knowledge
> Too high beyond my reach." *(Psalm 139:1-4)*

I find it so comforting to know that God is always seeking me and my good and that His seeking me has only one purpose, to make me His. He does not look at our sins.

"The Lord is tender and compassionate
slow to anger most loving
His indignation does not last forever
His resentment exists only a short time.
He never treats us never punishes us
As our guilt and our sins deserve." *(Psalm 103: 8-10)*

"He chose us in Christ before the foundation of the world, that we should be blameless and holy before Him… determining that we should become His adopted sons, through Jesus Christ." *(Ephesians 1: 4-6)*

We belong to Him whether we like it or not. Why should we want to escape from Him, who alone wants our total good? God made us in such a way that 'instinctively' we long for Him. We grope in the darkness as St. Augustine says: "Our hearts are restless till they find God." Even our happiest moment is tinged with longing.

The Psalmist constantly prays:
"God, You are my God, I am seeking You,
My soul is thirsting for You
My flesh is longing for You
like a dry weary land without water.
I long to gaze on You in the sanctuary,
To see your power and Your glory." *(Psalm 63:1-2)*

Again the psalmist prays and we join with him as we, too, long for Him: "My soul thirsts for You my God the God of my life, when can I enter and see the face of God." *(Psalm 42: 2)*

The greatest Messianic Prophet, Isaiah, exhorts us to seek God in conversion of life, that we may experience a change of lifestyle, and reap the benefit of living a holy life.

"Seek God while He may be found
Call to God while He is still near
Let the wicked man abandon his way
The evil man his thoughts.
Let him turn back to Him who will take pity on him,

To our God who is rich in forgiving
For my thoughts are not your thoughts
My ways not your ways, It is the Lord who speaks,
Yes, as the Heavens are as high above the Earth
As my thoughts are above your thoughts
My ways above your ways." *(Isaiah 55:6-9)*

God is always giving us 'another chance'. Doesn't the Offertory hymn put it well? 'The chances we have missed, the graces we resist, Lord, in this Eucharist, take and redeem'. *(Celebration Hymnal, Kevin Nichols)*
Aren't these comforting words! It is sad to think that we possibly begin to search for God only because we no longer know where else to go, and only when we feel 'let down' by life, by our lost beauty, by health, by our shattered dreams. Often it is only then that we open ourselves to God, to the One who still loves us.

Sometimes it takes a tragedy or we have to be 'broken to pieces' and reach 'rock bottom' before we love ourselves enough, to come to Him, who stands by us, and who alone can bring us peace. "He will be Peace" the prophet Micah foretold. And St. Paul tells us: "He alone is our Peace."
(Ephesians 2:14)

When suffering weighs heavy upon us, it is only then perhaps that faith in Jesus lights up our night and instead of trusting ourselves, and our powers and abilities, we're forced to seek His face, and call upon His help. He never turns away. He never turns *us* away. He is *always* waiting, longing, hoping, ready to help and to rescue us and lead us onwards towards His peace which "surpasses all understanding."

The Cross, the sign of our redemption, takes on new meaning then, and perhaps for the first time in our lives, we'll meet Him there beneath the Cross, and we won't want to run away any more, conquered at last by His overwhelming love.

Can we stay there now awhile and comfort Him? "Lord, my heart is Yours". Can we let Him comfort us? Can we keep his Mother company? Can we identify with her Motherly suffering heart, as the sword of sorrow pierces it? Have we no words of comfort for her Beloved Son, except to stay there watching awhile as He breathes His last? Do we hear Him say to us, "This is your mother?." Isn't closeness to the Crucified the only thing that makes sense, as you sit by the bedside of the dying, as they struggle to breathe their last breath, preparing for Home? "This day you will be with Me in paradise", Jesus promised the 'good' thief. Imagine how he must have felt, after his wayward life, to be so rewarded by Jesus!

Why not pause here a moment to meditate a little on the scene. Imagine the 'Good' thief, Dismas, with Jesus Crucified. Who is seeking who at this moment in time I wonder? Does it not speak for itself that God pursues us till we draw our last breath? He is the prime mover, always ready to reveal Himself, to forgive us, and to call us to Himself in order to give us new life.

So we can make His sacrifice our own, His sorrow on the Cross our own.
Being with Him, we can lead others to Calvary, and there, together, share in the fulfilment of the Cross, the completion of His Sacrifice.

Listen, let your heart keep seeking
Listen to His constant speaking
Listen to the Spirit calling you
Listen to His inspiration
Listen to His invitation
Listen to the Spirit calling you......

St. Luke writes in the Acts of the Apostles:

"Since the God who made the world and everything in it is Himself the Lord of Heaven and Earth, He does not make His home in shrines made by human hands. Nor is He dependent on anything that human hands can do for Him, since He can never be in need of anything. On the contrary, it is He who gives everything including life and breath to everyone.
From one single stock, He not only creates the whole human race, so that they could occupy the entire earth but He decreed how long each nation should flourish and what boundaries its territories should be. And He did this so that all nations might seek the Deity, and by feeling their way towards Him, succeed in finding Him. Yet in fact, He is not far from any of us, since it is in Him that we live and move and exist, as indeed some of your own writers have said 'We are all His children'."
(Acts 17:24-28)

God has no 'special' place. He's always popping up when you least expect it, and when you can't go any more, He

is there for you, carrying you. The poem 'Footprints' by
Margaret Fishback Powers sums it up so well:–

One night
I had a dream.
I was walking
along the beach with
the Lord, and across the
skies flashed scenes from my
life. In each scene I noticed two
sets of footprints in the sand
and, to my surprise, I noticed that
many times along the path of my
life there was only one set of
footprints. And I noticed that it
was the lowest and saddest times
in my life. I asked the Lord
about it: "Lord, you said
that once I decided to
follow you, you would
walk with me all the
way. But I noticed that
during the most trouble-
some times in my life
there is only one set of
footprints. I don't
understand why you
left my side when I
needed you most."
The Lord said: "My
precious child, I never
left you during your
time of trial. Where
you see only one set
of footprints, I was
carrying you."

He will come to you in the presence of a friend, in a surprise gift of a holiday, in the remembrance of a happy memory, or some unexpected happening for the best. Perhaps you will consider it a co-incidence, but I believe there are no such things, only *God* incidences, for I believe God is *in charge* twenty four hours a day!

When both my parents were dying together in 1981, I must have reached 'rock-bottom', (though nobody around noticed) I was exhausted and my heart was breaking. I tried to put on a brave face. I didn't know where to turn. My family was so traumatized at the shock and suddenness of everything happening that they behaved 'out of character'. My Community at that time was insensitive and seemed uncaring. Only God, the steadfast Rock, sustained me! I desperately needed to sleep and rest. I used to spend day and night by my mother's bedside. It's possible to get very worn down at times like this - one doesn't eat or sleep properly. My dad had just died in another part of the city, and I just felt I could go on no longer without sleep.

I booked in for a weekend Retreat at the Reparation Convent in Limerick simply with the intention of sleeping and resting and doing nothing else. Unfortunately the Retreat House was full. The secretary sent me down the road to ask the F.C.J's for a bed. These sisters did not know me, but one old sister recognised me from a prayer meeting in August, when I had asked for prayer for my sick mother. They welcomed me with open arms amidst 'sobs' of exhaustion, and they opened wide their doors and took me in to the heart of their Community, thus giving me a 'Home'. They kept me for two weeks, treated me like a 'queen', with breakfast in bed every morning, (I could sleep and sleep here as it was very quiet and peaceful). They never charged me one penny! Such love and hospitality and generosity I shall never forget.' Surely God saw my greatest need and arranged that "there was no room at the first inn", so that He could bless me with abundant love and the rest I desperately needed, beyond my hopes and dreams! Such is our God, always doing the best thing. These sisters were indeed my 'good angels' at a time of desperate need. I find that, no matter what I need, whether for myself or others, God gives it to me. Thank you, Jesus.

Try to sense His Presence and companionship, to share your life and all that is happening with Him – your daily efforts and set backs, talk to Him as to your Beloved Friend, tell Him your joys and sorrow, your difficulties, your hopes and dreams.

Express your love and trust in the silence of your heart, as you go about your daily tasks. Learn to see Him everywhere, in all things, in the beauty as well as in the squalor, in the sorrows and in the joys, and in the sin of humanity.

Ask Him to help you see as He sees, with compassion and tenderness:

Listen, let your heart keep seeking.....

He's in the sound of thunder
In the whisper of the breeze
He's in the might of the whirlwind
In the roaring of the seas.

He's in the laughter of children
In the patter of the rain
Hear Him in the cries of the suffering
In their moaning and their pain.

He's in the noise of the city
In the singing of the birds
And in the night time the stillness
helps you listen to His word.

Listen, let your heart keep seeking....

I found that little song sung in a church recently and was quite moved by the words as it was sung at Mass. I had never heard it before, but I liked its thought and simplicity.

Don't waste time seeking Him in power and wealth, prestige and glamour. He's with the poor and lowly, with those who know their need of Him, and who seek Him in humility, like Mary, Our Mother, that wonderful Jewish Virgin, who sought Him always and who lived for Him alone. She was so ready with her 'fiat' when the Angel came from God, and she responded to God, her Creator, amidst great perplexity and sheer human impossibility, with results that will have effect throughout history and beyond into Eternity.

"My soul glorifies the Lord
My spirit rejoices in God my Saviour
He looks on His servant in her lowliness
Henceforth all ages will call me Blessed.

The Almighty works marvels for me
Holy is His Name
His mercy is from age to age
On those who fear Him.

He puts forth His arm in strength
And scatters the proud hearted
He casts the mighty from their thrones
And raises the lowly.

He fills the starving with good things
sends the rich away empty
He protects Israel His servant
Remembering His mercy
The mercy promised to our fathers
To Abraham and his sons forever.
(Luke 1: 46-55)

This is Mary's song of gratitude, God did not disappoint her, but revealed Himself to her in the most astonishing way. Her gratitude oozes out like fine oil....

I add here the following little poem I found many years ago and liked, as it expresses sentiments well worth considering. I believe that things do not just happen, if we want to have a full and happy life; we ourselves have to help 'to make' them happen by having the correct 'mind set'. Seek the Kingdom of God, seek His face, seek His ways, set the sails correctly, detach your heart from earthly things, and all these things will be added unto you, for remember Scripture says rightly, "Where your treasure is, there is your heart too." *(Matthew 6:21)*

One ship drives East, another West,
With the self-same winds that blow;
It's the set of the sails and not the gales,
Which decide the way to go.

Like the winds of the sea are the ways of Fate,
As we voyage along through Life.
It's the will of the soul that decides its goal!
And not the calm or the strife.

(Anonymous)

Daily set the sails for Him and when there's no wind, row!
Someone once asked a sailor, "How does the wind work?"
"I know how my sail works" he said. So, let 'us' know too
how our sails work, only by the power of the Holy Spirit,
as we continually try to set our hearts on the things of
God.

In seeking God, Julian of Norwich suggests:–

(a) That, by His grace, we should seek with deliberation and diligence without slackening and do it moreover gladly and cheerfully without moroseness or melancholy:

(b) That we wait steadfastly on Him in love and do not grumble or gird against Him in this life, which is not very long anyway.

(c) That we trust Him wholeheartedly and confidently. This is His will.

Sometimes in our seeking God, we get discouraged when consolations are absent and God seems very remote. Here Julian and John of the Cross and other great mystics, would suggest that these feelings of loneliness, depression, futility, may be nothing other than God being present in a special way. He is prompting us and leading us to see, that something deeper is needed than these doubtless pleasant feelings to which we would like to cling. We are being weaned off these and are invited to search deeper to discover God in the depths of our being. "Seeking," Julian says, "is as good as seeing."

Anthony de Mello, in his wonderful contemplative prayer book 'Sadhana' gives a very effective 'symbolic fantasy' exercise, for seeking God and finding Him. I have used it so often with several groups, and I find it never fails to give the desired effect, a greater sense of who we are, and of where we find God. I include it here, as you too might like to lead a group or you may even speak it onto a tape and replay it for yourself, in the cool of the evening.

Now, close your eyes and relax. Be still and silent. Take a few minutes to attain peace. You are now going on a journey.

"I want you to imagine you are sitting on the top of a mountain that is overlooking a vast city. It is twilight, the sun has just set and you notice the lights coming on in the great city ... Watch them coming on until the whole city seems a lake of lights ... You are sitting here all alone, gazing at this beautiful spectacle ... What are you feeling?... After a while, you hear footsteps behind you and you know they are the footsteps of a holy man who lives in those parts, a hermit. He comes up to you and stands by your side. He looks at you gently and says just one sentence to you. "If you go down to the city tonight, you will find God." Having said this he turns around and walks away. No explanation. No time for questions ...

You have a conviction that this man knows what he is talking about. What do you feel now? Do you feel like acting on his statement and going into the city? Or would you rather stay where you are?

Whatever your inclination, I want you to now go down to the city in search of God... What do you feel as you go down? You have now come to the outskirts of the city and you have to decide where to go to search for God and find Him... Where do you decide to go? Please follow the dictates of your heart in choosing the place you go to. Don't be guided by what you think you ought to do or where you ought to go. Just go where your heart tells you to go.

What happens when you get there?... What do you find there?... What do you do there?... What happens to you?… Do you find God?… In what way?… Or are you disappointed?… What do you do then?… Do you choose to go somewhere else?… Where?… Or do you just stay where you are?…

Now I want you to change the fantasy, whether you have found God or not. I want you to choose some symbol for God… anything you want that, for you, symbolises God best; the face of a child, a star, a flower, a tranquil lake… What symbol do you choose? Take some time choosing… Stand reverently in front of your symbol… What are you feeling as you gaze at this symbol? Say something to it… Imagine it speaks back to you… What does it say?… Remain awhile contemplating… Then say goodbye to your symbol… Take a minute or two for this… Then open your eyes… and end the exercise."

You could, if you do it with a group, then invite the group to share experiences. If it is a large group, divide into smaller groups of about five. This gives a chance for each one to share if they wish. If you do it alone, with a tape, you could write down your journey, and dwell on it awhile.

You will find you'll discover amazing things about yourself, your attitude and relationship to God, and where you find Him most easily. It is comforting and life-giving. I always find that most people want to stay with their experience and are reluctant to open their eyes quickly. They just want to stay enjoying the peace.

I believe that if you are sincere in your search for God, you will always find Him and, of course He will always find you, no matter where you think you can hide from Him. Seek out people who know Him and love Him.

"Avoid pointless philosophical discussions. They only lead further and further away from true religion. Talk of this kind corrodes like gangrene, as in the case of Hymenaeus and Philetus, the men who have gone right away from the truth and claim that the resurrection has already taken place. Some people's faith cannot stand up to them." *(2 Timothy 2:16-18)*

Go to places like Mount St. Bernard's Abbey, Coalville, where He is honoured and adored and where He lives among the Cistercian monks dedicated to Him. They rise at 3.30 a.m. to pay Him homage and their whole day is devoted to Opus Dei ('the work of God'), in simplicity, prayer, and work. You might like to experience their hospitality and stay for some time in their guest house. To enter this order there is only one question asked: "What are you seeking?." The only answer, which many could not make is, "I seek God." Places like this speak of Eternity. In the beautiful church (built by the monks) you will find a light burning perpetually, night and day, signifying the presence of Jesus Christ in the Eucharist. For Catholics this is the focal point of their faith, and their most precious gift. They believe Jesus is truly present in the Tabernacle under the appearance of bread. This is the mystery which lost Jesus many followers. That's why it's a wonderful custom to pop into church during the day to greet His Presence, as He waits silently for you. It is a tragedy that many of our Catholic churches have to be locked nowadays because of vandalism, and so many people are deprived of these wonderful 'special' contact times with Him.

I risk being sent to the Vatican dungeons, but I pray that many fervent Catholics may soon be allowed to keep the Blessed Sacrament for veneration in their homes, at least for a few hours adoration each week. Some parishes have, in fact, begun to do this in Advent and Lent, with great blessing to the families, homes and parish. I feel that the Lord longs for this great privilege to be shared among His chosen ones.

Nuns and Religious have always been privileged in this way. In the Community in which I live, when we have a very special request to make to God our Father we spend long hours in adoration before Him in our home. Once we spent from 8 p.m. to midnight on four consecutive nights praying for His will to be made known. At the end of these four days it was revealed miraculously.

An all-night vigil also brings many graces. When Sister Regina Collins needed the law regarding the sale of property in Hungary changed, her lay community did an all-night vigil of prayer, resulting in a phone call to say that the law had been changed overnight.

The Eucharist encapsulates everything – the Cosmos, the whole of life, Scripture, work, and prayer. Through it one can join oneself to all the prayers, works, sufferings and joys of the day, through every Eucharist offered throughout the world.

The Eucharist brings the closest possible contact in this life with Jesus Christ Himself. It is the 'heart to heart' time of the day. "Anyone who eats this Bread shall live forever." Jesus said. *(John 6: 58)* "Nothing can separate us from His love made visible in Jesus Christ." *(Romans 8:38)*

It is good to remain silent and adore ...

> O Sacrament most holy.
> O Sacrament divine;
> All praise and all thanksgiving
> Be every moment Thine.

Why not find a place in your home where you can meet Him and seek His face daily? Make it your special 'oratory'. I have lovely friends, a young couple, who have made the cupboard in their bedroom their 'little cathedral', where they both just about fit in together! Here they meet Him every day. Wonderful to find homes where He is honoured and where the sign of the Cross is given a place of honour.

In many homes in Ireland the Sacred Heart lamp burns night and day before the picture, a constant reminder of His care for us. Make your home 'His dwelling place'. "If anyone loves Me, he will keep my word, and My Father will love him and we will come to him and make our home with him." *(John 14: 23)*

An Exercise for a Group or on your own:

1. Think of the impact Jesus has had on
   a) human history   b) your life.?
2. What is it about Jesus that appeals to you?
3. Which part of your life are you giving Him, and which part are you withholding?
4. Which of His words appeal to you most?
5. Who are the people who have helped you to seek and find Him?
6. Where does your search for God feature in your joys, your problems?

And so, he who seeks, always finds. Sometimes we have to admit that we seek the wrong way or the wrong thing, but let's keep seeking. Never give up the search! Just as the Apostles on Mount Tabor saw "only Jesus" in His Transfiguration, we too must struggle on, for that purity of vision that will seek only Him in everything until "In His light we see light" *(Psalm 36: 9)*. We pray that all our darkness might fade and become light in Him, and that everything not of God in our lives may be transformed in His light.

"Seek ye first the Kingdom of God
And all these things shall be added unto you."
(Luke 12:31)

"I call you to hope in Me, for I am the only Hope of the whole earth. So few really know this in their hearts! Do not be among them. Let Me alone be your one true Hope, as you witness to others My unfailing love for you."

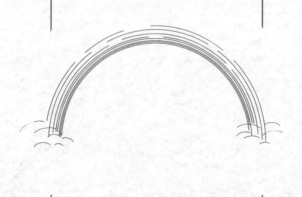

A CALL TO HOPE

For me, one of the greatest messages of hope comes in the Book of Genesis.

After the Fall, God promised to rescue mankind from the snares of the evil one. Our first parents had lost their innocence and were lost in their sin of disobedience. They had offended their Maker and, of themselves, they could not reach God. They were so ashamed that they hid from their Creator, as they recognised their sinfulness, their helplessness, their nakedness.

"Sin entered the world through one man (Adam) and through sin, death; and thus death was spread through the whole human race, because everyone has sinned." *(Romans 5:12)*

But God is always restoring, promising better things. Could our first parents have learned immediately how to call on God their Father, in their sin and shame? 'My God, why have I forsaken you?'

> *"But now, I have acknowledged my sins,*
> *my guilt I did not hide",*
> *I said: "I will confess my offence to the Lord,*
> *And you Lord, have forgiven*
> *The guilt of my sin."* *(Psalm 32:5)*

Scripture tells us that even before a word is on our lips, God knows it through and through, and so the message of hope for the whole of mankind, rings out clearly in the most wonderful promise ever made by God, addressed to Satan (the prince of darkness and despair) immediately after the Fall of man, thus giving hope to fallen humanity.

God said:
"Be accursed beyond all cattle, all wild beasts. You shall crawl on your belly and eat dust everyday of your life. I will make you enemies of each other; you and the woman, your offspring and her offspring. It will crush your head and you will strike its heel." *(Genesis 3:14-16)*

So, our hope in God brings us through every attack of the Evil One. As regards the woman, we know, of course, that the woman is Mary, Mother of God. Her offspring is Jesus, the Saviour of the World, the Son of God, the Son of Mary. Jesus' death on the cross crushed Satan's head, and freed mankind from the snares of the Devil and every human being without exception, has been paid for and ransomed by the death of Jesus on the Cross. 'Life's own Champion slain yet lives to reign. Christ my hope is risen; Christ our hope is risen! Alleluia!'

In November 1972 Pope Paul VI said: "One of the Church's greatest needs is to be defended against the evil we call the Devil. Evil is not merely an absence of something but an active force ... a living spiritual being that is perverted and that perverts others. It is a departure from the picture provided by Biblical and Church teaching to refuse to acknowledge the Devil's existence ..."
In Jesus today, we can overcome all the snares of the

enemy and all forces of evil. Jesus alone is our hope. He offers everyone new life. Thanks to Him, we can begin again to live, so could our first parents, and so, with the Church on Easter Night, we can cry out "O, happy fault. O, necessary sin of Adam!" Christ has conquered the power of evil, with the power of love, Christ is risen, Alleluia! "Man has only to pray and God will give life to the sinner." *(John 5:16)* "Behold! I bring you News of great Joy. Today in the city of David a Saviour is born. He is Christ, the Lord." *(Luke 2:10-11)*

We can replace 'city of David' with our own home 'town' name; our own 'home'; our own 'life'; and know that Christ is born again today and lives to reign in us.

"Adam prefigured the One to come but the Gift itself considerably outweighed the Fall. If it is certain that through one man's fall so many died, it is even more certain that Divine grace, coming through one man, Jesus Christ, came to so many as an abundant free-gift. The results of the gift also outweigh the results of one man's sin: for after one single fall came judgement with a verdict of acquittal.

If it is certain that death reigned over everyone as a consequence of one man's fall, it is even more certain that one man, Jesus Christ, will cause everyone to reign in life, who receives the free gift, that he does not deserve, of being made righteous. Again, as one man's fall brought condemnation on everyone, so the good act of one man brings everyone life and makes them justified. As by one man's disobedience many were made sinners, so by one man's obedience many will be made righteous. Just as sin reigned wherever there was death, so grace will reign to bring eternal life, thanks to the righteousness that comes through Jesus Christ Our Lord." (Romans 5:15-21)

Mary is a key figure in God's plan. One wonders what would have happened had she not cooperated with Him. She is the second Eve. From the beginning she has been a sign of hope, 'the maiden with child', foretold by the prophets:-

> "A woman, clothed with the sun,
> The moon beneath her feet
> And on her head a crown
> Of twelve stars.' *(Revelation 12:1-2)*

She is much loved in the Catholic Church, for we owe her an enormous debt of gratitude for her wonderful 'fiat', as she cooperated fully in God's Plan for her. Sometimes

Catholics are wrongly accused of worshipping her. There is a difference between honouring and worshipping. We worship God, but we honour Mary, the Mother of God. And who would not love and honour a mother like her? Apparitions of Mary, in the world today, must surely be a 'sign of hope' for countless people. She seems to always appear when some country is in trouble. She came to Knock on the west coast of Ireland in 1879, when the country was in a dire state of misery, poverty and hopelessness, when people did not know where to turn for the next meal, when the crops failed and unemployment was rife. Only trust in the Mother of God's powerful intercession brought any ray of hope to the helpless Irish people.

In the vision she appeared in the skies, like a beautiful rainbow after the storm. Central to the vision was the Lamb that was slain upon the altar and the Cross. On each side of Mary stood St. Joseph and St. John.

"See the rainbow and praise its maker,
So superbly beautiful in its splendour.
Across the sky it forms an arc
Drawn by the hands of the most High."
(Ecclesiasticus 43:11)

She obtained for the Irish nation many wonderful blessings, miracles and cures, and above all she gave them hope for a better future, and she still does!
Pilgrims flock in ever-increasing numbers to her shrines, for example, Fatima and Medjugorje. In Guadaloupe, in Mexico, as many as twenty million visit the shrine annually. Though the Church sometimes withholds approval, the

simple faithful have a way of deciding for themselves, by sheer weight of numbers, by evidence of signs and wonders and genuine conversions, what is of God and what is not! Worth mentioning here are the beautiful celebrated anthems and litanies we recite in Mary's honour:– the Salve Regina, the Hail Holy Queen (our sweetness and our hope); the Hail Mary (our Mother of Mercy, our Queen of Peace). What hope Mary gave us in pronouncing her 'fiat', thus raising up a fallen world to the light of hope for two thousand years!

The reformed liturgy of the Catholic Church today gives out a clear message of hope. The 'Prayer of the Church' and the readings for the daily Mass, are a constant source of encouragement and hope. Have we deafened our ears to the bells of hope that ring daily through these inspired texts, through the reconstruction of the Mass by Vatican II, through the reform of the sacramental rites, through the daily regular nourishment of the Eucharist? The living Word of God, especially at Mass and daily readings, is sure ground for our hope. Consider the two dejected men on the road to Emmaus. In reply to Jesus' question they spoke of their hope that now seemed extinguished. "Our own hope had been that it was He who would set Israel free." (Luke 24:21) So Jesus set about rekindling their hope. Then starting with Moses and the Prophets, he explained to them the passages throughout the Scriptures that were about Himself.

At the heart of society today, there lies a hidden self-induced despair, the very opposite of hope. We witness evils of violence in all its forms:– abortion, euthanasia, aids, drug addiction, sexual perversion, exploitation, greed, poverty, loneliness, unemployment – all are but symptoms of prevailing sickness.

This beautiful planet is being destroyed. The forests, the lungs of the earth, which breathe in carbon dioxide and give out oxygen, are being cut down mercilessly. The ozone layer, that protective layer for living organisms, from deadly radiation, is being destroyed by aerosols and aeroplanes. And man, the primate of all animals, made in God's image and likeness, is destroying mankind with fear, hate and war. This is the world from which Jesus came to protect us. Everything in His Father's world is made for Him, and through Him. This is the better world of love, peace, justice, brotherhood, hope; the world of flowers, of trees and blossom, of mountains and waterfalls, of streams and rivers, of birds and animals, of beauty and grandeur, of stillness and silence, the world of simple and lovely things like the honey bees, locusts, and the wild flowers.

Let us look more carefully at these beautiful things and find hope in our world rather than despair. Faith helps us to see. It is a way of seeing, an eye for looking out on Life and on the Universe. Michel Quoist once said, "To look upon a world in faith is to discover there new and unexpected dimensions that link the world with God. Such discoveries can open a path to prayer, to life. *If only we knew how to look at life, all life would become a sign, all life would be a prayer.* No longer can we say we have no power to change ourselves or the world, for God's power gives us gifts of life. God's saving power gives us a new vision; it enables us to live in Him, to live as human beings, to give each other hope and dignity, as we open up more and more in trust and love to one another.

"Love one another," Jesus said, "as I have loved you." *(John 15:9,17)* God's saving power enables us to go beyond the harrowing horizons, to persevere when faced with tasks that seem impossible ... "My grace is sufficient for you." God's grace enables us to try when all seems dead. It enables us to 'hang in there' when we feel like opting out.

Hope means a conscious *decision* to see the world in a different way than others see it. To hope is to look through the eyes of faith to possibilities for the future, a future not determined by the oppressive circumstances of the present. To hope is to know that the present reality will not have the last word! God can always turn good out of evil. How you know this from your own life! Nothing can separate us from His love. God is always our refuge and strength, a very present help in times of trouble.

When the poet, Hopkins, looked for an antidote to the decay of hope in his day, he found it, as Paul had found it, long before him, in the Resurrection of Jesus.

> "Enough! The Resurrection!
> A heart's Clarion! Away grief's grasping,
> Joyless days, dejection

Across my floundering deck shone
A beacon, and eternal beam."

Our ultimate hope, grounded on faith in the Presence of God in our lives, is the confident expectation of the Beatific Vision of God. That hope is nourished most effectively by continually sounding the note of thanksgiving in our prayer.

A practical mantra to keep us living and travelling in hope on our Pilgrim Way comes at the end of the great hymn of praise and thanksgiving, the Te Deum, "In te Domini speravi, non confundar in aeternum." "What," asks St. Augustine, "can be hoped for which is not believed?" The author of Hebrews in his famous celebration of the faith of the ancients puts the relation between faith and hope cogently: "Faith is the substance of things to be hoped for, the evidence of things that appear not. It was for faith that our ancestors were commended". *(Hebrews 11:1)* Abel, Enoch, Noah, Abraham, Isaac, Jacob, and so many others died in faith before receiving any of the things that had been promised. So, too, for Gideon, Baruch, Samson, Darius, Samuel, and the later prophets. All these 'heroes of faith' died without seeing their hopes fulfilled. Trust in God and His promises, finds daring expression in the oracle that the prophet Habakkuk received in a vision.

> *"For even though the fig tree does not blossom,*
> *Nor fruit grow on the vine*
> *Even though the olive crop fail*
> *And the fields produce no harvest;*
> *Even though flocks vanish from the folds*
> *And stalls stand empty of cattle*
> *Yet I will rejoice in the Lord and*

Exult in God my Saviour.
God the Lord is my strength."
(Habakkuk 3:17-18)

And again Isaiah keeps us on our toes!
"Those who put their trust in the Lord,
renew their strength,
they put out wings like eagles.
They run and do not grow weary,
walk and never tire."   *(Isaiah 40:31)*

For us, in the new dispensation, that joyful expectancy has given way to the reality of possession. We can receive Jesus in Holy Communion. We have entered into the fruition of all that they had hoped for. The object of their yearnings was the One who was to come: We have touched the hem of His garment, we have listened to His voice, we have stood by His Cross and have in a manner been witnesses of the glory of His Resurrection. Yet, we too wait in hope for the coming of Our Lord in Glory on the last day. Recollection of a divine intervention, of an unforgettable spiritual experience, acts as a perennial incentive to hope.

All three synoptic writers describe the Transfiguration on Mount Tabor. For Peter, it was a shattering experience, which he recalls in his second epistle, long years after the Ascension:

"It was not any cleverly-invented myths that we were repeating, when we brought you the knowledge of the power and the coming of the Our Lord Jesus Christ; We have seen His Majesty for ourselves. He was honoured and glorified by God the Father when the sublime glory itself spoke to Him and said; 'This is My Son the Beloved, He enjoys My favour'; We heard this ourselves, spoken from Heaven, when we were with Him on the Holy Mountain." *(2 Peter 1:16-18)*

And Paul, that great Evangelist and Apostle of hope, far from keeping secret his experience on the road to Damascus, proclaims it again and again, in the hope that his hearers (even such as the unlikely Agrippa), might come to have a share in the light that shone for him that day. Agrippa said to Paul: "A little more, and your arguments would make a Christian of me." "Little or more", Paul replied, "I wish before God that not only you, but all who have heard me today, would come to be as I am, except for these chains!" *(Acts 26:28-29)*

Paul, too, recounts the visions and revelations of the Lord, though he is driven to this by the idle boasting of some pseudo-Christians in Corinth *(cf 2 Corinthians 2:1-10)*, and in the Mamertine prison, where Paul awaited the sword of the executioner, his hope shone out like a beacon, communicating itself to countless thousands of Christians, down the long centuries:

"As for me, my life is already being poured away as a libation, and the time has come for me to be gone. I have fought the good fight to the end; I have run the race to the finish. I have kept the faith; all there is to come now is the crown of righteousness reserved for me, which the Lord, the righteous judge, will give to me on that day and not only to me but to all those who welcome His appearing." *(2 Timothy 4:6-8)*

Not all, of course are favoured with raptures, visions, revelations; but few who strive to live the Christian life in its fullness, are left without clear intimations of the loving Presence in their lives of the God they seek and serve.

Recollections of these past experiences of the divine, carry us forward on the path of hope, with varying degrees of certainty. For the martyrs, hope was stronger than death, so too for martyrs of desire. When Teresa of Avila cried: "I die because I cannot die", there was no shadow of lingering doubt about the glory that awaited her in death. Ruth Burrows, in her commentary on The Mansions, ('The Interior Castle Explored') , writes of its author:
"Here is a woman who surely knows. She isn't speculating or merely deducing. She isn't relying on what others have said. Here is one with a well of living knowledge within her. Her complete certainty is overwhelming. She knows, she is certain, that what Jesus was proclaiming, what Paul, John and others have tried to express of man's ultimate destiny of being with Christ in God, one spirit with Him who is Spirit, has become, even in this life, a living reality in her."

And surely, in the light of such brightly shining hope, we, too, can travel despite our mundane preoccupations, our anaemic, wistful longings.

Without hope we would be lost. We couldn't live. Life would be impossible. When tragedy strikes, what would we do without hope? An accident that takes your husband on the way home from work, leaving you with five young children – the youngest two months? The death of your fiancée two days before you marry him? The sudden death of your husband just after he retires? The death of your baby, with no hope of another? The loss of your partner or friend through foul means? The home that you have taken years to build up repossessed? Reaching rock bottom and nowhere to turn?

I remember once driving home at ten o'clock at night, and for some reason the car just wouldn't turn into our gate. I then felt compelled to visit Maggie in a village, five miles away. She was a young married mother with two children, one ten, and one eight. I did not know her marriage surname, or her address, but I knew she was away from her husband, as she just couldn't cope. But someone was praying for her! I walked up and down a few streets in this village, knocked on some doors and asked if they knew a Maggie who had just moved into the village and who had two children. Only in Ireland would one do such a thing at that hour of night!

After knocking on several doors, I eventually hit on the right house! I knocked at the door. A little boy opened it and I recognised his face. "Is your mummy in?", I asked. "Yes," he said "Come in." There she was, sitting in the kitchen crying, having decided that that night she certainly had had enough and was going to take her life. "I don't believe it," she cried, as she saw me, "I don't believe it. What made you come here?" I said, "I tried to turn into our gate, but the car wouldn't; I had to come and find you. God told me to come." Well, we sent the little boy to bed with hugs, having assured him I would look after his mummy for him. "There must be a God," she kept crying, "I've begged Him to help me as I couldn't cope. Tonight was the night I'd planned to do it, as I can't go on any longer, I have everything ready for it. I don't believe it", she cried, "There just must be a God!" (She had planned to take an overdose that night and the pills were all ready)

I stayed with her till 1.30 a.m. We talked and prayed, drank tea and listened, and out of the depths of despair came a beautiful ray of hope, a light in the darkness of the night. It was a new beginning! It was not long before Maggie returned to her husband with the children and life became better than ever before. Thank You Lord!

Studies have indicated that hope persists right through illness, even very serious illness, as I've experienced often when praying with our dying sisters. Even the most accepting patients hope for a remission, a cure, the discovery of a new drug or a miracle of healing. When hope is dropped in a state of final acceptance, death is close. We must always share a person's hope, all the little efforts to hope, point to a greater Eternal hope of life continued in Heaven. Death is not the end. Life is changed not ended, as we move into the life of the Resurrection. Our greatest Hope, as already said, is Jesus Christ, who said; "I am the Resurrection and the Life. He who believes in Me will never die." *(John 1:25)*

We cannot deny the fact that there is a radical change between this life and the next. Death is only a step towards fuller life with God. This is what we are preparing for all our life: "What no eye has seen or ear heard nor has it entered into the heart of anyone, what things God has prepared for those who love Him."
Paul writes to the Colossians: "When the true message, the Good News, first came to you, you heard of the hope

it offers. So your faith and love are based on what you hope for, which is kept safe for you in Heaven." *(Colossians 1:4)*

We must not allow our hope to dwindle away; on the contrary, we must pray for it to increase. The theological virtue of hope helps us to trust that God will give us eternal life and all means necessary to obtain it, if we do what He requires of us. Hope is a gift of God. We must receive it, accept it and help it to grow by *being* hopeful. Hope begets hope. The Oxford Dictionary defines hope as a feeling of expectancy; or a desire for certain things to happen; or a person who gives cause for hope, sometimes even hoping against hope for something barely possible.

I have seen miracles of hope come true, e.g. a baby born to couples who have tried for fourteen, fifteen, even sixteen years for a child. I have seen alcoholics, drug addicts, healed of their addictions through the power of prayer and a desire for a better life. I have seen others saved from the torture of intended suicide and self-destruction, I have seen people delivered of demons that were destroying their lives, I have seen hope against hope (isolation, loneliness, hopelessness), transformed into service and love for others.

Hope helps us to keep going, to receive what we do not yet possess. We should never be afraid to trust the unknown to the God Who is omniscient (knows all). With hope, we can start again. "No need to recall the past," God says in Isaiah *(43:18)*. "Trust in God forever, for He is the everlasting Rock." *(Isaiah 26:4)* Psalm 121 reminds us "Your protector is always awake, He will not let you fall, He will protect you from all danger, He will keep you safe now and forever." Again in Haggai *(2:4)* God says, "Be strong, I will accompany you." And again he says; "I am with you to save you." One of the most comforting quotations in Scripture I find is:

> *"He proved Himself their Saviour*
> *In all their troubles*
> *It was neither messenger nor angel*
> *But His Presence that saved them*
> *In His love and pity*
> *He redeemed them Himself*
> *He lifted them up, carried them*
> *Throughout the days of old."*
>
> *(Isaiah 63:8-10)*

If we read about the prophet Elijah in one of his worst moments, we see how God is constantly trying to give us hope as He looks after us. It is high time we took His word seriously and trusted Him more. I believe if God does not come to us directly, He will always send us a 'good angel' (Himself disguised!). We see this happening all the time.

"Elijah went into the wilderness, a day's journey, and sitting under a furze bush, wished he were dead."

(Do you know the feeling? Ever been near to giving up?) 'Lord', he said, 'I have had enough. Take my life. I am no better than my ancestors.' Then he lay down and went to sleep.

But an angel touched him and said: "Get up and eat". He looked around, and there at his head, was a scone baked on hot stones, and a jar of water. He ate and drank and then lay down again. But the angel of the Lord came back a second time and touched him and said: 'Get up and eat or the journey will be too long for you'. So, he got up and ate and drank and strengthened by that food, he walked for forty days and forty nights, until he reached Horeb, the mountain of God." *(1 Kings 19:4-8)*

What hope this word gives me. "Whatever things were written, were written for learning, that through patience and comfort of the scriptures, we might have hope." *(Romans 15:4)* We hope in Him but His hope in *us* is greater. Jesus has hope in us, He never gives up on us. His hope in us turns into certainty for us. His word goes forth from His mouth and never comes back to Him empty. His word always fulfils His purpose. *(cf Isaiah 55:11)*

So when Jesus says: "I have prayed for you that your faith will not fail you" *(Luke 22:32)*, we know that He is at the same time placing His hope in us. Not to hope in someone is paramount to death! Hope makes the best of the circumstances of life, indeed of every catastrophe. Douglas Bader, in the film 'Reach for the Sky', showed great hope and courage as he learnt to pilot a plane again after his flying accident where he lost both legs! Hope knows that suffering is often the price of redemption and new life.

When he was in the concentration camp at Auschwitz, a prisoner escaped. Some ten or twelve prisioners were randomly selected by the guards to die by starvation as a reprisal. One of the men being marched away cried out in anguish: "But what will happen to my wife and children?" Maximilian Kolbe, prisoner No. 16670, stepped forward and offered to die in his stead. He was a Franciscan priest. In the starvation bunker he gave hope to his companions by praying with them, singing and keeping their spirits up. When Maximilian was canonised in Rome on 12th February 1985 there was a man and his wife and their children in St. Peter's Square who had a very special reason for being grateful to him for giving up his life for them.

When Maximilian was a young boy he had a vision of the Blessed Virgin offering him two crowns, one red the other white. She asked him which he would prefer. The red symbolised martyrdom; the white, purity. He chose them both. Little did he realise God's plan for him.

People's courage in face of suffering often amazes me, and gives me much hope. One has only to visit a hospital to see hope in action, or to pass by a prison at visiting hours, where relatives never give up hope that the sentence will be shortened! Hope and trust go hand in hand. We often hear of great international figures who have abundance of hope, like Terry Waite, the Pope, Martin

Luther King, Nelson Mandela, Br. Roger of Taizé, Mother Teresa, Bishop Desmond Tutu, Missionaries everywhere, founders of Orders and lay communities. Just watch the London marathon on Television and you're amazed by hope as you see the large numbers of wheelchair contestants racing for the goal! We are all called to be bringers of hope. Even a phone-call, a letter, a card, a thought, a prayer, to light a candle for someone's intentions, can bring a blessing of hope when life is dulled. "May the God of hope fill you with all the joy and peace in believing that you may abound in hope in the power of the Spirit." *(Romans 15:13)*

Today we hear much about Celtic Spirituality; it is a great rediscovery! The Celts were a people of hope. They lived in such close communion with the work of God in His Creation, that there was little room for doubt about His existence, His Presence in their world of work as in their world of Prayer, His love, His Providence, His readiness to help in every need. Every aspect of their life and work had its appropriate prayer and blessing. Before a woman plied her task at the loom, she invoked a blessing on warp and woof and wool and finished product. For them, the Trinity presented no mystery. The 'three in one' was an ever present reality in their lives, an unfailing source of help in need and light in darkness. Out of the Celts' long experience of living under threat, the Celtic nations always had a promise of hope, reminding us to expect the morning light. Light in darkness, hope in despair, life in death is their constant theme. The wisdom of the Spirit found expression in poetry, in song and in saga; they realized for themselves that word of Paul to the unbelieving stoics on the Areopagus:

"In Him we live and move and have our being." *(Acts 17:28)* "We are saved by hope," St. Paul tells us, "This hope does not disappoint us because God's love has been poured into our hearts by the Holy Spirit, who has been given to us." *(Romans 5:5)*

We must never give up hope. Continually 'spark off' a movement of hope for a better world. We must try to fight obstacles to hope (like pessimistic attitudes to life, not letting go of things like memories that hurt, people, children, that need freedom, even precious moments!) The more we look on everything as gift the easier it will be to 'let go'.

Despair is a sin against hope, as is also presumption i.e. man hoping to save himself without God, or man presuming God's mercy is his, without conversion. Lord forgive my sins against hope. Forgive the times I've doubted you and not trusted You for the future. Forgive my depression and despair. Lord, thank you for all the signs of hope in our lifetime, for the breaking down of the Berlin Wall, for the death of Communism, for all efforts for peace, for medical and scientific progress according to Your will, for communities of reconciliation like Taizé, Coventry Cross of Nails, for the use of Television (when it brings the brotherhood of man together and widens our horizons to the needs of other countries). Thank You for our dear Pope John XXIII who opened the doors of Vatican II, thus releasing the Spirit of Hope upon the Church, bringing the laity a deeper spirituality and bringing the liturgy alive in a new way. We pray that the love of Christ, victorious over sin and death, may grant everyone the courage of forgiveness and reconciliation, where despair will give way to hope and where hatred and bitterness will melt in the love and power of the Risen Christ. Don't give way to discouragement, for Christ our Hope is Risen.

Pope John Paul II said in his Easter Message 1998: "This is our hope, this is our life's work, this is our challenge." "Proclaim the Good News; welcome or unwelcome, insist on it." *(2 Timothy 4:2)* "Make the preaching of the Good News your life's work in thorough-going service." *(2 Timothy 4:5)*

Salvation begins with each individual, with human dignity, with saving every human life. Jesus died for all. He has no favourites. He alone is everyone's hope in sickness or in health; in riches or in poverty, in captivity or in freedom, in death or in life. Let those who struggle against evil today, those who try to defend life and save it from every peril, let them pause, and wonder at the Risen Christ. He is the Hope for those who see the future threatened by war, by disaster, around the world. Those who are called to create harmony and peace need our prayers to be guided by the power of Christ to create values obtained at the cost of great sacrifice.

"I was in the underground train, a crowded train in which all sorts of people jostled together, sitting and standing, workers of every sort going home at the end of the day. Quite suddenly in my mind, I saw more than that: not only was Christ in every one of them, living in them, dying in them, rejoicing in them, hoping in them, sorrowing in them, but because He was in them and because they were here, the whole world was here too, here in this underground train. Not only the world as it was at the moment, not only all the people in all the countries of the world but all the people who lived in the past and all those yet to come.

I came out into the street and walked for a long time in the crowds. It was the same here, on every side, in every passer-by .... Christ." *('A Rocking Horse Catholic' by Caryll Houselander)* Pause for a moment and dwell with these thoughts, as you see a sea of faces in front of you, all needing to be inspired by your hope for them. Pray too to their guardian angels, who see the face of their Father in Heaven. Never underestimate the presence and powerful help of your own guardian angel, and you may even ask your angel's name! Know that there is always a good angel watching over you when life becomes unbearable.

I recently heard of someone who had moved to Blackpool, after his marriage had broken up. He was made redundant and hope was at a very low ebb. He couldn't settle or find peace so he decided that the only solution was to walk into the sea and drown himself and his sorrows. On his way down to the sea he met a gypsy lady, who asked if he wanted his palm read and if he could give her a few pounds. This was his only human contact that day. He was so surprised at her that he gave her his last twenty pound note, turned on his heel and walked back towards the town. On his way back he was invited for a cup of tea at the Salvation Army hostel and since then he has never looked back. He was saved by the gypsy woman, and perhaps his guardian angel! He gives his testimony in a very moving manner and his story, which is true, has given hope to many people. God can use anyone, or any situation, for his purpose. When all seems lost, He alone is our Hope.

"Never let life's disappointments, and My seeming lack of

response to specific prayers, cause you to doubt My absolute sufficiency. Even in weakness, I take you forward if *desire* is constant. I am ceaselessly at work for you. Remember that trust in My power to change situations... a trust which you will know has not been made in vain. Your fears are groundless."

('I Am With You', Fr. John Woolley, p 123)

Gerard Manley Hopkins in his great poem, 'The Wreck of the Deutschland', describes for us a very authentic hope. The doomed ship which went aground in the mouth of the Thames, had among its passengers five nuns fleeing from religious persecution in Germany, bound for the New World. As human hope appeared to die, the poet witnessed the birth of a greater hope, a hope stronger than death:
"Hope had grown grey hairs,
Hope had mourning on.
Trenched with tears, carved with cares,
Hope was twelve hours gone;
And frightful a nightfall folded rueful day
Nor rescue, only rocket and lightship, shone,
And lives at last were washing away:
To the shrouds they look, they shook in the hurling and horrible airs." *('Selected Poems', Gerard Manley Hopkins, p 7)*

Then a voice was heard above the tumult, The 'tall nun' gave shrill voice to a hope that was stronger than death "O Christ, Christ come quickly!" *(ibid p 10)*

It was the cry that gave the poet his inspiration, carrying as it did, an echo of the cry heard on the sea of Galilee "Lord save me or I perish", earning for Peter the reproach "O man of little faith, why did you lose hope?" When bidden, after a night catching nothing, to 'launch out into the deep and let down the nets for a catch', he might well have asked, 'What's the use?' But, he built a fragile hope on his faith in the power of Jesus' word and the hope was richly rewarded.

You will be encouraged by these comforting words of hope given by the Lord to Fr. John Woolley:

"My love must *always* give you hope... hope born of conviction about Me; hope which no-one on earth can give to you. Hope placed, even tremblingly, in Me, becomes more than hope... There grows a sureness about the underlying *safety* of your existence... no matter how threatening passing events might be.

Hope without substance is a pitiable thing. But hope based on a permanent reality is wise... and is rewarded many times over." *('I Am With You', Fr. John Woolley, p 122)*

"Always true to His promises, Yahweh shows love in all He does. Only stumble and Yahweh at once supports you. If others bow you down, He will raise you up." *(Psalm 145:14)*

"Rest in God alone my soul.
He is the source of my hope.
With Him alone for my rock, my safety
my fortress, I can never fall,
In God I find my shelter, I rely on Him.
People, at all times, unburden your heart to Him
God is a shelter for us" *(Psalm 62:5-8)*

Awareness of the future:
Start with the present moment. Go over events of the day so far as you anticipate them (e.g. work, meals, journeys, prayer time, people you meet) Just try to observe each event as it is likely to happen.
See yourself behaving (thinking, feeling, reacting) the way you would like to behave.
Just use the gift of imagination for this.
Then see those events as you would like them to be.
Try believing that God is in every event, no matter how good or how messy.
Try to look at the events, people, places, journeys with God in them.
Be aware that not even a sparrow can fall to the ground without your Heavenly Father knowing it and that every hair of your head is numbered.

('Sadhana', de Mello, p. 95)

"Bear in mind, yesterday is but a Dream
And tomorrow is only a Vision
But today, well lived
Makes every Tomorrow
A Vision of Hope.
Look well, therefore, to this Day."
Anonymous.

Hold fast to dreams
For if dreams die
Life is a broken-winged bird
That cannot fly.

Hold fast to dreams
For when dreams go
Life is a barren field
Frozen with snow.

('Listen to Love' - Langston Hughes)

"Lord, the future frightens me. I need Your constant help. I want to see You in everything that will happen to me, especially the worst. I want to trust You Lord but I am afraid to put my hand in Yours. Where will it lead me? I want to see You in people today, in the least attractive as well as in the most beautiful. I fear death and the process of dying. Lead me from Despair to Hope. Help me to find Your holy will in all circumstances today, especially in my suffering. Lord, increase my hope, You alone are the Hope for the world."

"Hope springs eternal in the human breast'
(Alexander Pope)

"I call you to share My suffering, as we meet at the foot of the Cross every day. Give Me your heart. Receive My Love. This will be your continual source of strength and healing at all times. All suffering borne with My Love makes everything possible."

A CALL TO SHARE HIS SUFFERINGS

Is there anyone, anywhere, who hasn't suffered?

I think not! Is there anyone in the whole world who likes pain and who would choose it? I have yet to meet such a person! A humanist might disagree but it strikes me that suffering only makes sense in the light of our faith in Jesus Christ, the Crucified One.

How a non-believer copes with suffering, or how he can find an explanation for it, without God, I do not know. To him, suffering, like any other good or bad circumstance of life, is merely a matter of chance. But is it? God cares for him too!

The sufferings of Jesus must surely find a place in each person's life, and in today's society, which seems to be haunted with fear. Fear is only conquered through perfect love (Christ's death). This is the love-story of Jesus, the Son of God, the Tremendous Lover.

"What *proves* that God loves us is that Christ died for us while we were still sinners." *(Romans 5:8)*

Jesus was a human being like us in all things except sin. In His agony in the garden, Jesus began 'to be sorrowful and to be afraid'. *(Mark 14:34)* He experienced a depth of pain no one has ever known or will ever know, to the end of time. No one could possibly have suffered more than Jesus. The utter darkness of sin, the loneliness and 'aloneness' of the night, *(the Apostles asleep)*; the kiss of Judas His friend, *(in betrayal)*; the fear of the suffering, *(He foresaw even unto His death)*; the knowledge that for some He would suffer in vain − all made Him cry out to His Father in agony "Father, let this chalice pass from Me, yet not My will, but Yours be done." *(Luke 22:42)*

This was a cry, not of despair, nor lack of hope, but of His struggle with total acceptance and obedience to His Father's Will. St. Luke tells us that an angel came to strengthen Him. "An angel appeared to Him coming from heaven to give Him strength. In His anguish He prayed even more earnestly, and His sweat fell to the ground like drops of blood." *(Luke 22:43-44)* His cry of anguish became one of total acceptance: "Thy will be done, not my will, if this cup may not pass but I must drink it." *(Matthew 26:42-43)*

This prayer to His Father, in the stillness of the night, brought Him the strength to accept His Father's will, enabling Him to overcome His fear and dread of His death. On Calvary, Jesus said: "It is accomplished, and bowing His head He gave up His spirit." *(John 19:30)*

The 'Hour' had come; the 'Hour' of Redemption for us; for the whole human race; the 'Hour' of His saving grace; which enables *us* to say, also, to the Father when our 'hour' comes: "Your will be done in us. The work You gave me to do is over; into Your hands I commend my spirit; Father forgive me for those things I have done without realising how much they made You suffer. Amen."

Such a prayer, we hope, can become our own prayer, now, and at the hour of our death.

"And when I think that God,
His Son not sparing,
sent Him to die,
I scarce can take it in
that on the cross,
my burden gladly bearing
He bled and died
to take away my sin."
Karl Boberg (1859-1940)

Old age can bring with it much suffering for ourselves and our family and life can become heavily burdened.

"Old age comes from Him
Old age leads to Him
Old age will touch me
Only in so far as He wills."
('Hymn of the Universe', Teilhard de Chardin, p12)

Death will come to us at His appointed time
    In the night watch or in the day
Inside the house or outside
    Alone or with another
In youth or in old age
    As His will permits.
Blessed be God forever.

"If we search for a solution to the problem of pain, we can find it only in the divinity of Christ, only in the tears of God. God so loved the world, that He sent His only Son. God was willing to allow the horror of sin and the suffering that comes from it, because, then, by becoming man, Jesus could share in the suffering and so He could reveal God's deep mysterious love for mankind in a way He could never have done. We in our turn could become, as a result, something deeper, richer, than we should ever otherwise have been.

So what seems like ultimate tragedy is, in fact, love unfolding itself, *and here is the answer to all our suffering*. He *was* despised and rejected, He *is* despised and rejected, and for many it is as though the Crucifixion had never happened and for many Christians, it is, in practice, as though it had never been.

Yet, though the sense of futility is woven into the texture of the agony, the agony itself is still only a moment of the Passion. Jesus approaches it not with hopelessness but with joy, and it ends not in hopelessness but in the ringing triumphant cry: 'Consummatum est' (it is consummated); the perfect work is achieved; and there follows, not darkness and emptiness, but the spearpoint of light of the

Resurrection; the New Day.

Nor is it that joy succeeds sorrow, as sorrow had succeeded joy; the sense of futility is creative of what is to come. Without it, the Passion would not have been so perfect; for love is greatest, when it is stripped of all sense of achievement, all return, and is sheer naked self-giving. That is what we watch in the garden; the divine self-emptying, which alone could annihilate the self-centredness of man. He was despised and rejected, left utterly alone, that His acceptance of His loneliness and His lovelessness, might deliver us from ours."

('The High Green Hill', Fr. Gerald Vann, O.P., pp 31-32)

Watching with Him, teaches us everything there is to know about suffering – the why, the how, the creativity, the value of it; the sense of our own futility in the face of it; our utter dependency on Him in the midst of it; our brokenness, our desolation; our sheer frustration; our courage, our fears, our hopes. And as we bring Him not only our own suffering but that of the world also, we see His redeeming omnipotent love, flooding out over the whole world. At once our hearts are enlarged, and we grow closer to Him in hope and expectancy, as we learn acceptance and obedience from staying close to Him. We learn that obedience to God's will is the key note of the whole Gospel story and of Jesus' life on earth.

And so we look at Him who died for us, and thank Him for allowing us to *share* in His suffering and His Cross, which redeemed the World.
Let us always remain close to Him. "They treated Him with contempt, and made fun of Him" *(Luke 23:11)*

"As you can see, the man (Jesus) has done nothing that deserves death, so I shall have Him flogged and let Him go" *(Luke 23:15)*

"They stripped Him and made Him a scarlet cloak and having twisted some thorns into a crown, they put this on His head and placed a reed in His right hand. To make fun of Him, they knelt to Him saying: 'Hail King of the Jews!', and they spat at Him and took the reed and struck Him on the head with it. And when they had finished making fun of Him, they took off the cloak, and dressed Him in his own clothes and led Him away to crucify Him." *(Matthew 27:31)*

"Some of them, started spitting at Him, blindfolded Him, began hitting Him with their fists and shouting, 'Play the Prophet!' and the attendants reigned blows on Him." *(Mark 14:65)*

"They led Him out to crucify Him.
They enlisted a passer-by, Simon of Cyrene, father of Alexander and Rufus, to carry His Cross." *(Mark 15:21)*

"The passers-by jeered at Him" *(Mark 15:29)*

"For My part, I made no resistance, neither did I turn away. I offered my back to those who struck Me, My cheeks to those who tore at my beard; I did not cover my face against insult and spittle. The Lord comes to my help so that I am untouched by the insults. Who dare condemn me?" *(Isaiah 50:5-9)*

"And at the ninth hour, Jesus cried out in a loud voice 'My God, My God, why have you forsaken Me?' " *(Mark 15:34)*

"Jesus knew that everything had been completed, and to fulfil the Scripture perfectly He said 'I am thirsty'." *(John 19:28)*

"The 'Hour' had come for Him to pass from this world to the Father." *(John 13:1)*

"He had always loved those who were His own in the world, but now He showed how perfect His love was" *(John 13:1)*

"It is accomplished, and bowing His head he gave up His spirit." *(John 19:30)*

"And when I am lifted up from the Earth I shall draw all men to myself." *(John 12:32)*

Such utter desolation! Jesus won the victory over all evil on the cross. This is the Victory Ground we should frequent. From here flow all graces. Stand with Him and pray. It would put your suffering into perspective! If it is very terrible suffering why not pray the Passion with Him from one of the four evangelists. The strength you receive from this will surprise you.

"And so it is a privilege to suffer for Him." *(Philippians 1:30)* Don't we love to share our friend's sufferings, and if they don't share them, are we not hurt? There is no greater 'honour' than to be 'with' your friend in sorrow and tragedy. It is often this love which sustains us in trials and keeps us going..! "If you do have to suffer for being good, you will count it a blessing." *(1 Peter 3:17)*

If we truly love, we suffer, just as He did. The more we love, the greater our suffering. There is no suffering we can undergo that He does not know about. The old saying goes "No cross, no crown!" Just as the whole human race was saved by the suffering of Jesus from the clutches of the evil one, so too "our suffering wins for us a crown that the Lord has promised to those who love Him" *(James 1:12)* However incomprehensible suffering is, it is somehow part of the divine plan, and we must accept it. "If you can have some share in the sufferings of Christ, be glad, because you will enjoy a much greater gladness when His glory is revealed. It is a blessing for you when they insult you for bearing the name Christian because it means that you have the Spirit of glory resting on you." *(1 Peter 4:13-14)*

"Think of what Christ suffered in this life, and then arm yourself with the same resolution that He had. Anyone who, in this life, has bodily suffering, has broken with sin because for the rest of his life he is not ruled by human passion, but by the will of God." *(1 Peter 4:1-2)*

"That is why there is no weakening on our part and instead, though this outer man of ours may be falling into decay, the inner man is renewed, day by day. Yes, the troubles which are soon over, though they weigh little, train us for the carrying of a weight of eternal glory, which is out of all proportion to them. And so, we have no eyes for things that are visible but for things that are invisible, for the visible things last only for a time and the invisible things are eternal." *(2 Corinthians 4:16-18)*

"Realizing the unseen, gives a sense of proportion to the experiences which temporarily elate or crush the human soul. To see My kingdom as the reality of this existence, and every other manifestation as transient, wonderfully gives courage and steadiness in the dark places. Life's passing phenomena are transformed by the reality lying behind them. Find in the world's experiences a spiritual gain… kept secure for you in the realm of My love."
('I Am With You', John Woolley, p 13, §3)

To me, our suffering, and the suffering of those around us, shows the horror of the Original Sin, which must have been quite horrendous against a God of love, who showered nothing but love upon Adam and Eve. The consequences of their actions are felt by the whole human race to the end of time. It was a man and a woman who first disobeyed God. They chose to sin. We can choose to sin, and our sin is also a breach in a loving relationship with God.

There is no doubt but suffering has a hidden power to bring about good out of evil and to draw out the best in us. Sometimes, I've heard parents say that they wouldn't be without their handicapped child who had brought them such love; others will tell you that it was a tragedy that brought them back to Church or gave them a new lease of life. Sorrow can be so creative (often, however, not when we're going through it, but afterwards!) Out of suffering can be borne a deeper love, greater compassion and understanding, patience, a deeper 'philosophy' of life and even a greater motivation for living. I have seen people's lives totally transformed through suffering 'accepted', though not without struggle! Suffering is challenging! purifying! Every tragedy is a unique experience for those who suffer; for those who can accept it, it is life-giving, transforming. "In my own body, I make up all that has still to be undergone by Christ". *(Colossians 1:24)*

All our suffering can be offered in atonement for sin; I hear people so often say, "Thank God for my suffering; I would not have chosen this cross and at the beginning I struggled to accept what's happened, but now, I feel I have a new life and I feel liberated, I am so changed. I can hardly believe myself." Sometimes they say, "You told me so. I could not understand then, but I do now."

How we view suffering (even if we want to run a mile from it) is vital as to how we accept it, especially if it's a situation we cannot change.
A woman was praying seventeen years for her husband to change, but when she decided to stop praying for him and prayed for herself alone, she began to see changes in him! Our attitudes to problematic situations can change and thus make them bearable if not changeable. Correct attitudes could lessen our suffering.

Helen Keller, was blind, deaf, and dumb, from the age of eighteen months (died at 87 years). Yet she lived a more exciting life than most ordinary people. She learnt to read, write, talk, and she could say in later life, "I thank God for my handicaps, for through them I have found myself, my work, my God." She toured the world with her teacher, and gave nearly two hundred and fifty talks in churches, synagogues, town halls, clubs; she raised a million dollars for charity and she inspired all blind and sick people with hope and courage.

What a friend God gave her in her teacher Anne Sullivan, who taught her everything, with such love and patience, (though with discipline – not easy to accept when Helen was young!) "The most important day I remember in all my life, is the one on which my teacher came; this was my soul's birthday!!"

Tragedy often makes a person more sensitive and receptive to the needs and agonies of others, and sometimes a whole new mission for the world develops, as it did for Helen.

Just as God sent an Angel to comfort Jesus, His Son, in the Garden of Agony, I believe God always sends us 'good' angels, to comfort us in our hour of need. We may never know it!

"I make Myself dependent upon your faith, and upon your concern for others at the human level. Even when much is uncertain or threatening, know that you are much used - because of My moulding you ... which is why you experience a sense of refreshment after I have met someone's need through you

.

Let Me develop the gift of uplifting others - simply by your presence. Cultivate the *will* to show love ... even at times when your own heart may be breaking."
('I Am With You', John Woolley, p 145)

God never waits till we are perfect to use us as good angels for others!

Only today, I received a letter from my friend in Canada, saying that my letters always arrive when she is feeling down and in need of a friend. At the moment she has been 'off work' sick for the past five weeks. I had been praying for her and thinking of her, and no doubt it was the Holy Spirit who prompted me to write at that particular time.

To be there for someone! This is grace! This is sharing the Cross! To be a friend in need, is to be a friend indeed. Everyone needs a friend! Thank God for our friends who make life bearable when all else fails, when troubles come, when we don't know where to turn. Thank God for those who help us to win through suffering – 'good' angels who appear sometimes 'out of the blue', then disappear almost as quickly (like Philip who was there at the right time to help the Eunuch with the Scriptures). *(cf Acts 8)*

God knows everything. "Not even a sparrow falls without His knowing it" *(Luke 12:7)*. He sorts out even the smallest detail to the point of it being almost unbelievable.

"A faithful friend is a sure shelter
whoever finds one has found a rare treasure
A faithful friend is beyond price
There is no measuring his worth
A faithful friend is the elixir of life
And those who fear the Lord find one
Whoever fears the Lord makes true friends
For as a man is, so is his friend."

(Ecclesiasticus 6:14-17)

It would be good if we could see our suffering as a share in Christ's very own.

"Lord, what is there in suffering that commits me so deeply to you? Why, when you stretch out nets to imprison me, should I thrill with more joy than when you offer me wings?

It is because, among your gifts, what I hanker after, is the fragrance of your power over me, and the touch of your hand upon me. For what exhilarates us human creatures more than freedom, more than the glory of achievement, is the joy of finding and surrendering, to a beauty greater than man, the rapture of being possessed.

Blessed be the disappointments which snatch the cup from our lips; blessed be the chains which force us to go where we would not" *('Hymn of Universe' , Teilhard de Chardin, p 106)*

"The sense of continuity is one of the priceless gifts of life shared with Me.

You have found the great blessing, and the great stability for your character, of My unchanging presence, in a bewildering succession of circumstances.   This may not be fully appreciated until, perhaps, a sense of that presence is temporarily lost, during a painful period of doubt.

Life can rob you, in a moment, of every familiar support, and of all your sources of being sustained.   You then look for any fixed point, anything resembling what once sustained you.   You look in vain until it dawns upon you that there I am ... still loving, still guarding you.

How much the world loses in a sense of identity and of stability if I am not there at every turn of the road ... You know that the closer you are to Me the safer will be your walk!"   *('I Am With You', John Woolley, p 132.)*

I've met so many amazing people in my life, who make me feel so 'tiny' because of their 'greatness' in accepting and coping with their cross.   Some struggle with forgiveness in a 'broken' relationship; others don't know how to relate; others, again, believe they are homosexual and wish they weren't; others are burdened with financial difficulties, house repossession (which may turn out to be blessing!) and they try always to look 'bright'.

Others again suffer as a consequence of their own choices, while others are maligned, their names even 'unjustly' appearing in the headlines.   Others again cope with unbearable loneliness after the death of a loved one (child, parent, partner or friend) some become so burdened with physical or mental illness, which they struggle to accept bravely. If God isn't in all this pain, where would the world be?

When I look at the plight of innocent refugees in the camps in Bosnia which I visit, the unwanted children in Romania, the street children in Bolivia, the victims of war and hatred everywhere, I can only pray and help in some small way, daily bringing them to Jesus at the foot of the Cross, so that I might help them, knowingly or unknowingly, to carry their daily cross, and become their friend.
Can you help in any way? Some help by fasting for others' relief.

The phone often brings a call for prayer for yet another person; many times too the 'travellers' ring from all round the country; their faith is amazing, as they finish their request and 'phone' prayer, with the little refrain: "With the help of God and Our Lady of Lourdes, Sister."

I once visited an 'adult' home for spastics, and was left speechless, and in awe, at their cheerfulness and acceptance, as they painted with their mouth, or their foot, producing wonderful pictures, or using an antennae on their foreheads to send 'Morse code'; quite amazing! We were shown round by a gentleman in a wheelchair, such joy he exuded! I shall never forget it. Our own Sister Anne woke up one day 'deaf' and within a short time went totally blind as well. What a little saint – always so cheerful and lovely. We spelt everything out on her hand to communicate with her. Such redemptive suffering – specially chosen like St. Thérèse, I would imagine!

Read the 'Snow Goose' by Paul Gallico – thoughtful, delightful, inspiring at all times! I read it regularly. Read it especially if you feel life has been cruel to you and you will find comfort in the thought that, though outside appearances may be harsh, the inner spirit of a person is indomitable.

Suffering can be literally a matter of life or death, it can ennoble or embitter; it can be a source of change, new life, growth. It can lead us to heights of awareness, sensitivity and compassion never dreamed of before. Those who cannot endure it any longer, unfortunately opt out, sometimes by suicide. They see no way out. God in His mercy regards their suffering, the depth of their pain is swept up into the Agony in the Garden.

Only by sitting beneath the Cross of Jesus, with His Mother (of Sorrows) can we face the horror of some situations. Here we will always gain inner strength and a peace the world can never give. "All I want is to share His sufferings".
(Philippians 3:11)

It's amazing what suffering borne out of love can do for us. It often takes suffering to draw out our best. It purifies us like the refiner's fire. Alcoholics change only when the pain is bad enough. Sometimes through suffering we receive transforming insights. Our suffering can lead us to a change of heart, a 'new heart'. "Your suffering led you to repentance." *(2 Corinthians 7:9)*

Paul himself knew much about suffering, since he himself had many hardships to bear for the Kingdom of God. He bore them bravely. His love for Jesus spurred Him on, so that he could accept every trial.

"Five times, I had the thirty-nine lashes from the Jews; three times I have been beaten with sticks; once I was stoned; three times I have been shipwrecked and once adrift in the open sea for a night and a day. Constantly travelling; I have been in danger from rivers and in danger from brigands, in danger from my own people and in danger from pagans; in danger in the towns, in danger in the open country; danger at sea and danger from "so-called" brothers. I have worked and laboured, often without sleep; I have been hungry and thirsty and often starving; I have been in the cold without clothes. And, to leave out much more, there is my daily preoccupation, my anxiety for all the Churches. When any man has had scruples, I have had scruples with him; when any man is made to fall, I am tortured."
(2 Corinthians 11:24-29)

So, our dear St. Paul suffered so much for the Lord Jesus. He would not have wanted it any other way after his conversion, as his love was so great for the Lord Jesus. He wanted to bear in his body the suffering of Jesus' death. He reached such 'wholeness' in his person.

"I have learnt to manage on whatever I have. I know how to be poor and I know how to be rich too, I have been through my initiation, and now I am ready for anything, anywhere; full stomach or empty stomach, poverty or plenty. There is nothing I cannot master with the help of the One who gives me strength." *(Philippians 4 :11-13)*

Would that we all had such love for Jesus, such faith, such conviction in times of suffering!

May God grant us this grace to have, to have not, to accept sickness or health, with love, so that in all things we may learn to praise Our Lord Jesus Christ, and remain united with Him in His suffering for us.

> "All you who pass by this way,
> Look and see;
> Is there any sorrow
> like the sorrow that afflicts Me?"
>
> *(Lamentations 1:12)*

One of my friends found that her husband had gone off with his secretary. She was, of course, devastated, and did not know where to turn. She rang me in a state of turmoil; what on earth was she going to do? The man she loved had deserted her. What shock, what pain! What next? Only her faith sustained her in those days, keeping bitterness and revenge from her door.

After six weeks, he wanted to come home. With difficulty she took him back, welcomed him, though her heart was breaking. Home a few weeks and then off again twice, so what then? Of course, after months away, he wanted to come back for good. Each time she forgave and loved, forgave and loved again and again and again. Such heroism! What grace has come to them both now through the channel of forgiveness, as they are back together as a couple, like Derby and Joan, more in love than ever before

and to crown it all, he has become a Catholic. A miracle of God's healing power; what reward for suffering, borne bravely in union with Christ!

"Even in sorrow, My world must be seen as one which can *give* to you. Those agencies of beauty, with power to uplift, are not robbed of their power when life becomes shadowed. As you allow My love to heal the spirit in life's almost unbearable misfortunes, allow it, also, to reach you through the untarnished aspects of My creation." *('I Am With You', John Woolley, p 169)*

One wonders how some people cope with pain. We can't transfer our 'cross'; what might be a cross for me, may not be a cross for you. 'God fits the back for the burden', the saying goes. God in His wisdom gives us a share in His suffering. All our suffering, then, is surely redemptive. "Take up your cross, daily," Jesus says "if you want to be my disciple." We all have a share in His Crucifixion.

One of my favourite Old Testament characters is Job, who lost all his possessions and family; eventually, bereft of children, impoverished and without even a roof over his head, he ended up on a dung heap covered in sores, and understandably feeling very sorry for himself. His wife begs Job to curse God and so bring about his own death through God's anger.

The advice offered by her is not unlike those who today advocate euthanasia as a merciful release from their suffering. In a secular age, modern man turns to the doctor to do what Job's wife wanted from God. However great the suffering, Job prefers life. His suffering came to him because he was an upright, God-fearing man, and Satan asked God if he could thwart this 'holy' man. Everything began to 'go wrong' for Job (as happens sometimes in our lives, at least it looks that way!) God gave Satan permission to tempt Job but "he forbade him to touch his person." *(Job 1:12)*

Job found his suffering so unbearable that he cried out to God; cursing the day of his birth; bitterly regretting that he saw the light of day:-
"Why did I not die newborn, nor perish as I left the womb?" *(Job 3:10-11)*

Do you ever feel like that – so low, so helpless, with nowhere to turn for an explanation of life's events, except to God? Job deplored his state, He wished he could descend into Sheol, where he would at least have rest and an end to his suffering. Job's story is applicable to all who suffer tragedy. It is timeless. We can see ourselves in him!

"Save me God!
The water is already up to my neck!
I am sinking in the deepest swamp
There is no foothold
I have stepped into deep water
And the waves are washing over me
Worn out with calling; my throat is hoarse,
My eyes are strained, looking for my God".
(Psalm 69:1-3)

This might well be our prayer at times. Job asked God for an explanation for his suffering. God's answer to Job is very interesting.
He certainly does not give Job the answer he might have expected, but in no uncertain way he lets Job know 'who he is' before Him, the creature in the presence of the Creator: a lesson for all of us!

"Where were you," God said, "when I laid the foundations of the earth?
Who decided the dimensions of it?
Do you know
Who laid the cornerstone
when all the stars of the morning were singing with joy?
Who pent up the sea behind closed doors

> when it leapt tumultuous out of the womb?
> Have you ever given orders to the morning
> or sent the dawn to its post?
> Have you an inkling of the extent of the Earth?"
>
> *(Job 38:4-18)*

We would all like to go through life without suffering but it does not seem to be God's plan for us. We all try to avoid pain; if all the 'pain killers' were thrown to the bottom of the sea, I wonder how much water would be left? It is consoling, however, that, even Jesus himself, the God-Man, asked His Father to relieve him of pain before a strengthening angel came. *(cf Luke 22:43)*

"You will always have trials, but when they come, try to treat them as a happy privilege ... so that you will become fully developed, with nothing missing." *(James 1:2:4)* This suggests that our trials have value for our 'wholeness'. "To suffer in God's way, means changing for the better and leaves no regrets, but to suffer as the world knows suffering, brings Death." *(2 Corinthians 7:10)*

No matter what we suffer, Jesus is always beside us. The stronger our faith in His Presence, the better we will be able to cope.

Some of the great old Irish mothers had a great sense of God in their sufferings. Many of them had large families, with little money to feed them, but they had much to teach about 'carrying the cross' heroically sometimes, and of keeping cheerful amidst tribulation. "Do not worry about tomorrow," Our Lord's words: "tomorrow will take care of itself. Each day has enough troubles of its own " (Matthew 6:33-34) seemed to have been their motto!

The cross comes the way we would not usually choose. Things might turn out worse if we were allowed to choose our own cross! I would have a problem in choosing, wouldn't you? Let's be strong for Him, remembering His love for us!

When we suffer 'with love', we can bear any pain. To suffer with Christ, is a privilege and a joy. Companionship with Christ on the Cross gives a new focus on suffering and a strength beyond us. "Offer Him your crosses and sufferings, as a gift to God, so they become a most beautiful flower of joy.
Pray that you may understand; suffering can become joy and the Cross can become a way of joy. Thank you for having responded to my call." (Medjugorje, message of Our Lady, Sept. 25, 1996)

"Nothing can come between us and the love of Christ, even if we are troubled or worried or being persecuted or lacking food or clothes or being threatened, even attacked... These are the trials through which we triumph by the power of Him who loved us." (Romans 8:35-37)

A 'Fiat' Litany

Let go the past
Let in the new
Let suffering teach
Let in the true

Let down? forgive
Let pass life's cares
Let die the deep
Let live *l'Esprit!*

Let go the fears
Let joy appear
Let sadness of years
Let grudge disappear
Let love divine
Let beauty shine
Let harmony
Let live *l'Esprit!*

Let His Peace flow
Let comfort come
Let new doors open
Let work be done
Let suppressed pain
Let it surface again
Let dark be light
Let live *l'Esprit!*

Let hunger feed
Let thirst be quenched
Let hurts of life
Balm of Spirit drench
Let Jesus reign
Let His word prevail
Let Go, let God
Let live *l'Esprit!*

(J. Walsh, Olney, 1998)

Into your hands O Lord, I commend my sorrows, my pains, my sufferings, my joys.

I commend my fears, my hopes, my dreams, my successes, my failures, my mistakes, my frustrations, my tears, my weaknesses, my sins.

Lord, help me to thank You for my joys as well as my sufferings. Thank You for giving me a share in Yours.

All that I am and have, I give to you. Thank You, Jesus, for suffering and dying for me. Amen.

"Come to Me, all who labour and are over-burdened and I will give you rest. Shoulder My yoke and learn from Me, for I am gentle and humble of heart and you will find rest for your souls. Yes, My yoke is easy and My burden light"
(Matthew 11:28-30)

"I call you to forgive. I have shown you by My example how to forgive. Never waste a second of your life for Me, by living in unforgiveness. I will give you a big and generous spirit. Ask Me to keep your heart tender and compassionate so that you may live in the nobility of My Word."

A CALL TO FORGIVE

Without forgiveness life is cruel and sad.

Forgiveness is one of the greatest virtues in the spiritual life. Without it, life can be joyless, uncomfortable, and diminished. With it, life can be full, happy, healing, harmonious, hopeful and generally life-giving; with a promise of a contented future.

Forgiveness is the foundation of all inner healing and wholeness in Jesus our Lord. In my experience of praying with people for healing, and in particular for praying for healing of memories, I find the greatest block to healing is unforgiveness. The consequences are destructive, and I would say that the start of some mental and physical illness may have a root in unforgiveness! It chains people up, makes us ugly, grumpy, ungrateful, tense, unpleasant, diseased, unapproachable and even prematurely old! A sour or bitter look, wrinkles of hardness and unforgiveness, can spoil a once beautiful face! We are responsible for how we look. The eyes are the windows of the soul and our faces are tell-tales. St. Teresa of Avila used to say "Deliver us, O Lord, from sour faced saints."

People say to me, sometimes, that they can't forgive; they'll never forgive, and so in a sense they may be right. "Well,"

I say to them, "you can't forgive and no one can make you forgive." Forgiveness is of God and only His grace can help you to forgive. You won't manage at a purely human level. It is divine to forgive. The desire must come from within you. No one can force you to forgive, even God doesn't do that. But since it is so difficult, why don't you give God permission to forgive for you? Can you agree to that? God knows how you are feeling, He sees what happened. He loves you to bits. He is all compassion and He wants you healed, freed of your burden, big or small. It is He who forgives all our offences.

You may feel like blaming Him right now for not intervening in your situation; perhaps the hardest thing to believe is that He does not take away our free will (yours, or the person or persons who have hurt you). Dostoievsky says, 'The worst thing God did was to give man free will.' Don't worry just now about how you are feeling towards God. He doesn't mind if you are angry with Him and blame Him. He knows you will understand more one day. He knows your struggles to come through all this. Just, try to concentrate on His unconditional love for you right now even though this may be very difficult for you if you have been let down in love. Give Him a chance to free you and help you. After all, He is the one person who can help you. Pause and ask God to pour into you His tender love and His healing gift of forgiveness. Allow a few minutes to open your heart to Him.

I haven't met many people who are good at forgiving. Most of us, if we are honest, will admit how extremely difficult it is. However, if forgiveness is to work, God must have our co-operation. I have found when praying with people who won't yield to forgiveness, that they find little relief for themselves or their situation. Forgiveness is paramount! It is like banging your head against a brick wall when it is lacking. People wonder why healing or new life is not happening for them, yet they will not even try to forgive, or pray to forgive. Sometimes they are waiting for the other person to forgive first, thinking that there lies the source of the problem.

We must never forget there are two sides to every story, and we both need to say "sorry". If we persist in unforgiveness, the peace we are seeking will not come. We can rely on God's help here since forgiveness is one of His greatest commands to us. Many of us know this, but we seem trapped in emotional hurt, and we hug the hurt to ourselves as a 'false' security. Circumstances are extremely difficult sometimes, and we don't know how to start or where to start, but let's start by saying, "I'm sorry for my part in it."

The *will* to forgive is what is most important, much more than how we feel. Our feelings can be so misleading. You may feel great anger on the surface but deep down you still love the person and want to forgive them. Sometimes one partner makes forgiveness dependent on an apology from the other.

God can actually make up the feelings when our hearts are hardened and cold, as He did for Corrie Ten Boom when she had to forgive the cruellest guard from Ravensbruck Concentration Camp, where her sister, Betsie, died and from where she escaped herself; a miracle! She met him afterwards when he had become a Christian, though she did not know this at the time. All she could see before her, was his dreaded clothes, overcoat, brown hat, blue uniform and a visored cap, with its skull and crossbones. Now he was in front of her, hand thrust out, seeking her forgiveness. She couldn't do it in her own strength. She begged God urgently to supply the feelings. "And so woodenly, mechanically, I thrust my hand into the one stretched out to me. And as I did, an incredible thing took place. The current started in my shoulder, raced down my arm, sprang into our joined hands. And then this healing warmth seemed to flood my whole being, bringing tears to my eyes. 'I forgive you, brother!' I cried, 'with all my heart.'

For a long moment, we grasped each other's hands, the former guard and the former prisoner. I had never known

God's love so intensely as I did then. But even so, I realised it was not my love. I had tried and did not have the power. It was the power of the Holy Spirit, as recorded in Romans 5:5, 'because the love of God is shed abroad in our hearts by the Holy Spirit, which is given to us'" *('Tramp for the Lord', Corrie Ten Boom, p 57)*

"When you experience the joy of reconciliation, when love and affection can flow again, you are very close to the mystery of My love, which is its essence. Hurt to Myself, or ethical failures, cannot affect the burning desire for an out-pouring and a receiving of that love.

True reconciliation is one of life's highest experiences ... one in which you have come near to the heart of the love which many still fail to realise or to understand. Always seek to be reconciled; My prompting also means My strengthening!" *('I Am With You', John Woolley, p 44)*

In prayer with 'wounding' couples, I have found that God's love melts the emotions and restores the tenderness, warmth and trust to even greater depth than before. It is so helpful and necessary for both sides to want to forgive, or it may take time for full healing. Very difficult struggling on your own! Wounded feelings take time to heal and a trust once broken needs a miracle of grace to be restored. I have seen couples forgive each other the most difficult and sometimes horrendous things, but what growth and new life as a result! I have seen couples where one partner has been unfaithful, (not just once), restored to a greater depth of love. Humanly speaking, impossible!

I have also seen individuals desperately ready to make up but the other partner cannot let go and forgive. When trust is gone, how do you start again? Only by the miraculous grace of forgiveness. The bowels of mercy must always be kept open, especially in families, and it is here in the heart of the home that children learn first to forgive. Parents have a huge responsibility in this area towards their children – to foster a desire for forgiveness deep in the heart.

Hosea waited and waited for his unfaithful wife to come back; a bit like our Heavenly Father waiting for the prodigal to return. We all need to constantly give and receive forgiveness. Some are minor hurts and irritabilities, some more serious and offensive things. It is because we let unforgiveness 'mount up' that it becomes so impossible in the end. In relationships, some things are better unnoticed and unheard; simply love, and keep loving is the answer. This means you keep things in your heart, as Mary did. And so your inner strength develops.

Sometimes we have to agree to differ and to let go in order to survive life, and when the hurts go too deep for us to cope. But then we need to start loving again, especially ourselves. What a beautiful thing to behold when two people forgive each other and start again.

If only we would yield to forgiveness, all Heaven would open up to us. The Kingdom would come into our hearts and often-times into the hearts of those around us. We would feel much happier, lighter, rejuvenated in the almighty power of God's Holy Spirit. Our world would change into light and suddenly we would have a 'lightness to our step' and we would become more alive. Isn't this what we are all seeking? Why not begin today, even as you read this page!

Healing takes place when those seeking wholeness, forgive whoever they are holding a grudge against, even if that person be dead. I believe that even the dead are waiting for our forgiveness to loose them from their chains.

I remember once, my friends praying with someone who tried to deny that there was anything wrong in his relationship with his father, even though his father was dead. But there was unfinished business of unforgiveness, even at death. Through a 'word of knowledge' in picture form, it was revealed that this needed to be put right and the son's act of forgiveness was requested by the Lord before his leg could be healed. Once this person yielded to forgiveness (with great difficulty!) tears welled up and overflowed, forgiveness was given and the leg lengthened and was miraculously cured at the same time. Such is the power of forgiveness. It is truly of God.

Maria spent her whole life aware of her mother's disapproval of her fiancée, who could never come up to standard. Maria's marriage was in fact a very happy one, but it was only on her mother's death bed that she gave any affirmation at all to Maria. "You always were a good girl," she said, "and you have always had a very good marriage." What a pity any word of approval came so late from her mother! So much unnecessary suffering and heart-ache could have been avoided for Maria. But, better late than never with an affirmative word. That brought Maria such healing and peace. A darling lady!

Deirdre carried her 'secret' burden for years, for she had been sexually abused by her sister's boyfriend. And as a result she had a real fear of men and found it impossible to relate to them. She decided never to get married. Fortunately, after prayer for inner healing, forgiveness of her sister's boyfriend enabled her to relate to men again, and to receive and give love.
The good news is that she is now married; a happy mother and wife, with two lovely children. Abuse of this sort is always healed through inner healing prayer. The key is

always forgiveness. There are so many wonderful stories to relate that could fill another book to God's glory.

Other times the forgiveness needs to be directed at ourselves, sometimes just for little happenings that upset us temporarily and are soon gone. We carry huge burdens of guilt and self-condemnation at times and these do not come from God. We punish ourselves with them and bring false accusations against ourselves, like Jenny who thought that she caused her father's death because of an argument she had with him just before he died. She had never been able to accept God's forgiveness for these feelings of 'false' guilt. Now, after special prayer, she was able to do so, and she started again to love herself and her family in a new way. Such relief!

Carrie, who had had two abortions, felt dirty and unlovable and thought if she did get married, God would punish her by not giving her a child. Such healing flowed through her forgiveness of herself. Now she loves herself more than she did before. She has since become a Catholic, and has settled down to a lovely family life. Only Satan accuses the brethren, God never does. Jesus asked the woman taken in adultery, "Does anyone condemn thee?" "No one Sir," she said, "Neither do I condemn thee. Go in peace," Jesus said to her. *(John 7:3-11)*

Sometimes it is God Himself we have to forgive as He is constantly blamed for things that go wrong. We need also to forgive ourselves for blaming Him. With illness of a loved one, or accidental death, we blame Him for the suffering or for allowing the death to happen (especially in the case of someone beautiful and young). We so often hear people, almost in anger, saying, why didn't He stop it, if He is God?

One woman I know just can't forgive Him for taking her husband at a young age and leaving her with two teenage children who need him so badly. "If God were God, why did He do this? Doesn't He care for my teenage children who need their daddy?"
Yes, there is mystery in suffering and death and in the happenings of life, and the only way forward, with His help, is to accept His holy will. He did not want suffering but He allowed it for a purpose. God sometimes appears to be cruel, but on looking back over all the events in my life, which I didn't like, I see the mystery and purpose unfolding, and out of the darkness I can now see light. Time is gift. Forgiveness is the key. How could a loving God, who sent His only Son to save us, ever want to hurt us? I don't believe He could. We do not always see things in the light of Eternity.

We need constantly to acquire the habit of forgiveness. There are many little instances in a day, where life might grow tedious, without an 'open' attitude of forgiveness. There are so many injustices about, with people, Church, work, that if we do not learn to forgive, our whole life could be ruined.

What if you were made redundant unjustly? What if you were let down by a priest, or the Church? What if you heard you were a mistake? Will you allow your life to die? I hope not. Learn forgiveness in the school of suffering and you will never grow bitter, but you will 'rise above' whatever happens to you and then your happiness will not depend on events, but on knowing God's love for you in your heart. Nothing else really matters in this life – success or failure count as naught before Him. He seeks only your heart. Get the balance right. Don't look the wrong way. Always run to the Cross, remembering that we are, all of us, sinners.

"Grant me tears, O God, to blot out my sins
Grant me tears, O God, when resting
Grant me tears, O God, to moisten my pillow
So that my soul may be cured of all ills.
Grant me tears of compunction and sorrow
for my foolish deeds, my lying, my greed, my pride,
my arrogance, my unlove.
Keep me gentle, forgiving, tender-hearted.
Amen."
(Old Celtic Prayer)

We are sometimes shattered by the thought of what happened to us, and how those we once loved and trusted can let us down and even turn against us. "It is the one," Jesus replied, "to whom I give the piece of bread, that I shall dip in the dish." The one Jesus loved and called and befriended; one of His intimate friends who was with Him at His 'last supper' before He died, who betrayed Him for thirty pieces of silver, the one with whom it all 'went wrong', the one for whom He was to die, Judas Iscariot, who doubted His love and forgiveness.

There was another, Peter, who became Head of the Church, who also denied Him, claimed He didn't know Him at a crucial time in His life when Jesus desperately needed his friendship. One look from Jesus was enough to melt Peter and so forgiveness and healing flowed between them. There were no words, just the look of healing love and forgiveness. Words are sometimes a barrier to forgiveness. Trying to work out who said what, and how, and why, is often better left between lovers, or life becomes more bogged down and complicated. Better, at most times, the look of love and the touch of forgiveness.

Perhaps we have allowed others to take advantage of us and we are sorry. Perhaps we've given our friendship generously and we've been 'let down'. Perhaps we were not strong enough in our love for ourselves first. Perhaps we were not as wise as we could have been in dealing with certain situations, at home or at work. It is inconceivable and heart-breaking, to be at the receiving end of another's unlove and it is easy to want to take revenge or even to want to hurt them in return, to see them punished by God.

In broken marriage relationships, there is often deep hurt, so deep that it is hard to forgive. Often the children suffer most and they have to forgive. It is difficult and courageous to learn to love again, to trust again, but it is good to know the vulnerability of love. Love is a precious gift. Cherish it. Childhood hurts are often so suppressed that we don't even know there's a need to forgive until something pops up, say, at middle age.

The Psalms and Old Testament are very comforting. Here the Israelites were constantly asking God to take revenge for them on their enemies. Jesus refers to the Old Testament teaching of hating one's enemies and being justified in doing so. The maxim was "an eye for an eye and a tooth for a tooth". On the contrary, He encourages love and forgiveness even for enemies. "Forgive your enemies," He says, "love them and pray for those who persecute you." *(Matthew 5: 44)* He goes on to say, "When you are praying, first forgive anyone you are holding a grudge against, so that your Father in Heaven, will forgive you your sins too!" *(Mark 11: 25)* Again He says: "If you are offering your gift at the Altar and there remember that your brother has something against you, leave your gift there before the Altar and go and be reconciled with your brother first, and then come back and present your offering." *(Matthew 5:24)*

Christian forgiveness is the most beautiful gift; it is the foundation of healing. To extend Christian forgiveness to someone opens the flood gates of God's love.

To be able to say "I forgive you" breaks Satan's hold over situations and people. Jesus showed us His power on the

Cross when He won the complete victory over all evil.
St. Paul told us: "Jesus has over-ridden the law and cancelled every record of the debt we had to pay. He has done away with it by nailing it to the Cross and so He got rid of sovereignties and powers and paraded them in public behind Him in His triumphant procession". *(Colossians 2: 14)*

It is at the foot of the Cross alone that we learn the measure of forgiveness. Here alone, is the victory ground. "Father, forgive them," Jesus said on the Cross as He lay dying, "they know not what they do." Thus He prayed for the very men who murdered Him. No blame, no shame, no guilt, no accusation, but merciful love. "Everyone will see Him," St. John writes in Revelation 1, "even those who pierced Him and all the races of the Earth will mourn over Him. This is the truth, Amen. I am the Alpha and the Omega says the Lord, God who is, who was, who is to come, the Almighty". *(Revelation 1: 7-8)*

Let's not forget that *our* sins of unforgiveness crucified Him too! "Forgive us our trespasses as we forgive those who trespass against us", Jesus taught us to pray. It is very clear from Scripture what our attitudes must be towards forgiveness. It is a life long struggle to live up to the standard, and do we ever reach it in this life? Some people are fortunate to be able to forgive easily, like my lovely friend, Maura. They wouldn't dream of holding a grudge or not forgiving, while others think it is their right to be in a mood every few weeks and sulk when they like. Perhaps they don't realize how hard they are to live with. They may not yet appreciate how 'dead' they are, while they wrongly pride themselves in thinking they are so 'alive'.

"I'll make him realise what's what!" a woman said to me, as she became more and more embittered. What a waste of a life!

Forgiveness is always difficult for us, even when we love much. St. Peter must have been thinking how generous he was when he offered to forgive his brother seven times (W. Barclay explains that Jews were normally expected to forgive their brother only three times!). Peter must have thought Jesus would commend him, but Jesus' answer was that His followers must forgive seventy times seven times. *(Matthew 18:21-22)* In other words, there is no limit to forgiveness. It must go on and on.

Jesus goes on to teach the parable of the unforgiving debtor, who showed no mercy even though he himself had been forgiven much. He finishes the parable with the challenging and somewhat frightening words: "that is how My Heavenly Father will deal with you, unless you each forgive your brother from your heart." *(Matthew 18:35)*

The message is clear: we must forgive if we are to be forgiven. Nothing that we have to forgive could remotely compare with what we've been forgiven by God – a debt beyond price. It is sin that caused our Saviour's death on a cross. Do I need to take His words more seriously? Could I alleviate some of the suffering in my family by starting the 'forgiveness' ball rolling today? Dare I write a few letters saying "Please forgive me", and dare I send them? Why not try today? Write the letters even if you do not send them. This in itself is healing. Then, think seriously about sending them!

There is so much unnecessary suffering in families because of unforgiveness. We have all seen it, maybe we have experienced it, or even worse, maybe we have been the cause of it. Why not repent now as you read this chapter? Why wait till tomorrow?; it may not be yours. I have seen relationships ruined as a result of unforgiveness and potential friendships destroyed.

Forgiveness must be like love – unconditional. No use suggesting, "I'll forgive her if she apologises first," or "I'll forgive you if you stop drinking or gambling," or again "I'll forgive you if you promise not to do it again," or "Why should I forgive?; it's all his fault". etc.

Remember, forgiveness is not an emotion. It is less to do with feelings, and more to do with the will. There is a difference between the head and the heart. Forgiveness is a decision of the will.

For those who have been very deeply hurt it is important to remember that the head may have forgiven, but that the feelings and excruciating pain of the heart may last for ages. Complete forgiveness of the heart may take many years.

I remember once when I was a very young sister having to deal with someone in authority, who disliked me and treated me very unjustly. The struggle to forgive her was very difficult, as the incident was to affect my life. The sight of her was enough to set angry feelings in motion and the desire to avoid her at all costs, was, I suppose, quite understandable, under the circumstances.

God is merciful and He does give us chances, again and again. Many years later, she was obviously sorry for what she had done and tried to make up in quite an unusual way. She came to our house for a rest for two weeks and on returning home, she died almost immediately afterwards. But I later heard from another sister in her community, that on her return home, she spoke of no one but me: I was everything. There was no one like me. The same sister never addressed me thus in life!

However, to finish my story, I remember the guilt I carried over those feelings of anger. I confessed the same sin over and over again until eventually my confessor must have got tired of me and told me he didn't want to hear it mentioned again, that all was forgiven.

My will had forgiven her but my hurt feelings took a long time (in those days!) to catch up. We know how damaging negative feelings are if they remain in our spirits. They must somehow be transformed into positive emotion, otherwise they will 'eat us up' as the saying goes.

Don't you find, in the darkness, that there is always a light shining somewhere within, enough to light up the way and a friend will always turn up out of the blue. You will find that unforgiveness is often accompanied by hate, bitterness, even revenge. Feelings like these must be acknowledged, and dealt with. To suppress them is dangerous! We must always acknowledge how we feel.

I then realized, with the help of my confessor, that sometimes what we call unforgiveness is actually not unforgiveness at all, but only our hurt spirits trying to cope with the pain of what's happened to us, unable to heal the deep wounds as quickly as we would like.

Even when wounds are healed, scars remain, and they need gentle treatment. We must not be too hard on ourselves. Rest in Jesus' love and tell Him of our pain. We need patience with ourselves too. As I pray with people I often wonder how they could ever forgive the hurts committed against them. I've even wondered how some could face life again and live. Yet this is the wondrous miracle of forgiveness. We *can* begin to live again.

"Those who nursed their bitterness," writes Corrie Ten Boom, "remained invalids. It was as simple and as horrible as that. Those who were able to forgive their former enemies, were able to return to the outside world and rebuild their lives, no matter what the physical scars." Once she met a woman, sitting huddled in a corner of a big room. She was defeated by life itself. She had been a professor of music at Dresden Conservatory before the war but now she had nothing (so she thought!). These Gospel song words came to Corrie's mind, as she tried to lift this woman's spirits:-

> "Down in the human heart, crushed by the tempter,
> Feelings lie buried that grace can restore;
> Touched by a loving heart, weakened by kindness
> Chords that were broken will vibrate once more."

Corrie talked of her own pain and loss, of her love for Jesus and His forgiveness, of the music of her own being that no one could steal from her. "For," she said, "no one can steal what is in your heart. The ability to surrender our bitterness lies hidden within every human spirit. We have the ability with God's help to forgive even the worst enemies." *('Tramp for the Lord', p 57)*

How true! Although in healing of memories we see miracles, we find healing is blocked or postponed if there has been no forgiveness.

Jesus tells us that if we don't forgive we're incapable of receiving forgiveness ourselves, because we are resisting the Light. "To hate your brother," John says, "is to live in darkness." *(1 John 2:9)* We may not exactly hate our brother, but we could often wish him off the face of the earth!

Forgiveness should mean that we actually do wish our opponents well. No doubt we will struggle with forgiveness till we die. We hear people say, 'I'll forgive but I'll never forget or can't forget'. What would we do if our Heavenly Father treated us like this and kept a record of all our wrong deeds to bring against us? "Nevermore will I remember your sins," God says, "I have dispelled your faults like a cloud, your sins like a mist." *(Isaiah 44: 22)* "Though your sins are as scarlet, I shall make them white as snow." *(Isaiah 1:18)*

The big breakthrough in praying for healing of memories comes at the moment when someone says "I forgive.....". It is such a privilege to witness this occasion. One can see the fire of Christ's forgiveness dispelling the darkness of unforgiveness, as the fire of His love purifies the soul of the bitterness which has gnawed away at health and beauty. Love and forgiveness enable our hearts to open up like flowers to a new life. Far from becoming hardened because of their sufferings, those who forgive can love even those who hurt them.

St. Thomas More would often pray for those who opposed him:

"Almighty God,
have mercy on ... ...
and all that bear me evil will and would me harm,
and their faults and mine together,
by such easy, tender, merciful means as thine infinite
wisdom best can devise;
vouchsafe to amend and redress and make us saved
souls in heaven together,
where we may ever live and love together with thee and
thy blessed saints,
O glorious Trinity,
for the bitter passion of our sweet Saviour. Amen.

Can we ever judge another's pain? Corrie Ten Boom was lecturing on forgiveness, explaining how she suffered in the concentration camp during the war. She said that the only way to get rid of bitterness was to surrender it, but those who nursed their bitterness were unable to rebuild their lives. A man in a wheelchair, who had lost his legs in the War, interrupted, asking what could she know about bitterness, since she had two legs.

"I managed to survive the camp", she told him, "My father died on the way there, and my sister, Betsie, died there. The conditions were appalling. We were even made to stand naked in front of everyone for hours at a time. They took everything we had, but they could never take Jesus from my heart"

As Corrie turned to the man with no legs, he slowly said to her: "So you have hated also? What do you suggest I do about my hate?". "Ask Jesus to come into your life" she said to him. "He will give you riches no man can take away from you. Jesus can even use a legless man if he surrenders his bitterness." The man in the wheelchair thought carefully for a moment. "When you forgave your enemies, was the bitterness gone for ever?" he asked. "Oh, yes," she answered. "My bitterness has well and truly gone." "What do I do should my old bitterness return?", he asked. She answered, "Keep claiming the victory of Jesus over fear and resentment, and live in obedience to His word." *('Tramp for the Lord', pp 53-54)*

If we turn again to Scripture now, what an amazing example of forgiveness we have in the first martyr, St. Stephen, who unconditionally forgave his murderers. His glowing face was evidence of his surrender to the power of God's love, flowing into his soul. What a prayer of forgiveness, identical to his Master!

"And Stephen, filled with the Holy Spirit, gazed into Heaven and saw the Glory of God, and Jesus standing at God's right hand. 'I see Heaven thrown open', he said, 'and the Son of Man standing at the right hand of God'. At this all the members of the council shouted out and stopped their ears with their hands, then they all rushed at him, sent him out of the city and stoned him. The witnesses put down their clothes at the feet of a young man called Saul. As they were stoning him, Stephen said in invocation, 'Lord Jesus, receive my spirit' Then he knelt down and said aloud, 'Lord, do not hold this sin against them', and with these words he fell asleep". *(Acts 7: 55-60)*

There are always many witnesses to the Gospel of

forgiveness, e.g. Martin Luther King, Nelson Mandela and others. A young Lebanese man, after being ambushed, wrote this letter to his family just before he died. "I have just one request: forgive with all your hearts, those who killed me. Join me in praying that my blood, even though I am a sinner, may help to atone for the sins of Lebanon, mingled with the blood of all who have fallen, from all sides, and from all religious confessions. May it be offered as the price of peace, the love and the concord which have disappeared from this country and even from the whole world. Don't be afraid. What grieves me, is that you will be sad. Pray, pray, pray and love your enemies..."

Forgiveness Prayer:

Lord Jesus, I ask you to help me to forgive and to make me a loving person. I know that you want only my happiness and fullness of life and I know the way to obtaining these gifts is by learning to forgive. I now forgive everyone in my life who has ever hurt me. I forgive especially the person who has hurt me most... I forgive myself for the hurts I've imposed on myself, for the things I have said or not said, for things I have left undone... I am sorry for the times I've been angry with You and blamed You for illness... accidents... or death of anyone I love. Purify my life, take away my bitter and resentful feelings and attitudes and please give me a healthy outlook on life. I need You so much, Lord, to help me to keep loving, keep forgiving.

I need You to help me to forgive my mother or father for any lack of love or for anything lacking in my upbringing as a child, because of them.

(Spend some time praying through anything that comes to mind. Invite Jesus to be with you in the memories. Thank Him for your parents whether you know them or not).

Help me to forgive any one of my brothers or sisters, aunts or uncles that need my forgiveness now.

Help me to forgive any teacher, doctor, nurse, priest or any person who may have hurt me.

Help me to forgive my spouse or my children for any lack of love or co-operation on their part.

Help me to forgive my mother-in-law or father-in-law for their interfering in my marriage, for their prejudice against my partner and for causing division between me and my spouse.

Help me to forgive my neighbours for their lack of care and co-operation.

Help me to forgive my enemies who may have wished me or my family evil.

Help me to forgive the Church for not bringing me Jesus.

Help me to forgive all those who are arrogant and authoritarian in their dealings with me.

Help me to forgive my community for its lack of love for me.

Help me to forgive my employers for their unjust treatment.

Help me to forgive other Christians for their lack of understanding of my faith. Jesus, I now, with your grace, forgive them all.

Thank you Jesus for freeing me of the evil of unforgiveness. Fill me with your Holy Spirit and lead me always in your ways. Amen.

"The law of the Lord is perfect
New life for the soul...
The Commandments of the Lord are clear
Light for the eyes.

More desirable than gold
Even than the finest gold
His words are sweeter than honey
Even the honey that drips from the comb.

Thus your servant is formed by them
Observance brings great reward
But who can detect his own failings?
Wash out my hidden faults?

May the words of my mouth always find favour
And the whisperings of my heart
In your presence Lord –
My Rock, My Redeemer.   *(Psalm 19)*

Forgiveness is beautiful. It is God-like. It is worth cultivating at all costs. It is a task that needs to be lived out daily. If you are a parent, please try to bring your children up with forgiveness. God is faithful. His grace never fails us. He is with us forever. Take courage and live. Why wait until it's too late? Forgive *now*, and you will reap the rewards in this life and in the next. Keep your sense of humour and balance and always look up!

**"Father, forgive them,
they do not know what they are doing."**
(Luke 22:34)

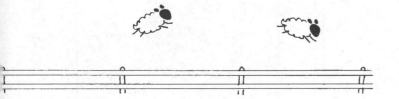

"I call you to healing, that you may walk before Me in holiness, truth and justice. I long for you to be free of fear, and of those things which dissipate you so easily. Believe in My healing love for you at all times and in all places. Wherever I am there is peace. I alone am the Healer. Trust Me!"

A CALL TO INNER HEALING
AND WHOLENESS

It didn't fizzle out with the early Church.

God still heals today! God's healing is not something that died out with the early Church.
Inner Healing is the healing of the inner person, body, mind and spirit, including the healing of memories and dreams.

By means of inner healing, hope is re-born (especially for those who have resigned themselves to living with unfortunate circumstances, bad habits, and traumas). As they begin to see the door to recovery opening before them, they gain inner strength and, gradually, they realise that they *can* start to live again…

If the call to Inner Healing is responded to, it is an exciting, though sometimes painful, journey.   It always leads to new life, increases happiness and gives a freedom of spirit, never known before. It is God's free gift to us and is there for everyone who chooses and desires it. The good news of course is that it works! It is absolutely free. It comes from above!

It could be compared to major surgery at times, with Jesus Himself as the Master Surgeon. The gifts we need for this ministry are the spiritual gifts of the Holy Spirit:

> *"There are many different gifts, but it is always the same Spirit; there are many different ways of serving, but it is always the same Lord. There are many different forms of activity, but in everybody it is the same God who is at work in them all. The particular manifestation of the Spirit granted to each one is to be used for the general good. To one is given from the Spirit the gift of utterance expressing wisdom; to another the gift of utterance expressing knowledge, in accordance with the same Spirit; to another, faith, from the same Spirit; and to another the gifts of healing, through this one Spirit; to another, the working of miracles; to another, prophecy; to another, the power of distinguishing spirits; to one, the gift of different tongues and to another, the interpretation of tongues. But at work in all these is one and the same Spirit, distributing them at will to each individual."*
>
> *(1 Corinthians 12: 4-11)*

I believe that at some stage in all our lives, we could do with a dose of inner healing. In fact inner healing is a process that should be happening all our lives through. There is hardly a person on the earth who does not seem to need it. We all have memories that affect us adversely. No one escapes the pain of life and sometimes as W.B.

Yeats wrote: "Too much suffering makes a stone of the heart". We know from Scripture that God calls us to change our hearts of stone into hearts of flesh instead. Inner healing certainly does this for us.

"I shall pour clean water over you and you shall live, you shall be cleansed. I shall cleanse you of all your defilement and all your idols. I shall give you a new heart and put a new spirit in you: I shall remove the heart of stone from your bodies and give you a heart of flesh instead." *(Ezekiel 36:25).*

This is truly what happens as a result of Inner Healing. As Christ implants His law deeper and deeper into our hearts, we become more and more whole, more healed, more joyful, more loving, in fact, more alive! "I have come" Jesus said, "that they may have life, and have it abundantly." *(John 10:10).* We need to let this word soak into our being so that it can come alive within us.

So few Christians seem to enjoy this fullness of life, even faithful churchgoers: they seem to lack the vitality associated with a living faith. I've often wondered why this is, why such faithful people, and even some of God's very specially-chosen ministers, so often seem to lack the joy of faith which must surely be associated with the Good News. If that is the effect of Good News, what on earth is the effect of bad news, one wonders!

The early Christian's faith was full, joyful, dynamic, contagious. Three thousand were added to the Church with Peter's first sermon. How many converts can our parishes boast of today? Where is the joy at our services, as we gather round the Lord's table? So many 'sad and stony' faces in Church; where is Christ's peace? Are we celebrating our faith, or are we, as it were, doing something out of routine? Do we hear the Gospel readings, or are we distracted with our own thoughts? Faith must be living and active. We are in the presence of the *living* Jesus, He is alive! He is risen today! Alleluia!

What has happened to the glorious, life-giving voice of Vatican II in our churches? If lived in its fullness we would become a church community bringing the spirit of Christ to the world.

It was only after I myself received the Baptism in the Spirit, followed by some inner healing of a childhood memory which unconsciously affected my life right up to about 1975, that I began to see the importance of Inner Healing, and its effect upon our lives. I suffered for much of my life from 'extreme' shyness, which prevented me at times from being myself, from speaking up at meetings, from reading at Mass, from meeting people; and which made me 'blush' easily especially if anyone mentioned anything had gone missing! This was a great burden to me as I was never guilty. I felt my true self was being stifled at times.

When I was about eight years old, I think, we had for a few years a sweet shop from which I started to steal sweets and later on sweets plus a few pence now and again. I don't remember much about it but I do remember my mother caught me 'red-handed' one day and she scolded me (rightly so) but it didn't work! So the next time, she threatened me with telling my dad. "You wait till your Father comes home," she said. Enough said! I tried to avoid him all evening but at one point, he called me and challenged me with this problem. "If you don't stop," he said, "I'll have to put you in the orphanage down the road." We all dreaded this orphanage, run by the Good Shepherd Sisters, for we saw those poor children in our school, all dressed in horrible green dresses, when no one else had a uniform. He also gave me a little hiding and made me sit on his bike in the shop for the rest of the evening. I was not allowed to move! He never touched me before or after that, and he never could forgive himself for punishing me; it must have been so difficult for him for I loved him dearly and he me!

Years later, when I went home as a nun, he referred to this incident with such sorrow, trying to tell me it was my mother's fault!! I could see he was deeply contrite and he found it difficult to forgive himself. I don't know who was more hurt! I think he never could let it go, bless him! We both forgave each other. I told him I might have been impossible if he had not corrected me and could have ended up a 'thief' and so I thanked him for being a good dad. But he was never consoled.

This memory was well forgotten but it popped up again in 1975 as I was being prayed with generally for inner healing. I was at a prayer counselling training course. It was amazing. What I recalled vividly was the woman's beautiful face and pure blue eyes. She came into our shop to buy something. She saw me sitting on my dad's bike crying, and as she left the shop, she came over to me with a big bag of sweets, and of course this made me cry all the more! Kindness when you are upset makes you even worse! I clearly saw her lovely face as I remembered the incident. As we prayed through the memory, we invited

Jesus into the whole situation. I forgave my Dad again. I repented of my stealing. I felt the warmth and forgiving love not only of my Dad but of my heavenly Father as well.

Since then my 'abnormal' shyness has disappeared. Thank God. I feel so relieved! Looking back, I seem to think I had a big conversion after this incident and began to help my mom in the house a bit more, being a good girl!! My memory is a bit remote and my brothers and sisters may not agree with this idea!!

My dad was the authority figure in my life and so this 'punishment' had other related consequences for me in later years! This was a deep root from which reaction behaviour set up so it became a pattern. I suffered because of this shyness for so many years. It prevented me from doing things I might have done. Those who know me now, don't believe I was ever shy!

When you see the connection with the past it is like a revelation from the Holy Spirit. It is very wholesome and healing. Once when I was a very young nun in Aberystwyth, just professed, the Superior (an old French Reverend Mother) lost her keys. She asked at table if anyone had seen them. Of course, I blushed (as usual) though I knew nothing about the keys. Later, in her office, she found them under papers on her desk. I happened to be standing there asking for a permission. "Next time you take something like that," she said "you'll own up, won't you?" I nearly died at such an unjust accusation!

I share this because for me it was a key incident in my life and it may help you to see incidences in your own life that have affected your pattern of behaviour, and so, it may help you understand inner healing. Jesus brings the memories to mind as required so that they can be healed simply, quickly, and the pattern becomes obvious and is broken. It's truly wonderful to experience and it works so gently and the healing comes so faithfully. I certainly have thanked God many times for this healing in my own life, as it liberated me so much, as you can imagine.

Another example may help here, of a slightly different nature. A few years ago, I had a 'bad' experience that certainly needed healing of memories. One of our school teachers called Katherine (whom I hardly knew, having met her only twice) committed suicide and unfortunately I was the one who found her hanging. Lord have mercy on her. The horrible memory haunted me for days until I was prayed over by a holy priest, for healing of the memory, as he invited Jesus into it. I was healed instantly. That night, as I thanked God in our little chapel and prayed for Katherine's soul, I became overwhelmed by an indescribable peace I have never experienced before or since. I could have stayed in chapel all night praying. However, I did eventually go to bed and was awakened at 3 a.m., only to sense her presence in the room. I had put a photograph of her on my wall in my room to remind me to pray for her. She had on her a white jumper on which were purple stripes; all I know is I sat up in bed in the middle of the night, and saw these rays coming towards me from the picture, right across the room. I just lay back and fell asleep peacefully knowing she was O.K. It was wonderful how healing and peace came to the pupils and teachers after the Holy Mass was celebrated in this non-Catholic school (where we taught) for the repose of Katherine's soul. The Mass always brings healing.

During those sad days that followed, I received much consolation just by sitting at the foot of the Cross with Jesus in His suffering. There was never a time when Our Lady, Mother of Sorrows, was not present to me. She was such a tower of strength and comfort to me. I could shed tears with Her, which brought release and healing. Important never to suppress tears because they do bring deep healing. Sometimes you must give yourself permission to grieve.

I had tried to do my best for this dear teacher when she told me of her depression. It is hard to know what to do sometimes in people's sadness. I offered to take her home to her parents but she did not want to worry them. She had just begun to eat when she met me, and was beginning to feel a bit better and she said she would be fine. However, doctors told me afterwards that the dangerous time for those depressed and threatening suicide is not when they are depressed, it is when they are coming out of it, and beginning to feel stronger in themselves. This was I believe the case with this teacher. She was suffering from a broken love affair, her 'boyfriend' had told her to look for someone else; that he could not marry her, but she could not accept this apparent rejection. She did not want to let him go. It's a mistake to let someone have a hold on your life to that extent, if they reject you in any way. This is where healing of the self-image is important. It's hardly worth breaking your heart over someone who would not give his heart for you! Anyway, what is one man's opinion?

It never ceases to amaze me how God works. Three weeks later, I was on the team to give a 'Choice' weekend in London, and there were no less than five young people at it who had attempted suicide and needed help. One girl I brought home with me for ten days. She was planning suicide by the age of twenty one. Her mother had committed suicide when she was four years old. She sent her off to the shops and when she arrived home her mother had gone. Dreadfully sad situation! I begged God to save her life and to restore her good sense.

She sat on the bed in our house, trying to slash her wrists. I was given 'spontaneous' wisdom to know how to deal with her. I slapped her hand, to help to bring her to her senses, telling her she could ruin her body if she liked but that I had no intention of watching her doing it. I tried to run out of the room but she grabbed my arm, from which I escaped! She shouted, "You don't care about me." "No," I said, "we don't care two hoots about you, that's why I brought you home; that's why I got our doctor to sign you off for ten days so we can look after you here. You can go home if you like. Your car is outside; why don't you go now ... !"

Well, I don't know how I managed to get to bed that night, but I knelt by my bedside and begged God to keep us all safe through the night, especially her, and not to let her do anything stupid. It certainly was a risky business; what could I do but trust God our Father, the Almighty, totally?

The following morning, she was keen for me to see her blood-stained wrist, but I refused to look at it. I felt this would not be right. I had prayed for wisdom and felt that sympathy at this stage would not help! She was looking for a plaster; I told her she'd find one in the kitchen. Next she wanted a pair of scissors, I told her she'd find one in the drawer. She wanted me to put on the plaster, I said I was sorry I had to leave for school, she'd have to do it herself. I wondered what state I'd find the house on my return. Would it still be standing, would she still be there? To our utter amazement she was still there, having hoovered the whole house and done all the ironing that I had left out on purpose! She was in good spirits, thank God! I was so relieved and thanked God profusely for His everlasting mercies and care for us. "He rescues me from the snare of the fowler who seeks to destroy me and He sets me free." *(Psalm 124: 7)* Today this lovely-looking girl is a fine young woman and a fully qualified district nurse. Praise God.

I am often called upon to pray for those who have had a suicide in the family. For them it is indeed often a great source of sorrow and sometimes even guilt. Above all, pray for the repose of their soul. Try to let the dead person concerned go back to God from whom they came. This will bring peace.

Suicide is an illness we really do not understand. You see, whenever there is a suicide in a family, if you look back over the family tree, you may find other members of the same family tree who have also committed suicide, albeit a long time ago. Suicide definitely does run in families. It is a well attested fact.

Dr. Kenneth McAll is an undoubted pioneer of this type of understanding, and it is very worthwhile reading his book "Healing of the Family Tree".

"See, it is inscribed in front of Me: I will not be silent until I have settled My accounts with them for their sins and their fathers' sins," said the Lord.   *(Isaiah 65:6-7)*

Illnesses, also, are passed in our genes down the family line, generation after generation: often a grandchild, through no fault of its own or its parents, inherits a certain illness from its grandparents. For example cystic fibrosis. A genetic weakness can often be cured medically by the discerning doctor, and future generations do not suffer in the same way.

Similarly, tendencies in families towards suicide, abortion, sexual abuse, alcoholism and violence can also be passed on down the family line. So pray for your ancestors.

In order to stop the chain of suicide being passed down the family line, you simply close the 'psychic door', or link, between any person thinking of committing suicide and any other person or persons in their family who have already committed suicide.

You close the 'psychic door' by saying: "In Jesus' Name, I close the psychic door between .... *(name the person who has already committed suicide)* and .... *(the troubled person thinking of suicide)*. You then bind the 'spirit of suicide' away from the family tree or line, by saying: "I bind you, spirit of suicide, in Jesus' Name, and I command you to go to the foot of the Cross, never more to trouble this person or family."

Then you pray the cleansing Blood of Jesus upon the family, by saying: "I ask You, Jesus, to cleanse this family line with Your Precious Blood, and protect it always with Your Holy Spirit."

And lastly you cut links between any member of the family (known or unknown, past or present) who has ever committed suicide and the present troubled person, by saying: "In Jesus' Name, I break any curse and I cut any links not of God between .... (the one who committed suicide) and .... (the present troubled person), and I ask that only the Love of Jesus be between them."

Tony, both of whose brothers had already committed suicide and who was about to commit suicide himself, is alive today thanks to this type of prayer. He lay on the couch at home unable to move or speak. As I prayed with him in the way I have described he was healed. He is doing very well today, thank God, and has his own little flat.

This type and pattern of prayer given above is very powerful when you are asked to pray with someone troubled by the memory of abortion or sexual abuse.

When you have been ministering it is very important, in the Name of Jesus, to cut all links between yourself and the person or persons with whom you have been praying. You want to make sure that whatever has afflicted the person doesn't attach itself to you, or attack or contaminate you. It also safeguards any wrong dependency.

We can be 'trapped' by our past, by our regrets, our bad memories, our omissions etc. As a result, certain areas of our life remain 'dead'. Many parents I'm sure have many regrets over how they've reared their children. They did their best at the time, but in retrospect they know they could have done better. Regrets are only useful for change and learning!

Parents may not communicate deeply with their children, unfortunately, unless they are scolding them or unless there is something wrong. Even the best parents with the best will in the world injure their children 'unknowingly' by their lack of affirmation, by too many *'don't'*s, by not saying enough *'I love you'*s to them. We're bad at giving compliments, and we do not praise enough when praise is due. Children thrive on praise!

Nowadays perhaps there is more awareness of the need for affirmation and children have more confidence - sometimes too much! Some children are scarred by teasing. Too much teasing by people, especially brothers and sisters, can cause much repressed anger in later life. Nicknames are generally not to be recommended unless they are nice 'endearing' names, but again they can lead to suppressed anger and great annoyance that should never have been thought fun. Questions like, 'what's wrong with you now? You are so awkward; that's not the way to do it; why can't you do it right, why can't you be like so-and-so?' are always harmful, like poisonous darts, so destructive to those to whom they are addressed.

Scripture tells us wisely:
"Parents, never drive your children to resentment but in bringing them up, correct them and guide them, as the Lord does." *(Ephesians 6: 4)*.

Just as a child's 'self-image' can be damaged, so too can a wife's or husband's self-image be damaged – for example, the wife may be criticised constantly in front of the children or the children are loved 'first', or the husband is 'nagged' all the time and can't do anything right.

So many 'bad' habits can develop in relationships if one is not seen as a 'gift of God' each day and if each other's love is seen not as a daily gift 'given' but as one's due. Another's love, no matter how close people are, must always be treated as *'pure gift on their behalf'*. It must never be taken for granted. It's a miracle that anyone should love us! Receive love, courtesy, kindness graciously. Nothing is really 'yours'; all is gift each day even after years together. Cultivate a grateful heart.

I'm sure we can all take consolation from St. Paul, the great apostle, as we ask God even now, to forgive our mistakes, and to give mercy to those we have hurt in the past. On behalf of religious sisters, who have 'damaged' children, I would like to ask forgiveness and ask God's blessing on all the children whose lives religious have touched and maybe wounded. May God grant His pardon and peace. Trust the past to the mercy of God. Regrets like 'if only' are a waste of time, what is – is! What is done, is done! Change now! Make up where you can now, it's never too late with God. "The chances we have missed, the graces we resist", Lord please redeem today.

"I know of nothing good living in me, (that is, in my unspiritual self), for though the will to do what is good is in me, the performance is not, with the result that instead of doing the good things that I wanted to do, I carry out the sinful things I do not want. When I act against my will, then it is not my 'true' self doing it, but sin lives in me.

In fact, this seems to be the rule, that every single time I want to do good, it is something evil that comes to hand. In my inmost self I dearly love God's law but I can see that my body follows a different law that battles against that law of sin which lives in my body.

What a wretched man am I! Who will rescue me from this body doomed to death? Thanks be to God through Jesus Christ Our Lord." (Romans 7:18-25)

"Let your love be ready to console me", the Psalmist cries: "let your love come to me and I shall live, for your law is my delight. For with your precepts you give me life". *(Psalm 119:76)*

So many of our lives are broken, fragmented in certain areas. Too many people live in the past, digging up one memory after another, never experiencing the glorious light of the present moment. Some live their whole life under an illusion, thinking they're stupid, unattractive, horrid, lazy because someone has told them so. They never find themselves. They live, not under God's image of themselves, but under someone else's 'false' image of them. They allow Satan to hold them bound, to steal their joy and to rob them of the inheritance Jesus died to give them – a life restored in Him. Why should we allow this to happen to us? We are far too precious in God's eyes and life is for living fully in Him. I beg you to choose life. Conquer evil with good. Claim your inheritance in Jesus and enjoy the rest of your time on earth living in healing and forgiveness.

Psychologists tell us that we relate to others out of the experiences we ourselves have had. If others relate positively to us we tend to have a good self-image and vice versa. The quality of our love for others is coloured also by the quality of our love for ourselves and how true it is. It amazes me how beautiful-looking people think they're ugly and some brilliant people think they're useless.

We are witnessing many wonderful healings in these areas. What seemed impossible to overcome, or to live with, can become a 'driving force' for God in our lives. It is so encouraging for me to hear Jesus say: "Only the truth will set you free." *(John 8:32)* There is a great need for 'rescue' operations in this area, so that people can reclaim their spiritual inheritance, become themselves, and really know who they are. The transforming power of the Holy Spirit becomes obvious as He 'rescues us from all our foes'.

Every day becomes a 'good day', a 'God' day. Every experience can be a 'God' experience, wholesome and healthy, seen in His light, where we always see light. You'll find there are no such things as co-incidences but only 'God'-incidences. God is in charge! You begin to believe it. You learn that every hurt can be healed, the challenge is for us to "let go, let God", and to wager all that we have for Him; to allow His love to enter our heart as the greatest prize, the pearl of great price. Your self-image can be transformed by the truth, and the quality of your love can improve as you know who you are and as you begin to like yourself better, a sure sign you are growing in the Holy Spirit!

> *"I believe that nothing can outweigh the supreme advantage of knowing Christ Jesus my Lord. For Him I have accepted the loss of everything and I look on everything as so much rubbish if only I can have Christ and be given a place in Him. I am no longer trying for perfection by my own efforts. The perfection that comes through faith in Christ and is from God and is based on faith. All I want is to know Christ and the power of His Resurrection and to share His sufferings by reproducing the pattern of His death. That is the way I can hope to take my place in the resurrection of the dead. Not that I have become perfect yet; I have not yet won. All I can say is that I forget the past and I strain ahead for what is still to come. I am racing for the finish, for the prize to which God calls us upwards, to receive in Christ Jesus. We who are called 'perfect' must all think in this way.*
> *If there is some point on which you can see things differently God will make it clear to you; meantime let us go forward on the road that has brought us to where we are"*   (Philippians 3:8-16)

It is true that in all our lives, especially when we are hurting and vulnerable, a pattern of reaction or behaviour emerges. The pattern is usually 'triggered off' by a hurt we've experienced earlier in life; it could be childhood or adolescence or even as far back as our time in our mother's womb. We may only become aware of 'patterns of behaviour' years on, but unless we're aware of inner healing and how it works, we may not link present patterns with past hurts.

More and more the Holy Spirit is showing us the connections, sometimes very strong ones, between past and present. Many of us say we never remember dreams, yet when we begin to talk about dreams and dreaming, it's amazing how we begin to recall them to mind. Dreams are always part of us, as are the characters in our dreams. We synthesise in our dreams what we can't synthesise in our lives. God works in us all the time. 'He works in his beloved as they slumber'. *(Psalm 127:2)*

Our dreams can be so healing. They are worth working with, but it is beyond the scope of this book to deal with them. Nightmares can be healed when prayed through. They are often a sign of some suppressed emotion, as are recurring dreams. Sometimes people have their natural sleep restored after special prayer, and never again need to rely on sleeping tablets. Thank God; what a relief for them.

It is something similar, I think, that happens to us with inner healing. Once we become 'tuned-in', we begin to see links, to our great advantage and wholeness. If we start to observe our behaviour patterns when we're hurt, we'll probably find they are identifiable and there will be a predominant pattern of reaction when we find ourselves in certain situations. The Good News is that these patterns can be broken through the power of Jesus, during this special type of prayer for healing. We can be set free of them. The Holy Spirit often shows the 'root' cause which usually goes back to the 'first' time this particular hurt was ever experienced and it becomes healed. We try to protect ourselves against hurts by our reactions, and patterns of reaction set up. As we pray through and about the hurt Jesus is invited in and He heals us. "He is the same yesterday, today and forever." *(Hebrews 13:8)* Forgiveness is essential. Freedom comes through it. Afterwards you become more of an 'actor' than a 'reactor', and your 'wholeness' grows. You become more aware and more understanding of others' problems and hurts, by being healed yourself.

Praise the Holy Spirit for His graciousness to us in showing us how to pray like this, with such beautiful results. Sometimes the healing is not complete after the first session and it may need another prayer session to deal with the related circumstances. But when 'the snare is broken we are set free' in Jesus' name, for good.

A few examples may be helpful here. The names are disguised.

Rebecca often felt 'unwanted'. She came to a day of renewal I was leading. When it came to the session in small groups, she told me that nobody wanted her in their group. I told her she didn't even know the people and therefore to give it a try and join one group if she could. She found it very difficult. She had this preconceived idea that nobody wanted her. During the prayer session, I suggested she came to my group. The Lord showed clearly the root of her problem. She had been an unwanted child, her father never wanted her, and she carried this hurt up till now, projecting these feelings onto everyone even her dear husband. We helped her in prayer to forgive her parents especially her dad: "I forgive you, dad," she said aloud; "I love you. I know Jesus wanted me for He gave me life, so it is a lie that I was unwanted." We used some apt scripture quotations that reassured her of God's love for her. Satan's hold over her in this lie of thinking she was unwanted was conquered by her forgiveness and the truth of scripture. The healing process had begun. I know she's healed because two years later, she bounced up to me in Walsingham, telling me how healed she's been since that prayer, how she's never since felt unwanted and how her husband and herself are much happier now! Praise Jesus!

Another girl of twenty one, always felt 'second best'. She suffered because her boyfriends kept running off with other girls re-inforcing her feeling of being 'second best'. As I prayed with her, I felt the Lord telling me to ask her if she ever felt 'second-best'. She said she always did. "Let's see where it comes from," I said. As I prayed her through her early childhood the incident which was the 'root' cause of this pattern was brought to light. It happened when she was three years old and she began to recall it vividly. Her dad had been away on business and he brought a huge beautiful doll for her sister of five and brought nothing to her. Although she was only three years old she remembered it vividly. She was deeply hurt at the time, and felt her sister mattered more than she did; consequently she felt second-best from then on. The pattern was 'triggered off'. Having understood what happened, forgiving her dad, and inviting Jesus into the situation she is healed completely. Her parents say she is a 'new' girl and best of all she is getting married very soon now. Praise Jesus!

I recall the healing five years ago of a beautiful young married woman who could not forgive her dad for childhood wounds and hurts. She asked me to pray with her. I said "Certainly, let's ask God to bless us and let's thank Him for His love." She told me she had tried several times to forgive her dad, but she just couldn't. She would never again go back home to Ireland; she had no peace of mind. She had this 'love-hate' relationship with her dad but she didn't ever want to see him again.

"Forgiveness is the key," I said, "if you want peace of mind you must forgive everyone who has ever hurt you. Don't bear grudges. Is there anyone you need to forgive?" I asked; "Yes," she said, "my dad. I'll never forgive him." "Well," I said, "then I can't pray with you."

I stood up as if to go home, She felt bad as I had driven a few miles to see her. "What must I do, then?" she asked. "Well," I said "Let's pray for the grace of forgiveness for a while." When she was ready, I asked her again if she would forgive her dad, telling her she would block the family healing if she did not, and her dad needed her compassionate love. "Can you forgive him now?" I said, "for if you can't, at least you can give Jesus permission to forgive him for you. Can you do that?" She cried as she said softly, "Dad, I forgive you, I'm sorry, I love you." "The snare was broken and she was set free." Satan's power over her was conquered with these words. Praise Jesus!"

"Please take them by the hand Lord," I prayed, "and give them a renewed relationship of father and daughter." God filled her heart with compassion towards her dad. Then she gave her life to Jesus again, had Baptism in the Holy Spirit and has never looked back, peace was restored.

Afterwards her daughter wondered what had happened to her mom and she said her Aunty Margaret who had been a 'pig', was nicer recently! All the family were healed. 'Interflora' arrived at the house with a beautiful bouquet of flowers sent from Ireland some weeks after this "with all our love Mom and Dad." They did not know what had happened, but Jesus cleverly popped over to Ireland and prompted her mom and dad to make this lovely gesture. She keeps the little card in her handbag as a reminder of God's healing love. Years later, God gave her the grace to be with her dad at his deathbed. All restored and healed! Thank you Jesus!

Sometimes a hurt sends us into a state of 'self-pity'. I find this is one of the worst 'demons' to root out, because we indulge in 'false' comfort, and Satan is a deceiver, and wants to trap us in misery. We become like little children seeking attention all the time. It's so sad to see people selfishly making themselves the big 'I am' round which the world and everybody else has to revolve. I've seen people psychologically sick through self-pity. I have seen others who have developed physical symptoms of illnesses doctors can't discover. I know of one man who spent his whole married life in bed, supposedly ill, but since his wife died, he's as right as rain! He's up and about all the time, doing all the cooking, cleaning, ironing, shopping, and he has never been better. Extraordinary!

There's a difference between 'self-pity and self-love. We have a duty to love ourselves and if you're tired, be good to yourself. No use 'running yourself into the ground' for whatever reason. You must protect your own integrity, being even more kind to yourself when you feel low. One of our sisters always bought herself something nice when she was 'down'; this cheered her 'up'! People sometimes punish themselves when they're tired by getting 'more' tired, working harder than ever. Somehow they seem unable to stop and take stock of what is happening to them. They allow pressures and stress to steal their health, becoming more and more blind to their own basic needs. This is no good! People do it all the time. God doesn't approve! He says 'love yourself' so you can love others.

So, if you're 'low' why not treat yourself really well? If you enjoy cooking perhaps you could lay the table nicely, with flowers, table cloth, candle, and have a good meal! In fact, you must become better than ever to yourself, when life is hard on you.

"If you're feeling low, don't despair.
The sun has a sinking spell every night,
but it comes back up every morning".   (Anonymous)

Self-pity demands everyone around you focuses on 'you', and makes 'you' the focus of attention. Much-loved Princess Diana, in her struggle to love herself, looked outwards to others' needs, and spent much of her energy on others. It was surely God's plan to bring her and the saintly Mother Teresa together, and He even took them home together, the great mother of the 'poor' dying almost in the 'shadow' of her beloved, much-inspired 'spiritual' daughter. Like Padre Pio, and St. Thérèse, they will both make 'much noise' after their death, Diana's untimely death helping to restore the 'soul' to the nation! 'By your wounds, you will be healed...'

Being unsure of parents' love unfortunately creates insecurity and leads to feelings of rejection and lack of self-love. Our deepest need as human beings is for self-esteem, self-worth, personal dignity. Many drug addicts have told me that they were never loved as children. For some reason communication of love has broken down. Some parents have been very troubled at this because they did their best to show love to their children.
In God's presence and with healing prayer, the masks that were worn 'for protection' for years, can come down and we can be free to become ourselves. With prayer through childhood memories, God's ever present love can and does restore the love that was never felt as a child. No more need for compensations, like drugs or anything else. One can live again believing one is loved and lovable.

I was asked once by a nun to pray with a woman whom I'd never met. I was told she had problems with horrible feelings of something mauling her body. She felt quite disturbed and quite unclean. She was, in fact, a beautiful looking woman, in her mid-forties, with lovely children. Her poor husband was nearly demented with her, and told her to go to the priest, who suggested she needed a psychiatrist.

On hearing her story I felt she only needed inner healing. I went before the Blessed Sacrament (as I usually do) and I asked God to tell me what was wrong with her. He said immediately "it happened in a field with a fifteen year old when she was four." I thanked Him for telling me the possible 'root' of her problem. I was so thrilled. I told Sr. Helen to keep praying, that God had shown me clearly how to pray. I couldn't wait to see her healed! I rang her and made an appointment to see her. She had already requested this. (Incest often causes distress in later years)

Over a cup of tea she told me the problem she felt, and how unhappy she was. After letting her speak, I told her God wanted her healed and He had told me what was needed. "It happened to you in a field with a fifteen year old when you were four years old", I said. "How could you know that?" she cried, as she put her head on the table sobbing, "I've never told anyone in my life, I'm so ashamed." "God wants you healed at all costs", I said, "so He told me to tell you what was wrong in order to heal you."

She just couldn't believe it. Often we do not link the past with the present problem, but when the Holy Spirit gives a 'word of knowledge' like this you know for sure the person is going to be healed completely. I asked God to bless her and protect her family and I told her I would collect her on Wednesday of the following week and take her to the nun's convent where we would pray with her together for healing.

I never usually pray for deliverance for someone on my own, and I never tell the person that they need deliverance.

We prayed in the usual way, asking God to surround all of us, including her family, with His love and protection. We asked her if there was anyone in her life she hadn't forgiven. Then out came the deeply-suppressed memory, the incident of the field, the haystack, the other children playing, the fifteen-year-old uncle taking her aside to another field and the sexual abuse. She forgave him there and then, having bottled this memory up for forty years! We bound the spirit of incest in Jesus' name, cut links between her and her uncle which were not of God, asked Jesus to give them a new relationship as His presence filled the whole memory. I met the nun a few months ago, though I've never met this lady again and would not even recognise her I'm sure; the sister assures me that she's been 'perfect' since this prayer five years ago. Praise Jesus! No more worries! "Jesus is the same yesterday, today and forever." *(Hebrews 13: 8)*

If you've been raped, you need a similar kind of prayer. You need to be cut off from the person concerned and the spirit of rape must be bound in Jesus' Name and sent to Jesus. Forgiveness is always of the essence even though this is humanly extremely difficult to do. With God all things are possible. You can, as I have said before, give Jesus permission to forgive the person for you. Psychyiatry and counselling may help a great deal to heal this type of trauma but, in the final analysis, we are dealing with spirits, and spiritual ministry is needed for complete healing. This includes forgiveness, which is the only way forward if people are to start life again.

Compassion is needed all round. Compassion for the abused: compassion for the abuser: compassion for the family of the abused, and also for the family of the abuser. However difficult, and indeed impossible, it might seem to you, the only way ahead is forgiveness all round. How can the abused forgive? How can the abuser forgive himself or herself? How can either family forgive? How can you forget or even forgive where a treasured life is ruined or lost? Your instinct is to want to retaliate – to kill if you could get your hands on the culprit! How can life start again? How can you ever trust again? How can you ever feel clean again? And, for the abuser, how can you ever be forgiven again? Yet, with God, it is possible.

The only way I know is through compassion. Compassion leads (albeit sometimes slowly) to forgiveness. And forgiveness eventually leads to a new Freedom and Peace. And you *can* start life afresh. It is in this connection particularly that Inner Healing comes into its own, and works miracles where psychiatry cannot.

Sadly, we come across some people today who have been used in Satanic worship, either as children or adolescents. It is heartbreaking to see the effects. These children or adults need very special prayer, for whenever a person has been sacrificed to Satan in satanic ritual the rite has to be revoked. If the person has been baptised the baptismal promises have to be remade. To break Satan's power over them they have to be consecrated or reconsecrated to God. They have to forgive their offender. Jesus alone makes this possible. He alone can give them the grace to do this. Otherwise the effect is horrendous on their own lives and even on the lives of their very own children.

In cases of Satanic ritual or where an adult has sold his or her own life to Satan similar prayers are usually needed with liturgical exorcism by a Catholic priest appointed by the Bishop. This must be accompanied by intense prayer and fasting.

Fortunately true 'possession' is rare. To be freed the person has personally to choose Jesus as their Lord and Saviour. Nobody else can do this for them. You may have to help and encourage them but, to be truly free, they have to say the words of renunciation themselves. The bondage with Satan is so strong that the person completely loses his or her own free will. They can't escape his clutches. Hence they have to revoke Satan's claims on them and renounce their consecration to him. Renewing Baptismal Vows, or making them for the first time (if they are unbaptised) is their saving grace. Unclean spirits can return later as Jesus warns us in Luke 11:24-26. In each Diocese a priest is appointed as Exorcist by the Bishop for this very important and demanding ministry.

The gift of Discernment of Spirits is a gift from the Holy Spirit and is essential for anyone who will work in healing ministry today. On the one hand you must never go into this ministry lightly, but on the other hand, once you are called to this ministry, the Holy Spirit will never let you down. Effective deliverance can only be completed within the context of evangelisation. God's Word is vital!

You must never pray in this way on your own, and you must always be backed up by as much supportive prayer as possible. It is not good to have more than one or two people praying with you for deliverance. The prayer should be done in private as much as possible. Discretion and confidentiality are essential here. You must always safeguard the sacredness of the person to whom you are ministering. God wants His people healed at all costs, and sometimes we see the most wonderful of miracles.

Another very important area where people are very deeply hurt is the area of abortion. Those who've been involved in abortions suffer greatly; they think God will never forgive them and that He will punish them by not giving them a child later on. Of course abortion is a terrible thing, and a grievous offence against Almighty God. It brings its own retribution. Circumstances surrounding an abortion are often not the best, and there is much stress, pressure, heartache associated with it; the mother often not realising what she is doing to her unborn baby.

Sadly, many who are temporally 'reassured' by a doctor or nurse to proceed with an abortion suffer huge remorse a little later. I often encourage mothers, as they receive God's pardon to forgive themselves, to baptise their baby and give their baby a name whether a boy or a girl. We always thank God for the child and ask blessing on the mother and any brothers or sisters.

The joy of repentance and contrition that follows for the mother can only be of God, and life can begin again for them. "Jesus is the same yesterday, today, and for ever' *(Hebrews 13:8)* God's love and forgiveness always heals.

For those who actually perform the abortions there is sometimes much regret and trauma of spirit. Our sympathy goes out to our Christian doctors who suffer more and more because of their stand against abortion. Our prayers are with them daily.

Carlo Carretto has written a wonderful book called 'Journey into Life', where he describes his vision of Aborted Babies. He describes how he was brought round to the back of a hospital in a big city, and shown all the aborted foetuses in a huge dustbin. He felt sick, he was so upset. He asked if he could spend the whole night in the Cathedral of that city, praying in reparation. He found at midnight, that the whole Cathedral came alive with hundreds of cherubs (all aborted foetuses). One hopped on his lap, the others were all over the chandeliers, and on the benches, altar etc. They spoke to him and told him to tell their parents they were O.K. They had gone ahead and were happy but it was their parents who needed help. What a night!

Natural miscarriages are very common. Where there is miscarriage or stillbirth, it is important to give the baby a name and offer the baby back to God from whom it came. The baptism and naming of the child brings great comfort to grieving parents and family.

Many a heart ache is caused by adoption. A mother suffers now or in later years in the giving up of a baby; an adopted child suffers because of hurts in the womb or early childhood, wondering about their roots; and the adoptive parents suffer, because, despite their efforts, the adoption doesn't always work out well. This may be due to these earlier hurts, and the child is then unfortunately unable to receive their parents' love. Inner healing is the answer where there is unhappiness. Of course, many adopted children settle down well and are happy and normal.

I have spoken earlier of being 'baptised in the spirit'. I now need to introduce you to the experience of being 'slain in the spirit' or 'resting in the spirit' which is different from the experience of being baptised in the spirit which is very scriptural and was common in the early Church *(cf Acts 2:1-13; 9:17-22; 10:44; 11:15; 19:6-7)*

Baptism of water is the Sacrament of Initiation into the Christian Faith - and obviously can only be received once. When you are baptised as a child or adult, remember that you receive all the gifts of the Holy Spirit.

Baptism of the Spirit is a reawakening in a person of the spiritual gifts, *(cf 1 Corinthians 12:4-11)* which, of course, are already there, albeit dormant. It is an experience of a person (usually baptised, but not necessarily so) who wishes to renew his or her commitment to Jesus as Lord of their life.

Sometimes, for example, after Holy Communion or after being prayed with, you will have a religious feeling, which is so intense that you don't want to move (rather like the apostles who didn't want to move down from the mountain after the experience of the Transfiguration - they just wanted to stay there).

Often, misunderstood by bystanders, to be 'slain in the spirit' is a wonderful experience of deep inner peace and closeness to God, as a result of being prayed over for a deeper commitment. It could be that a person will feel so much at peace that he or she has to 'rest in the spirit' and just can't keep upright, sometimes needing to sit down or lie down on the ground. The experience can be short or last half an hour or even longer. During this time the person is receiving deep inner healing and is being restored and renewed, and should on no account be disturbed. Just leave the person alone to the Holy Spirit. They are still fully conscious, and will 'return to normal' when God's work in them is done. Misguided people feel compelled to disturb them too early. Just leave them be, sitting or lying down, and support them with your prayer as they 'rest in the spirit'. You don't have to worry about them – they are deeply happy!

If the person is not at peace, it is a sign that there is a need for inner healing, and they should seek further ministry. If they don't, it could be that they will end up feeling worse than before.

One day I prayed with a woman who thought she had been 'slain in the spirit' but I could see she was not at peace. It was late and we had to round off the prayer meeting. On the way home in the taxi, I asked God what was it that was troubling this woman. He told me that it was a spirit of murder. I thanked Him but wondered how on earth I would be able to tell her that. I knew, of course, that God would make it possible and that it would be the right time for her! I rose next morning early to go to pray at the shrine; to my utter amazement I met the woman who needed the prayer and who had, in fact, asked me to pray with her again.

We talked a little about the night before "You weren't at peace last night," I said. "You mean when I was slain in the Spirit," she said. "Yes," I said. "I don't think you were slain in the Spirit, you were not at peace, were you?" "No," she said, "I wondered why I wasn't." "Well," I said, "I asked God to tell me how to pray with you and He told me to tell you there's a spirit of murder troubling your family." "Really?" she said. "Yes," I said, "that's what He said, and He wants you to repent for your family." I couldn't believe how truthful she was because immediately she said, "Yes, I've had an abortion (we couldn't afford another child) my mother had an abortion and my grandmother had an abortion." "And," I said, "your daughter will have an abortion too unless we pray for healing in your blood line on your mother's side."

I prayed with her with a priest friend. She repented on her own behalf, on her mother's and grandmother's behalf. We bound the spirit of murder in Jesus' name, plus any other associating spirits. We forbade them, in Jesus' Name, ever to affect the blood line again, or to return to her family. We prayed the healing blood of Jesus on the family line. We cut links not of God in the family and begged the spirit of life and respect for life to flood it. We asked her to name all the babies and we baptised them in turn in the name of the Father, Son and Holy Spirit. Praise Jesus! Aborted babies need their own mother to give them their name, and to baptise them. Healing always follows.

Another time I prayed with a lady who felt very 'low' at the time, and who'd had a very deprived childhood which left its mark. Her parents could never afford the presents other children had; above all she desperately wanted a bike but her parents could never have bought her one. As I prayed through her memories, asking God to highlight the memory that needed the most healing, her face suddenly became radiant! "What are you doing now?" I asked, "and what age are you?" "Twelve," she said. "It's wonderful. I'm cycling up and down the boreen in Ireland; the fields are lovely with flowers." "Is anyone with you?" I asked. "Yes," she said, "Jesus is on His bike, cycling beside me!" This woman was experiencing present problems in her marriage, but this prayer brought her deep healing and peace.

What a Lord! What a restorer! He is the best 're-cycler'. Only He could do it. She went home so happy!

We've had wonderful prayers answered for couples who long for a child and can't have any. One couple has four beautiful children, another has triplets, and others have one precious child, all total gifts of God, with whom all things are possible. Little Joseph is one such treasure; his mother was told for seventeen years by medical experts in Harley Street that there was no hope. God knows better! Praise Jesus for the gift of life!

Joseph's grandmother was at a sale of work and I was trying to sell her a baby blanket. "I've no grandchild," she said wistfully, "otherwise I would buy it." "Sure," I said. "If you buy this baby blanket you will have a grandchild. I'll ask God for you." She did buy the blanket, and a few months later her daughter conceived little Joseph, having given up all hope of ever having a child. I was at the baptism. What joy!

The divine 'helpline' is open twenty four hours a day for God neither slumbers nor sleeps. We are encouraged in St. James' words to pray for healing, so if you haven't already done so, why not start now. Begin at home if a child is sick.

When the rulers saw the man crippled from birth healed at the Temple Gate, they asked Peter the Apostle, "By what power and by whose name have you done this?"

"It was by the name of Jesus Christ the Nazarene, the stone rejected by the builders but which has proved to be the Keystone; for of all names in the world given to men, this is the only one by which we can be saved." *(Acts 4:11)* The Apostles continued to testify: "We cannot promise to stop proclaiming what we've seen and heard." *(Acts 4: 20)* Neither can those stop witnessing who have experienced God's power today. "The man who was miraculously cured was over forty" *(Acts 4: 22).* We find that people around the age of forty quite often experience a need for inner healing. (Was this the 'noon-day devil' they used to talk about when we were young sisters, I wonder?) They become restless, dissatisfied, and may begin to feel the ageing process, feeling less attractive, more sluggish than when young.

The suppressed hurts of childhood often begin to show their head, without it being realised, and current problems at work, home, relationships, even panic attacks, could well have their root cause in a childhood hurt. Woundedness from the past can affect wholeness in the future and in the present. It is like a revelation when this dawns on you and you begin to see the link with the past.

To have been brought up with too many negatives in early life can lodge deep frustration within the spirit, leading to all sorts of problems later on. Negatives are to be avoided at all costs! Watch yourself! An insecure childhood may lead to an insecure adulthood, though this is not always the case. Teasing causes deep resentment and suppressed anger lasts for years and needs forgiveness.
Inner healing teaches us to live with pain, sorrow, set-backs, without becoming bitter, as we see all in the light of

Jesus' own suffering. Nothing will then destroy our inner peace, and all will tend towards our good in the end. We must try to see things 'in balance' and not let our whole energy and attention be absorbed by what's been happening to us. Life is too short to waste any of it! Closeness to the Cross of Jesus is a great help in times of difficulty and there you will always have the company of Mary. Everything – joys and sorrows, dreams and desires, can all be brought safely to the foot of the Cross. Here, at least, you know for certain that something can be done about them. It is the place of victory. Leave all your tension and hurt here too, your rejection, rebelliousness, self-hate, anger, greed, depression, injustice, bitterness. Surrender it all here. "In the Name of Jesus we have the Victory". *(Acts 4:12)*

The Christian faith is a priceless treasure. I don't know what I would do without it, do you? We have the power to live or die, to accept or reject. *The choice is ours.* Inner healing is a choice. If only people knew what God is offering them with this gift, they would jump at it and be healed. It works; it does not cost fifteen pounds or more a session; it is absolutely free from God, through His Holy Spirit; it doesn't take years! One or two powerful sessions of prayer can take you towards complete healing and new life follows.

Persevere in seeking wholeness, and the healing I suggest here will come to you. Do not be afraid of what God might want to do for you. Try it. Just give Him a chance! "If only you knew the gift God is offering you ..... and who it is who is saying: 'Give me a drink', you would have been the one to ask and He would have given you living water. The water that I will give will turn into a spring inside you, welling up to eternal life." Jesus said. (John 4: 14)

Inner Healing is like this spring, a spring of hope. With these resources problems take on a new look and can be coped with, no matter what they are. There is a new enlightenment. You will never despair even if you're on the brink of it. God is always there somewhere in the background like He was when the apostles were out at sea and were almost drowning with the tumultuous wind and waves. Jesus made "as if to pass them by" until they themselves called out to Him for help, and then invited Him into their boat, and there was a great calm. The presence of Jesus always brings calm.

Martin Luther King, worn out with struggle against prejudice and injustice, writes: "I am at the end of my powers, I have nothing left. I've come to the point where I can't face it alone. Threatening telephone calls and letters keep coming to our home. Only faith in God can transform bleak and desolate valleys into sunlit paths of joy, and new light into the dark caverns of pessimism. Only God is able." In a state of utter exhaustion one day, when his courage had almost gone, he determined to take his problems to God. Head in hands on the kitchen table, he prayed aloud that he was at the end of his patience and could not go on any longer.

"At that moment," he said, "I experienced the presence of the Divine, as I had never experienced Him. It seemed as though I could hear the quiet assurance of an inner voice saying: 'Stand up for righteousness, stand up for truth; God will be at your side forever!' Almost at once, my fears began to pass from me. My uncertainty disappeared. I was ready to face anything. The outer situation remained the same but God had given me inner calm ...

My experience with God had given me a new strength and trust. I know now that God is able to give us the interior resources to face the storms and problems of life. When we're rock bottom, and broken, God is able to make a way out of a no-way, and transform dark yesterdays into bright tomorrows. This is our hope for becoming better people. This is our mandate for seeking a better world."
('Strength to Love', p 114, Martin Luther King)

God seeks us out to comfort us. Sometimes 'He tests our faith in the furnace of distress'. *(Isaiah 48:10)*

"God found him in a wilderness in fearful desolate wastes. He surrounded him. He lifted him up. He kept him as the apple of his eye. Like an eagle that watches its nest, that hovers over its young, so He spreads his wings; He took him, placed him on his outstretched wings. The Lord alone was his guide and no other god was his." (Deuteronomy 32:10-12)

Each one of us is called to holiness, to wholeness, to love. We are called to: 'Walk before Him in holiness and justice all the days of our life, in His Presence, free from fear and saved from the hands of our enemies'. *(Luke 1:74-75)* I love this 'Nunc dimittis' prayer. To live in holiness must not be confused with living a sort of 'holy Joe' life, over-pious and sanctimonious. It is to live a real practical down-to-earth faith, with Gospel values that show in our life, where we 'cry the Gospel with our lives.' It has to do primarily with knowing your status as *a child of God, His beloved child,* while believing firmly that *'nothing'* can happen to us without God's permission, at least His 'permissive' will for us. God is in charge in spite of what appears to be wrong in our lives and in the world. It is a life of trust, a life of faith, a life of truth, a life of love to which we are called.

"You will learn the truth and the truth will make you free". *(John 8:32)*

Now our enemies could be our nearest and dearest (and sometimes are!) our very own close family or community. For example, Cain was jealous of his brother, Abel, as were Joseph's brothers. Jesus warns us that "our enemies would be those of our own household." *(Matthew 10:36)* We all know this from time to time . "Daily I counter their malice with prayer" *(Psalm 141:6)*. This is the way forward! Our enemies may be our memories that haunt us. We know how to deal with those now so they won't ever be a problem or trouble us again. Try it! Our past sins, too, may hold us in bondage, but Jesus' Resurrection broke these prison gates. Why not talk to a priest and unburden yourself. Never let your past sins haunt you. Jesus always wants to bring you peace of mind. God never ceases to show us His love and mercy though we at times alienate ourselves from Him by our sins. All sin alienates us from God; it causes a 'breach' in our relationship with Him. Repentance restores! The Sacrament of Reconciliation is such a wonderful gift.

God, our heavenly Father wants us to know the circle of His love enfolding us twenty four hours out of every day. It is what He has given us as our inheritance. His love is like a complete circle round us. Nothing can break it or take it from us. I feel so secure with this love. Hurts of life just fade away within it, as they lose their power when overwhelmed by the power of Jesus' love. Our wounded circle is always held within the unbroken circle of God's love, where we're ransomed, healed, restored, forgiven.

I love to sing the following Celtic prayer of St. Patrick to myself or with others, as I imagine His love around me like an unbroken circle of protection.

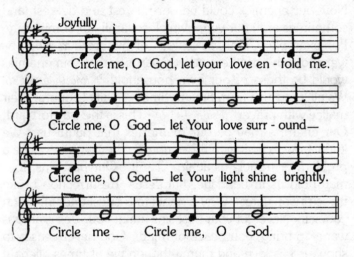

Circle me, O God, let your love en-fold me.
Circle me, O God — let Your love surr-ound —
Circle me, O God — let Your light shine brightly.
Circle me — Circle me, O God.

Circle me, O God, when I'm weak and weary
Circle me, O God, when despair is near.
Circle me, O God, let Your peace surround me
Circle me, Circle me, O God.

Circle me, O God, when I'm tired and restless
Circle me, O God, be my hope and strength
Circle me, O God, let Your Presence guide me
Circle me, Circle me, O God.

And as I pray the 'Circle of His love' round me I know that nothing can hurt me. My 'enemies' have no power over me, whoever or whatever they may be.

So I sit, at peace, immersed in His wonderful love. I invite Jesus into any hurtful memory I may have. I'm not afraid of the pain with Him. I keep inviting Him to come, until the whole situation is filled with His all-embracing love. I'm aware He loves the people who have hurt me also. I re-live some events with Him, (the places, the people), and I ask Him to fill my heart with forgiveness and a 'new' love. I let go of the memory then and move on. To bask in the good memories with Him is like having a mud bath. It's very healing and psychologically very sound! "You can then go on your way rejoicing for no law can touch you" *(Galatians 5:18)* Wake up to His love! Be filled with expectant faith and praise God at all times. "God will live in us and His love will be completed in us" *(1 John 4:12)*

How do I know I would benefit from Inner Healing?

The answer must be that everyone could do with inner healing at one point or another in their life. Granted, some of us are more fortunate than others if our childhood was secure and we were well loved, but, even then, there's always 'a something' that can affect us adversely.

When people first come into charismatic renewal, they experience new life and a great 'explosion' of love and they often say to me "Why didn't I know of this before? I feel so much more alive now." Inner Healing is a bit like that. It helps everyone live more fully, especially spiritually! Satan is well aware of our emotional weaknesses and hurts. He is quite clever at 'trapping' us, and holding us in bondage, so we miss out on the inheritance God has in store for us and the sort of happy life we could be living now if only we knew how! There must always be more to life! God's life is abundant and when you've begun to experience it, you wonder how on earth you ever lived any other way.

If you think there's something missing in your life, look again. You've tried this and that and you're still not peaceful though you're at the height of your profession and you're still not fulfilled. You may be longing for more 'spiritual awakening'. If you feel you can't forgive someone, or you've forgiven and can't forget, or if you feel burdened with guilt and think you'll never be forgiven, then seek inner healing. If you're scrupulous and feel your sin is so great, that God will never forgive you or if you feel yourself a constant failure, no good to anyone, depressed, unlovable, full of tears, inadequate, oppressed, lonely and alone, then you will certainly benefit from healing of memories. If your life is good, there could be more – more love, more peace, more joys – prayer for inner renewal will certainly be of benefit to you.

I wish everyone experienced the fullness which God has in store for them and the peace beyond understanding which He gives to those who seek Him. Renewal and inner healing are two wonderful gifts of God's Holy Spirit. Remember Satan is a liar and deceiver *(John 8: 45)*. Whenever he accuses you or holds you bound, he is very happy.   He's out to rob you of your inheritance!

When you feel in need of something 'more' in your life remember: "Yahweh will guide you, giving you relief in desert places. He will give strength to your bones and you shall be like a watered garden, like a spring of water, whose water never runs dry. You will rebuild the ancient ruins, build up on the old foundations." *(Isaiah 58: 1-12)* This way of living is not new. The early Christians lived in this 'Power'.

If you are carrying 'guilt' that is destroying you, seek inner healing. I prayed with a man who carried the 'guilt' of his mother's death for years. It 'ate' into him, destroying his peace and 'almost' making him very ill. It was of course a 'false' guilt from something that happened between himself and his mother. You hear people say sometimes 'I wonder what is eating him?' He felt, as a result, responsible for 'killing his mother'. He cried like a baby, as we prayed with him, with tears of deep healing! The same man could not have been a better son; could not have done more for his mother. He lived for her, even moved house to help her. What more could he have done for her? Yet, Satan cunningly trapped him in a lie. Since we prayed with him for the truth to prevail, that he loved his mother; that he was a good son, the best! and was not responsible for her death, he is a 'new man'.   Praise Jesus!

   If you have been traumatised by childhood experience of abuse, sexual or otherwise, or the loss of a parent, or if you have been separated from your home through illness, or if you had a serious accident or illness, had a punishment that did not fit the crime, or if you have a general feeling of being unwanted or unloved, then you would benefit greatly from inner healing. We see miracles! One person was told by an aunt that he was never wanted and that his mother was 'on the pill' when he was conceived; no wonder he has had a dreadful poor self image all his life and sought comfort in "the wrong areas" to his own detriment. Healing is in process. Praise Jesus!

Some hurts are deeper and take longer to heal. Cathy was locked in a dark cupboard as a child for punishment and had an inordinate fear of darkness and other things. Peter, who was beaten by his dad several times ended up beating his wife, and Tom, without meaning to, actually killed someone because of anger and violence and ended up in prison. Nothing is too difficult for God to heal and transform by his grace. William stammered for thirty years and when prayed with for the fear of dogs (one attacked him when he was three and his stammer began) his stammer disappeared. Another, who could not cry at the death of his father, believed it was unmanly to cry and so hadn't cried for thirty years. Now he has learnt to cry 'without guilt', bringing great physical healing to him.

All sorts of phobias can be healed so simply in this way. It is wonderful how quickly God works! We know from psychologists that the 'subconscious' records all experiences of our life, especially fears. "Jesus is the same yesterday, today, and forever." *(Hebrews 13:8)* and so there is no experience that cannot be brought to His eternal presence and healing power *now*. He still heals today if we let Him. Healing of the self-image seems to be a common need, and when it happens, the person begins to live. Even very 'religious' people have a poor self-image that truly damages them and their performance! Parishes could benefit from teams to minister inner healing and healing of memories. People often have 'nowhere to go' for the right help and they may be nervous of counselling or psychotherapy. So this kind of person would benefit from inner healing prayer, especially prayer for healing of memories, although we should remember also that normally prayer and medicine go hand in hand and complement each other.

I once led a healing service in Church and a woman was very moved and began to cry. She said she always felt there was something missing in her life but she did not know what it was. During the prayer, she sensed she may have been a twin. She could not wait to ring her mother that night to ask. Her mother confirmed she had been a twin, but that the other died at birth and they felt it was better to keep it a secret from her. But more! During that week a friend (unwittingly) had sent her an article on the 'loneliness of a lone twin'. She couldn't believe it. We were both amazed at the way the Lord healed the whole situation and brought her new found peace and wholeness. There are no co-incidences with God. He knows everything! His plan is perfect; His timing unbelievable!

How we deal with our fears is important, or they'll deal with us. De Mello says there are only two things in life: 'Love and fear; God and fear'. Fears can be 'gift'. It was no doubt fear of the dark that led to the discovery of electricity, fear of war brought the United Nations together, fear of illness has led to advancement in medicine, fear of ignorance has led to great educational developments, and scientific advancement. Fear can in fact be a good motivator, but misplaced fears can be powerfully destructive, and they can only be overcome by the opposite of fear. We're told in Scripture 'Perfect love casts out fear' *(1 John 4:18)*.

I meet many people who are plagued by fears (of heights, of flying, of rejection, of the dark, of crowds, of water, etc.) Unfortunately fears can become phobias that need to be conquered. The good news is they can be overcome.

One woman could not step on an escalator: after prayer she had no more worries. Another was frightened of flying, and now she can travel happily by air. Another young woman was terrified of swimming as she nearly drowned as a child , so her fear of water is quite understandable, but she has now overcome it through prayer and she can boast of being a good swimmer today. Others find it hard to relate to people or to hold friendships down for fear of rejection. All can be healed in Him. One friend who was convinced she could never marry, because of her fear of men (result of childhood hurt) now has a beautiful home, husband, children. And so, the Good News goes on and on. It has no limits. His mercies are eternal.

By allowing our fears to surface we may find them to be more imaginary than real. We need only courage to face them. Skeletons in the cupboard are best out, I think, not denied. In the presence of Jesus, the masks worn for years can be slowly removed and the more we know we're loved and accepted by Him, the more we become healed.

"I give them life, long and full, and I show them how I can save" *(Psalm 91:16)*

"Happy the people who learn to acclaim You!
Yahweh, they will live in the light of Your favour;
They will rejoice in Your name all day
and exult in your righteousness. "
(Psalm 89:15-16)

Blessed are we who know Your love Lord, and who are beginning to conquer fear and receive Your healing love, a love that knows no limits, that's always strong and active. May Your love grow in us, and spread to all those we meet. "Knowing these things you will be happy in carrying them out" *(John 13:17)*

I must now go on to mention something rather unpleasant but necessary – the occult. Jesus tells us to "Be wise as serpents but simple as doves" *(Matthew 10:16)*. This means that we must be aware, especially for our own protection!

If you have been involved in the occult, even innocently, you must renounce it and repent of it. Tell Jesus you are sorry. Confess it if you can. People wonder sometimes why they lack peace of mind, yet they are, or have been, involved in ugly things. I recommend to you Dom Benedict Heron's book, 'I saw Satan Fall' : basic, good, solid teaching on the occult, and also the books 'Jesus Lives Today' by Fr. Emiliano Tardif and 'Inner Healing' by Fr. Jim McManus.

Sometimes a person does not actually need a psychiatrist but deliverance ministry.
A priest brought a woman to me for special prayer. She was desperate for peace. As we prayed, she cried out, "No-one loves me, only the devil; I'm the devil's child." I silenced the demon in Jesus' name and forbade it to cry

out again. It remained silent for the rest of our prayer which was an extremely difficult session. I asked her to say the name of Jesus, but she couldn't – a sure sign of an ugly presence! There was much to deal with, links to cut and practices to be renounced. As she held the crucifix, Jesus Himself ministered to her. The peace that anointed her was exquisite. She gave her life to Jesus and has since had an amazing conversion. God is all-powerful. We must never worry about demons. In Jesus' name they have to flee. When forbidden to return in Jesus' name, they are held bound. "What you bind on earth is bound in Heaven, whatever you loose on earth shall be considered loosed in Heaven," Jesus said. *(Matthew 16: 19)*

I would love to quote more appropriate words from Fr. John Woolley, a very saintly Anglican priest. These are really remarkable words, given by Jesus to him over a period of more than fifteen years. They bring comfort and healing to many people round the world. Whenever you open this inspired book you will find the words on the page that you open are just meant for you, and for that particular day and time.

"If, in dark places, your dutiful expression of thanks to Me seems unreal, remember that your gratitude is not restricted to life experiences; your gratitude extends to mercies yet unrealised!

Nothing brings more joy to My heart than your fundamental trust in My activity, when you can see very little cause for thanksgiving. You are then sharing in My own anticipation of what is in store for you. When thanking Me that I cannot fail you, you have entered the dimension where plans are constantly made for your greatest good ... the dimension where present darkness is seen as scattered.

My child, a life of thanksgiving and worship in the midst of what at times, is totally discouraging, is something to which you are called. Thanksgiving reveals a human heart which understands, deeply, the faithfulness of the divine love."
'It is your faith which has saved you, go in peace'. (Mark 5:34)   *('I Am With You', Fr. John Woolley, p 84)*

Solo or Group Exercise:

a) Ask yourself seriously if you accept and like yourself as you are?

b) With whom can you be yourself?

c) What masks do you need to 'take down' in order to become your better self. Could you drop them?

d) If Jesus gave you permission today to change yourself, what would you change?

e) Are you prepared to 'let go', to start a new life with Jesus today?

f) Will you allow Him to be Lord of every area of your life?

g) Do you really want to be healed?

h) Will you allow Jesus to heal your memories?

I) Have you decided to grow in thanksgiving?

j) What are you doing with your anger? Where does it come from? Find out. Remember that Jesus says "Never let the sun go down on your anger" *(Ephesians 4:27)*

k) Have you ever dabbled in the occult? Do you need to be freed?

Some Blocks to Inner Healing:

1. Unforgiveness
2. Lack of self-acceptance
3. Guilt
4. Unrepentance
5. Over-seriousness
6. Negative attitudes
7. Lack of stillness
8. Self-pity
9. Lack of desire for healing
10. Lack of perseverance
11. Self-righteousness
12. Religiosity
13. Occult involvement
14. Oppression and Obsession
15. Freemasonry

1. Unforgiveness is a major block. I need to be forgiven! "I forgive" we say, but "I won't forget." Is this forgiveness? Only God can help us to forgive unconditionally. We need to develop daily and maintain a capacity to forgive. Keep struggling with forgiveness no matter how hard. God sees every effort we make. If only we could be the *initiators* of forgiveness. If we hold on to a 'bitter root', our lives can become poisoned and we will never reach the fullness God has in store for us.

"Always be wanting peace with all people and the holiness without which no one can ever see the Lord. Be careful that no one is deprived of the grace of God and that no *bitter root* should begin to grow and make trouble. This

can poison a whole community." *(Hebrews 12:15)*
"Real forgiveness" writes C.S. Lewis, "means looking steadily at the sin, the sin that is left over without any excuse, after all allowances have been made, and seeing it, in all its horror, dirt, meanness, and malice, and nevertheless being wholly reconciled to the man who had done it. That and only that is forgiveness." *('Inner Healing', Fr. J. McManus)*
"God's righteousness is never served by man's anger, so do away with bad habits" *(James 1:20)*. Being angry, aggressive, can almost be a cult! Deal with anger or anger will deal with you.

Bitterness, anger, aggression, are all signs of the need for forgiveness. Their effect, particularly on families, can be so destructive, and the damage done to individual lives can be irreparable. Forgiveness is very often the key to healing. The truth, of course, is that it is ourselves we damage. Shall we ask Our Father, even now, to forgive us our offences as we forgive those who offend us:

> *Our Father who art in Heaven*
> *Hallowed be Thy name*
> *Thy Kingdom come*
> *Thy Will be done on earth as is it in Heaven*
> *Give us this day our daily bread*
> *And forgive us our trespasses*
> *As we forgive those who trespass against us*
> *And lead us not into temptation*
> *But deliver us from evil. Amen.*

2. Lack of self-acceptance, together with a poor self-image, feelings of unworthiness or even self-hatred is a huge block to experiencing fullness of life. When we do not accept ourselves or love ourselves, there is always a 'root' hurt that needs healing. For instance: If people grow up thinking they are useless, fat, ugly, unattractive, stupid etc., they never attain wholeness in themselves unless healed of these ideas. Quite often the opposite is true. Psychologists spend long hours trying to help people appreciate the truth of who they are. Words from Scripture tell us the truth of who we are. Listen to them. Conquer the lie with the truth, as you become familiar with passages of Scripture about yourself. 'Journalling' is useful here.

"We are God's work of art, created in Christ Jesus to live the good life, as from the beginning, He meant us to live it". (Ephesians 2:10) "We've been carved on the palm of God's hand". (Isaiah 49:16). We're the 'sex' God made us. "God made them male and female", (Genesis 1:27) so there is no such thing as being the wrong sex. Neither can we say we are 'unwanted' for God wanted us - so there is no such thing as an 'unwanted' child. "It was You who created my inmost self, who put me together in my mother's womb, for all these mysteries I thank You, for the wonder of my being I thank You." (Psalm 139:13-14)

We must learn to believe the Words of God, and live by them. The more we believe these truths, the more healed we become in our innermost being.

3. Guilt is a killer and is unfortunately a very 'Catholic' thing, though Catholics are blest with the sacrament of reconciliation! 'False guilt' is even worse and very destructive, i.e. taking on the responsibility for something, e.g. someone's death or an accident which was not your fault. Panic attacks can be the result of not being there for someone's death and you take on the guilt of it. The event would have happened without you!

Scrupulosity is one of the worst spiritual ailments and hard to cure, i.e. blaming yourself and thinking almost *everything* is a sin and can't be forgiven. Shakespeare says that "conscience doth make cowards of us all." This is the secret voice within each one of us, by which we know before God our sin. Conscience passes judgement on our sinful actions. It makes us aware of God's law, hence the need for quiet reflection. "Let us be sincere in heart and filled with faith, our minds sprinkled and free from any trace of bad conscience." *(Hebrews 10:23)* Feelings of guilt and shame can be the direct consequence of sinful behaviour; God's forgiveness alone frees us. We need to come to Him in repentance and simply receive His healing. If the dustman came on a Monday and took away all our rubbish, we'd hardly be too pleased if he brought it all back on Tuesday. Yet that's what we sometimes do with our guilt and sin. People often punish themselves with guilt, even for forgiven sin. Clinging to unrepented or unconfessed sin, blocks the experience of God's healing love. Thinking you will never be forgiven can destroy your peace of mind totally. Thoughts like these are *never* from God.

"Come now," God says, *"let us talk things over."*

Good evening! Lord,
Hold my hand,
Hold it tight.
Let's talk.
The sun has set,

Stay by my side
Tonight
And everywhere I walk.

I don't have to speak aloud, Lord
For You know my heart.
You've been with me from the beginning
Never changing from the start.

Praise and Glory to you, Lord!
Thank you for our talk.

('Evening Prayer' by Jacqueline Rice)

4. Unrepentance, an unyielding spirit, alienates us from God, from others, and it disjoints us, so we are not 'together' as a person. The first message of the Gospel is 'Repent' *(Mark 1:15)*. Every unrepented sin strengthens our aversion to God. All sin is rebelliousness against God, who views all sin as singular. Beware of jealousy and anger.

Let His Spirit live in you! "The heart is more devious than any other thing." *(Jeremiah 17:9)* If I allow my emotions to run away with me, anger, lust, greed, jealousy, bitterness, etc., I end up in a 'sorry state'.

"God released them from the gloom and darkness, shattering their chains; breaking bronze gates open, smashing iron bars." *(Psalm 107:14,16)*

5. Over-seriousness about ourselves, about our spiritual progress, allowing 'stress' to dominate our life is bad. Often the beginning of an illness can be traced back to a time of 'unheeded' stress. Be awake always to the dangers of stress and do something about your life before it is too late! Try to cultivate a sense of humour. Pray for it. Take time out to relax, enjoy music, walk, enjoy God's world, and eat properly. Thank God for these good things. Likewise avoid over-complacency which can block our inner-healing (thinking that we're fine as we are); 'There's nothing needing changing in me! I'm O.K!' But am I?

6. Negative attitudes lead to doom! Joy, energy, spiritual growth are killed by negative attitudes. Test yourself frequently! Keep guard over your thoughts and avoid nonsense words like "I'm no good; I'll never make it. I can't do it; I don't need to change." etc. etc. We all tend to say things like this from time to time. "God made me ill" one hears sometimes or "Why did God let this happen to me?" etc. God never interferes with our free will and much of our trouble we bring on ourselves. God does not want us to be ill. If He did He would not be God. Don't blame God. He does not interfere with nature or with us! Remember Jesus spent His life healing the sick. We still suffer from the consequences of Original Sin; that's where all evil comes from. This is the root of sin in the world.

"Never when you have been tempted say: 'God sent the temptation'; God cannot be tempted to do anything wrong and He does not tempt anyone. Everyone who is tempted is seduced by his own wrong desire ... Everything that is perfect which is given from above, comes from the Father of Light; with Him there is no such thing as alteration, no shadow of a change." *(James 1:13-14,16-17)*

Recently I myself experienced new life in painting pictures. I've thought and said all my life that I cannot draw or paint;

that's not for me. After an art week I can 'boast' of three framed paintings, although my friend says the frames are the best part! What a miracle! Why not develop some more of your potential by learning a new skill?

7. Lack of Stillness. "Be still and know that I am God." *(Psalm 46:10)* If we give little time to God or prayer, then it's no wonder we lack healing and peace. We keep running away in our 'business'; we 'switch on' God when we don't know where else to go, when we're in trouble or upset. No one else can save our soul for us, so we ought to pay more attention to being still with God for healing. In the stillness of our prayer comes strength, and here, too, we'll find God and a 'new' heart. Once you've met God, you begin to change. "I will call her into the wilderness and there I will speak to her heart." *(Hosea 2:16)* Learn to pause or nothing will catch up with you! All good relationships need 'quality time' together and stillness and listening! God is always calling. Good to think that we're on call too.

8. Being full of self-pity. The 'nobody loves me' syndrome is one of the hardest blocks to overcome. Self is the centre of one's life and everything revolves round 'Me! Me!' What a pitiable attitude! We would get very angry if someone told us we were full of self-pity! But so often we are. Be brave to face it if you are. "Beware of self-pity." *(Micah 7:8)*
Self-pity can catch up on you without your realising it. Face it, recognise it, own it, do something about it, or it will do something about you! How often does self-pity put you in a mood? Be honest. Someone ignored you, so you're upset. Someone else was chosen, so you feel inferior, someone got

better results than you so you have a right to be jealous, moody. Someone was given authority and you weren't. (So what? God did not want you there!) Be content to blossom where He wants you and never be 'put out' by someone else's blessings. Rejoice in your own!

I have seen people become so ill as a result of self-pity, even to becoming seriously ill, and unable to work. The medical profession can find no reason for their illness. Satan loves us to wallow in self-pity and he loves it when our 'ego' is the centre of our 'small' world. ('Ego' is the abbreviation for '**E**ase **G**od **O**ut') We are admonished in Ephesians *(4:17)* "Not to give place to the evil one." "Resist the devil and he will flee from you." *(James 4:7)*

On the other hand, being the 'self-propelled', arrogant master of your own life, allowing only your own ideas to rule you, can cut you off from anything else, including the Lordship of Jesus Christ in your life. It can make you too 'egocentric' and unbearable, closed to any form of change or change of attitudes. A little humility helps! Balance is the key. No one is perfect, and most people admit to a need to change. Being very over critical of others, having high standards for them but not for ourselves can be a great hindrance to our spiritual growth. "See the mote in your own eye first," Jesus says.

Our attitudes to our specially anointed ministers must be life giving, not derogatory; otherwise we could be partly responsible for preventing God's kingdon coming in our parishes. Be kind and thoughful for your 'shepherds'. Remember they are always serving us, and they get tired, too, and they need our support. They are God's anointed.

9. Lack of desire for healing. God desires our healing but we ourselves do not long for it enough. God is greater than our lack of faith. We cannot impose our rules on God. He can heal us whether we want it or not. Lord, increase our faith. He did not work many miracles in Nazareth because of their lack of faith. If we have faith as small as a grain of mustard seed, we can move mountains!

10. Lack of perseverance, and patience with what God is doing for us and in us: giving up too easily when the going gets hard! Not only that, Scripture tells us, "let us exult in our hardship, understanding that hardship develops perseverance and perseverance develops a rested character. Sometimes that gives us hope and a hope which will not let us down, because the love of God has been poured into our hearts by the Holy Spirit which has been given to us." *(Romans 5: 3-5)*

11. Self-Righteousness: Jesus condemned pharisaical attitudes. "I've no need of conversion, I'm fine as I am." "God resisteth the proud and gives His grace to the humble." "Blessed are the poor in spirit; theirs is the Kingdom of Heaven". *(Luke 6:20)*

12. Religiosity or 'pseudo-religion', as it could be called, can cloud our minds to the truth of our faith, as we escape behind holy pictures, devotions of one sort or another. 'Devotionalism' can be a great danger and can take one away from practising one's faith in its fullness.

Don't misunderstand me, I am not 'against' devotions but 'collecting' devotions which can become a real danger and a trap of Satan, so that the message of the

Gospel is clouded, and inner-healing missed. We miss Christ and each other!

"Then we shall no longer be children, or tossed one way or another and carried hither and thither by every new gust of teaching or at the mercy of all the tricks people play, and their unscrupulousness in deliberate deception. If we live by the truth and in love we shall grow completely into Christ who is the Head." *(Ephesians 4:14)*

True holiness shows itself in the fruits of the Holy Spirit. *(Galatians 5:22-26)* Always worth pondering!

13. Any involvement in the occult. Witchcraft, spiritualism, astrology, fortune-telling, New Age practices, martial arts, pendulum swinging, ouija, tarot cards, etc. must be renounced and repented of, even if it was only in innocence you were involved. It leaves its 'ugly' stamp, and must be dealt with.

Many people are 'innocently' unaware of the number of horrible 'new age' and occult shops about today and blindly buy things in them. Be alert! Especially for your children. One knows the effect of occult things, such as disturbance, blackness, lies, coldness, unrest. Make sure your children do not wear pendants, rings or bracelets bought from such shops.

Beware, too, of listening to 'heavy metal' music. It can have disastrous consequences. Recently I met a boy who told me that all his troubles started after he had been to a heavy metal music concert, and that nothing has gone right for him since. Did you realise that in this music they blaspheme and curse God.

"The lamp of your body is the eye; it follows that if your eye is sound, your whole body will be filled with light. But if your eye is diseased, your whole body will be all darkness. If then the light inside you is darkness, what darkness will that be." *(Matthew 6: 22-23)* We must keep in God's light, letting our eyes dwell only on beautiful things, things of His world. Avoid anything that leads to darkness. "Avoid everything in your everyday life that would be unworthy of the Gospel of Christ." *(Philippians 1: 27)*

When confronted with evil I use frequently this powerful prayer of St. Irenaeus:

"Behold the Cross of Our Lord Jesus Christ.
Fly all hostile powers.
The Lion of the tribe of Judah,
The Root of David,
Has conquered.
Alleluia!"

Tapes are another manifestation of the occult.
You might have seen audio tapes strewn haphazardly across the road, on trees or on the outside of buildings. You may not realise that these are often put there by Satanists and indicate evil's willing of an accident or ill will against you or others. Whenever you see such tapes strung out, be careful, because in a few days time when you return you will usually find a terrible accident has taken place. If seen on a house or buildings it indicates a curse against God's work. Always, in Jesus' name, break this evil power and the curse of witchcraft three times saying: "In Jesus' name I break the curse of witchcraft and of all evil willing against ....*(here you name whoever, or whatever, it is)*. Nothing can then harm you. I say this prayer often

for protection. Carry blessed salt and holy water in your car and keep some in your home.

"He that is within you is greater than he that is in the world." *(1 John 4:4)*

"For it is not against human enemies that we have to struggle but against sovereignties and powers which originate the darkness in this world; the spiritual army of evil in the Heavens. That is why you must rely on God's armour, or you will not be able to put up any resistance when the worst happens, or have enough resources to hold your ground." (Ephesians 6:12-13)

"So that, by His death, Jesus could take away all the power of the devil, who had power over death, and set free all those who had been held in slavery all their lives by fear of death." *(Hebrews 2:14)*

"My grace is enough for you. My power is at its best in weakness." *(2 Corinthians 12:9)*

14. Oppression and obsession. Satan is God's great enemy and ours. We know he is a lying 'oppressor'. Sometimes he oppresses us by causing things to happen that upset and worry us, for example, things moving by themselves in the house, strange noises in the night, lights that go on and off without explanation. He can oppress us, also, with a spirit of illness, making us weak and ill with no energy, inexplicable to the doctors. The Gospels speak of the woman who had an enfeebling spirit which bent her over double so that for eighteen years she could not stand up. When Jesus cast out the enfeebling spirit she was totally healed. "Woman, you are rid of your infirmity, and at once she straightened up and glorified God." *(Luke 13:12-13)*

On the other hand people can suffer from an 'obsession' from the enemy, their minds being tormented with thoughts of suicide, self-mutilation or self-destruction. Sometimes it shows itself in abnormal feelings of unworthiness or scruples, so that the troubled person feels they will never be forgiven by God. This can become a permanent state and it has a power and an intensity which makes it impossible to overcome except with the type of deliverance ministry mentioned in this book.

There is no 'oppression' or 'obsession' from which a person cannot be delivered with Christ's power.

15. Freemasonry.

Like communism it is an evil affecting the Church and families today. Where the family has been involved, (whether in the present or previous generations), it is important to pray the cleansing power of Jesus upon the family line. It must be renounced and repented of and the curse of freemasonry must be broken in the name of Jesus Christ. It is the anti-Christ. Unfortunately this evil is unrecognised by many, even religious, people. It is in fact a spirit of blindness. Some Christian churches actually have freemasonry signs in the building unrecognised by the clergy. Usually they would have been put there by the builders. These signs should be removed.

"The Lamb is the Lord of lords, and the King of kings, and He will defeat them, and they will be defeated by His followers, the called, the chosen, the faithful". *(Revelation 17:14)*

All that God wants is our healing, and He will leave no stone unturned if we really want healing. And so:–

"This, then, is what I pray, kneeling before the Father, from whom every family, whether spiritual or natural, takes its name: Out of His infinite glory, may He give you the power, through His Spirit, for your hidden self to grow strong, so that Christ may live in your hearts, through faith, and then planted in love, and built on love, you will, with all the saints, have strength to grasp the breadth, the length, the height, the depth, until knowing the love of Christ, which is beyond all knowledge, you will be filled with the utter fullness of God.
Glory be to Him, whose power working in us, can do infinitely more than we can ask or imagine. Glory be to Him from generation to generation, in the Church and in Christ Jesus, for ever and ever. Amen" (Ephesians 3: 14-21)

Here are a few helpful thoughts and Scripture words for your Meditation. You could spend time taking one thought at a time and praying it through. Let these words ring in your ears. You could use some of these wonderful phrases as you would use a mantra, so that your mind becomes filled with God's word and it will become a living power within you. "God's message is still a living power among you who believe it." *(1 Thessalonians 2:13)*

1. "God is Love" *(1 John 4:8)*

2. " God's power lasts for ever" *(1 Peter 5:11)*

3. "Behold I give you power to tread on serpents and scorpions and the whole strength of the enemy. Nothing shall ever hurt you. Yet, do not rejoice that the spirits submit to you, rejoice that your names are written in Heaven." *(Luke 10:19-20)*

4. "Forgetting the past, and looking forward to what lies ahead ..." *(Philippians 3:13)*

5. "Helped only by His power driving me irresistibly..." *(Colossians 1:29)*

6. "All I want is to know Christ and the power of His Resurrection." *(Philippians 3:10)*

7. "My power is at its best in your weakness." *(2 Corinthians 12:9)*

8. "He that believes in me, the works that I do, he shall do also." *(John 14:12)*

9. "Nothing is impossible to God." *(Luke 1:37)*

10. "The Spirit of the Lord is upon me ... He has anointed me to bring Good News to the poor, to proclaim liberty to captives, and to the blind new sight, to set the downtrodden free, to proclaim the Lord's year of Freedom." *(Luke 4:18)*

11. "Whatsoever you desire, when you pray, believe that you have received it and you shall have it." *(Mark 11:24)*

12. "I have called you by your name, you are Mine." *(Isaiah 43:1)*

13. "There is nothing I cannot master with the help of the One who gives me strength." *(Philippians 4:13)*

14. "Whatsoever you ask in My name, I will do it." *(John 14:13-14)*

15. "Happy the one who does not lose faith in Me." *(Luke 7:23)*

16. "Unload all your worries on to Him, since He is looking after you." *(1 Peter 5:7)*

17. "Remain in union with Me and I shall remain in union with you ... Whoever remains in Me and I in him will bear fruit in plenty. Cut off from Me, you can do nothing." *(John 15:5)*

18. "May the peace of God make you perfect and holy and may you all be kept safe and blameless, spirit, soul and body, for the coming of Our Lord Jesus Christ. God has called you; He will not fail you."
(1 Thessalonians 5:23)

Take a look at Jesus, the only Healer, and His Healing Ministry.

Jesus is the Healer. He spent roughly one third of His public ministry healing the sick, casting out demons, restoring people to wholeness. He fulfilled the prophecy written of Him: "He took our infirmities and bore our diseases." *(Matthew 8:17)*

He healed because He loved. His healings were a sign that He was the Son of God, Saviour of the World. The same is true of His healings today. Jesus told His disciples to preach the Good News and to heal in His name, and so He generously passed on to them His healing gifts. "And He called the twelve together and gave them power and authority over the demons and to cure diseases and He sent them out to preach the Kingdom of God and to heal." *(Luke 9:1-2)*

Jesus gave them a commission: "Go into all the world. Preach the Gospel to every creature ... these are the signs that shall follow them that believe; they shall lay hands on the sick, and they shall recover." *(Mark 16:15-18)*

In the New Testament there is a close connection between the proclamation of the Gospel and the healing of the sick. It is still the same today. "The disciples went forth and preached everywhere, while the Lord worked with them and confirmed the message by the signs that attended it." *(Mark 16:20)*

There were many healings in the early Church and the healing power of Jesus was very evident in the Acts of the

Apostles. Why not start reading it again today? It is wonderfully inspiring and full of Good News. I was so bored with it when I studied it for 'O' Level and now I can't stop reading it. Perhaps we must ask ourselves if our faith is strong enough today. Lord, increase my faith.

Why do we not see so many healings? Is our obedience to proclaiming God's word as it should be? How I wish that each of our parishes had a trained healing ministry team available to all who desire inner healing. Jesus brought healing wherever He went. His very Presence healed people even before He actually touched them. He would heal the sick even while those who were concerned for them were on their way to Him – like the Centurion's servant, who was at home paralysed in great pain, and he was healed without Jesus even coming to him. The faith of the sick person often cured them, like the woman with the haemorrhage, who only wanted to touch the hem of His garment - Jesus noticed her even in the crowd. "Power has gone out from Me." He said. "Your faith has healed you." Jesus said to her "Go in peace." *(Luke 8:48)*

He shares His healing with the Church: "So many signs and wonders were worked among the people at the hands of the Apostles, that the sick were even taken out into the streets, and laid on beds and sleeping mats in the hope that at least the shadow of Peter might fall across some of them as he went past. People even came crowding in from the towns round about Jerusalem bringing with them their sick and those tormented by unclean spirits, and all were cured." *(Acts 5:14-16)*

It is recorded in the Gospels that Jesus cast out many different kinds of spirits, for example:– deaf and dumb spirits *(Mark 9:14-29)*; evil spirits *(Luke 7:21)*; perverse spirits *(Luke 8:2)*; impure or unclean spirits *(Matthew 12:43-45; Mark 1:23-27; 3:11; 5:2-20; 7:25-30; Luke 4:33-36; 6:18; 8:26-39; 9:37-43; 11:240-26)*. He ordered them to leave, never to return, "Never enter him again" *(Mark 9:25)*. He gave His disciples power to cast out spirits: "In My Name they will cast out devils" *(Mark 16:17)*. St. Paul uses a simple and effective prayer in Acts 16:18, "I order you (fortune telling spirit) in the name of Jesus Christ to leave that woman. The spirit went out of her then and there" *(Acts 16:18)*. We are told of deceitful spirits *(1 Timothy 4:1)* and of spirits of wickedness *(Ephesians 6:12)*

The power of Jesus deals with every evil spirit. In His Name alone are they bound and cast out.

Many others sought to touch Jesus. "When the local people recognised Him, they spread the news through the whole neighbourhood and took all that were sick to Him, begging Him just to let them touch the fringe of His cloak. And all those who touched it were completely cured." *(Matthew 14:35-36)* The touch of Jesus always cures. It is humbling when praying with people to see His touch still healing people today.

Sometimes the faith of the community is rewarded, like when the group brought the paralysed man to Jesus. But as the crowd made it impossible to find a way of getting him in, they went up on to the flat roof and lowered him and his stretcher down through the tiles into the middle of the gathering, in front of Jesus. It must have looked quite funny! Jesus was touched. "Seeing their faith, He said, 'My child, your sins are forgiven ... I order you: get

up, pick up your stretcher and go off home', and he got up, picked up his stretcher at once and walked out in front of everyone, so that they were all astounded and praised God." *(Mark 2:9-10)*
Can you imagine all the commotion? What would you be doing if you had been there? Which of the characters would you be?

Sometimes Jesus told people to show themselves to the priest before He cured them, like the ten lepers. *(Matthew 8:4)* Whatever the cause of the illness, He was always ready to heal. Nothing was, or is, impossible to Him *(Mark 9:24)*. He healed 'at home' as it were, also. We're told that Peter's mother-in-law was sick of a fever, and He touched her hand and the fever left her and she got up and began to wait on them. *(Matthew 8:16)*

Jesus showed tremendous compassion towards the sick and possessed. He did not spare Himself. His food was only to do the will of His Father, who sent Him. *(cf John 4:34)* "Power went out from Him everywhere and the power of the Lord was behind all His works of healing." *(Luke 5:17)* One of His most amazing miracles, I think, was the healing of the possessed man, the Gerasene Demoniac, who lived among the tombs, who wore no clothes, nor did he live in a house and he frightened everyone to death!

"It was a devil that had seized on him a great many times, and then they used to secure him with chains and fetters to restrain him, but he would always break the fastenings, and the devil would drive him out into the wilds". In the presence of Jesus, he became human again, "clothed in his right mind". Jesus delivered him of his many demons.

Up to now, no one had been able even to touch the man. Everyone feared his violence. The power of Jesus over the demonic forces helped the man "to sit at Jesus' feet, clothed in his full senses." The demons spoke out, called themselves legion, but were rendered silent, powerless in Jesus' presence. The man, when he was healed, wanted to join Jesus but He sent him away: "Go back home," Jesus said, "and report all that God has done for you." Thus this man would be the very first evangelist: "So the man went off, and spread throughout the town all that Jesus had done for him." *(Luke 8:35,39)* He was given an important mission by Jesus, to go home and witness to his healing, though the man himself wanted to go about with Jesus.

A footnote, as it were, here, regarding healing, especially after occult involvement, not to rush around laying hands on people for healing but to give oneself time for consolidation and growth in the ways of the Lord! "Do not be quick to lay hands on any man." *(1 Timothy 5:22)*

"Jesus made a tour of the towns and villages, teaching in their synagogues, proclaiming the Good News of the Kingdom and curing all kinds of diseases and sickness, And when He saw the crowds, He felt sorry for them because they were like sheep without a shepherd." *(Matthew 9:35-36)*

How often Jesus, in His risen body, must make a tour of the towns and villages, and how often He must long to heal! He has no hands but ours, no feet but ours, and so today, through our eyes, He can look with compassion again, as we offer Him the crowds in the underground, large cities, concert halls, football stadiums, prisons, refugee camps, the homeless, the disfigured, the abandoned, the street children of the slums, the market places, the hospitals, homes, churches, the sick at home; everyone (especially 'sheep without a shepherd') in need of His healing Presence. How He still must long to gather His children under His wings as He did in Jerusalem. "Jerusalem, Jerusalem, how often have I longed to gather your children as a hen gathers her young ones under her wings, but thou wouldst not." *(Matthew 23:37)*

Let us pray with St. Teresa of Avila *(1515-1582)* who writes:

'Christ has no body now on earth but yours, no hands but yours, no feet but yours. Yours are the eyes through which His compassion looks out on the world; yours are the feet with which He can go about doing good; yours are the hands with which He can bless.
Lord Jesus, I give You my hands to do Your work
I give You my feet to go Your way
I give You my eyes to see as You see
I give You my tongue to speak Your word
I give You my mind that You may think in me
I give You my spirit that You may pray in me
I give You my heart that You may love in me the Father and all humankind
I give You my whole self that You may grow in me
So that it is You, Lord Jesus, who live and work and pray in me. Amen.'

Do you pray with Him as you 'look out' on the world?
Do you long for His Kingdom to come in men's hearts?
Do you find Him still working in miraculous ways, mysteriously, through you?

Do you thank Him for sharing with you His healing gifts?
As you look around the supermarket, pray.
As you walk your dog, pray.
As you drive along the motorways, pray.
As you walk through the town or city, pray. Bring all to
Him for healing, whether you know them or not.

"That evening, they brought Him many who were
possessed by devils. He cast out the spirits with a word
and cured all who were sick." *(Matthew 8:16-17)* With a
word!
Let the horizon of your heart be enlarged as you become
an intercessor with Jesus. Bring them all to Him ... conquer
the darkness of sin and its consequences by becoming a
'full time' intercessor for the world. Pray with Jesus who
now intercedes at the Right hand of God for all of us.
"His power to save us is utterly certain, since He is living
for ever to intercede for all who come to God through
Him.' *(Hebrews 7:25)*

"Only an immense energy of Divine Love in the world
can scatter the darkness. You must pray and pray that
love be poured into your hearts and into the hearts of all
people. Pray for the world. More simply still, just pray
your love. Prayer is love-giving, healing. You know what
it is to pour out love on another human being, perhaps
with words, perhaps in silence. It is power that goes out
from you, then, as it went out from Christ when the woman
touched the hem of His garment, and in that giving-out of
power and life, you are yourself enlarged. So it must be in
your prayers . Send out your love in great shafts of golden
light, up to the heart of God, at your Mass, in times of
prayer, at odd moments through the day, and open your

hearts to the immense love that will be poured upon you in return; then your heart will be enlarged; you will be in the light that is life and others will see the light in you and will be able to enter it themselves." *('The High Green Hill', Fr. Gerald Vann, O.P., p 169)*

So we pray for healing, spirit, mind and body. We listen to God's word. We break Satan's hold through forgiveness. We pray for healing of memories. We trust the Lord to set us free as we cooperate with Him. We thank Him for all He is doing for us. We beg Him to fill us with His Holy Spirit that we may be recreated and rekindled in His love, renewed in our love and service of Him. Be certain that "anyone who tries to live in devotion to Christ is certain to be attacked." *(2 Timothy 3:12)*

We need to pray for each other against the wiles of Satan, because he is always trying to stop good being done, and he is certainly not happy with people receiving healing of this sort. So watch out for his cunningness, his lies against the good and his efforts to disrupt or mock God's work; but remember always that Jesus has won the victory and Satan has no foothold, unless we give him one.

Accept that Jesus uses us, broken as we are. It is He alone who does the healing through us. Each of us can continually be ministering God's inner healing to others. Ask Him: 'Lord make me a channel of your peace, your healing love'.
"May the God of peace Himself make you entirely pure and devoted to Him; and may your spirit and soul and body be kept strong and blameless until the day when Our Lord Jesus Christ, comes back again." *(1 Thessalonians 5:23)*

"We know we belong to God, but the whole world lies in the power of the Evil one. We know, too, that the Son of God has come and has given us the power to know the true God. We are in the true God, as we are in His Son, Jesus Christ. This is the true God, this is Eternal Life. Children, be on your guard against false gods." (1 John 5:18-20)

**"Let us wake in the morning
filled with your Love.
Make our future happy
as our past was sad."**

(Psalm 90:14)

"I call you home to My kingdom which I have prepared for you. Only then will My life in you come to complete fulfilment. Prepare zealously for the great day of homecoming. Remain faithful to My word until we meet in Heaven."

A CALL TO HOME

There's no place like home.

"For us our homeland is in Heaven, and from Heaven comes the Saviour we are waiting for, the Lord Jesus Christ, and He will transfigure these wretched bodies of ours into copies of His glorious body. He will do that by the same power with which He can subdue the whole universe." *(Philippians 3:20-21)*

The saying goes "There's no place like home, home sweet home!" How true this is! To be 'home'less must be a terrible thing, though our Saviour Himself experienced it. "Foxes have holes," He said, "the birds of the air, nests, but the Son of Man has nowhere to lay His head." *(Luke 9:58)* We know how sad it must have been at His birth in Bethlehem when Joseph and Mary found 'no room in the inn.' *(Luke 2:8)*

Our Founder, Fr. Dom Jean Leuduger, *(1649-1722),* must have had a very saintly mother, for she chose to have her baby to be born in a stable, to identify with her Lord and Master. Why not offer a prayer now for those who have no place they can call home, for those who sleep on the streets, for refugees who have had to flee their homes and for those whose homes are not happy places to be.

Home on earth is never permanent though it may mean everything to us, but our heavenly home must mean even more and it is ultimately what we are yearning for; a home that grows not old, where there is neither sorrow nor death, where there is only peace and happiness with God.

Everyone loves a place they can call 'Home', with one's own room, space, family, privacy, etc. After a holiday one often longs to get home. When my parents were alive, 'going home' was a highlight of my year, a very special treat. My parents were the 'heart' of the home. I couldn't wait to see them.

On reaching Limerick City my heart gave a throb with excitement and though my parents are not 'at home' there any more, there is still a certain anticipation and joy on reaching the outskirts of the City.

Roots mean so much and are important and although I do not consider Limerick my 'home' any longer, since I left it at the age of seventeen to enter the convent, I have a certain feeling for it as my family are still there and my sister, Betty and family now provide a home. Home now is where my heart is!
In some sense, I suppose, while my parents were there, there was a special sense of home, of belonging to them and they to me. Nothing or no-one could break this very special bond and strangely enough, though they are dead, it is still there and I sometimes feel them near.

To accept that they would not be there one day, was something I could not take on board. I could never imagine life without them, or could never imagine the day when they would not be sitting by the fire, until of course it actually happened. What a cross to lose both my parents together within two months of each other in 1981. All over Christmas of that year, they were both dying together in the same hospital, Dad died on January 8th (aged 90) and Mom on March 25th (aged 74). With such a big age gap between them we would have expected my mother to live longer (as was her wish), but God had other plans. She had done her work which was to mind my Dad in his old age and when he died, her work was done. I know they have both gone ahead of us to 'a home' that we too hope one day to reach.

I wrote the following poem after the death of both my parents. It flowed as one sentence and was, for me, a great healing.

I had never written a poem before but I found in the 'letting go', in being alone in solitude and loneliness before God, He comforted me through writing. Over and above the loss of my parents together, was the sad loss of my sister-in-law's stillborn baby. I felt grief like never before. Why not try to express your own pain in writing now?

On the death of my Parents (1981)

The dawn has come
Death's sting is hushed
And life is full once more
Not as it was, but in the Lord
The fullness won for all

No eye has seen
Nor ear has heard
What things God has in store
For those who love Him
Give Him all
On their last day of call

Serene now, resting in His love
Their presence is felt more
Than ever, on this pilgrim earth
Where they were once the core.
Their love inspires new ways, new life,
Their courage daunts our fears,
Their absence, filled now with new hope
To face the coming years.

Their work is done, ours yet to be
Fulfilled in God alone.
"Take hold my hand. Stay close to me
And know you are my child
I love you with eternal love
Be not afraid, I'm here
I'm cherishing, protecting you
Through every doubt or fear"

And so, life must go on and on
And we in Him must grow
Let go the past, live for today
And in His love, you'll know
The joy of pain, its sweet caress,
The peace no one can take
Except those, who in love with Him
Walk daily for His sake.

"So, whether life be glad or sad
Know well, 'tis in My plan.
In trouble or adversity,
I'm standing close at hand.
You'll never be let down, my child,
Take courage, I've passed your way
The Calvary road was full of pain
I've won, the Eternal Day."

(Sr. J. Walsh, Sept. 8th 1981)

There's no return in this life from the dead. It is so final. Neither would we want to call back the dead, and Scripture and the Church teach how wrong that would be.

I become increasingly anxious about some Catholics who in their grieving and ignorance, seek to communicate with dead relatives and think it is alright to do so   They go to places that are 'out of bounds' for example, spiritualist church seeking comfort, but it is a false comfort, and they need to repent and be put right with the Church.

Read Deuteronomy 18:9-13, to see what God is saying about all this:-

"When you come into the land Yahweh your God gives you, you must not fall into the habit of imitating the detestable practices of the natives. There must never be anyone among you who makes his son or daughter pass through fire, who practises divination, who is soothsayer, augur, or sorcerer, who uses charms, consults ghosts or spirits or calls up the dead, for the man who

*does these things is detestable to Yahweh, your God.
It is because of these detestable things that your God is
driving the Nations before you. You must be entirely
faithful to Yahweh your God."*

God Himself will be your comfort and your peace. Trust
Him, try to let your loved one go home to Him. If you
cannot do this immediately, don't be too hard on yourself.
Remember that Jesus wept, too, at the death of Lazarus.

This world is not our permanent home and we would
certainly not want it to be even though we may be very
happy in it and love life. There are so many injustices for
some, so much suffering that leaves us so helpless. We
are on the way "and death is the Express Way."

Death is the end of our earthly pilgrimage, of the time of
grace and mercy which God offers, so as to work out our
earthly life in God's plan. There is no re-incarnation after
death, though some religions think there is. This is not
Catholic teaching. We die once and once only. We must
try to live as we wish to die. If we're not fit to face death
today, we'll hardly be fit to face it tomorrow. The certainty
is that we all have to die.

Glad that I live am I
That the sky is blue
Glad for the country lanes
And the fall of dew
After the sun the rain
After the rain the sun
This is the way of life
'Till the work be done

> All that we need to do
> Be we low or high
> Is to see that we grow
> Nearer the sky
> *(Anonymous)*

Recently, I met a lady whose husband was dead. She told me they had just gone out to dinner with friends and they were sitting looking at the menu. When she asked her husband what he would like to eat, she noticed some change in his eyes, he was sitting there dead! What an enormous shock! There are so many who die suddenly and unexpectedly, including my own sister Frances' dear husband, Tom. At midday he thought he had 'flu, yet by 8.30 p.m. he was dead. Nothing makes up for her loss. It makes us realise we cannot hold on to life, once the Master calls, that's it. No money, nor anything else, can call us back. So He tells us to be ready, always, with oil in our lamps, waiting for the Bridegroom to call us 'Home'.

The sense of loss, emptiness, loneliness, finality, at death for those left behind is often very cruel, and leaves us wounded and broken. Where can we turn to, at times like this, but to our Saviour, who comforted the widow of Nain when she lost her son? The Apostles, too, felt lost after Jesus was killed, but what joy when they discovered, through His many appearances after the Resurrection, that He was well and truly alive, risen from the dead. He showed them His hands and His side, but now His body was not the suffering body but a glorified body that could never again experience pain or death. Thomas doubted Jesus' resurrection. So Jesus, in His kindness, came to reassure him after He had risen. "Put your finger here; look, here are My hands. Give Me your hand; put it into My side. Doubt no longer but believe." Thomas replied, "My Lord and My God!" Jesus said to him: "You believe because you have seen Me, happy are those who have not seen and yet believe." *(John 20:27-29)*

The Sadducees had real difficulty in believing in the Resurrection; they denied it outright.

"If Christ, raised from the dead, is what has been preached, how can some of you be saying 'There is no resurrection of the dead'? For if the dead are not raised, Christ has not been raised, you are still in your sins. And what is more serious, all who have died in Christ have perished.

If our hope in Christ has been for this life only, we are the most unfortunate of all people. Christ has been raised from the dead, the first fruits of all who have fallen asleep.

Death came through one man and in the same way the resurrection of the dead has come through one man. Just as all men die in Adam so all men will be brought to life in Christ; but all of them in the proper order: Christ as the first-fruits and then, after the coming of Christ, those who belong to Him.

After that will come the end, when He hands over the kingdom to God the Father, having done away with every sovereignty, authority and power.

For He must be king until He has put all His enemies under His feet, and the last of the enemies to be destroyed is death, for everything is to be put under His feet." *(1 Corinthians 15:12,16-26)*

They came to Jesus with a question about a woman who had had seven husbands, and they wanted to know whose wife she'd be on the last day, "To which of these seven husbands will she be wife?" they asked Him, "since she had been married to all seven of them." Jesus replied, "At the resurrection, men and women do not marry. No, they are like the Angels in Heaven; and as for the Resurrection of the dead, have you never read what God Himself said to you, 'I am the God of Abraham, the God of Isaac, the God of Jacob?' He is God, not of the dead but of the living." *(Matthew 22:29-32)* And His teaching, we are told, made a deep impression on them.

"I am the Resurrection and the Life," says Jesus, "he who believes in Me, though he die, yet he shall live, and whoever lives and believes in Me shall never die." *(John 11:25-26)*

So for us Christians there is no problem. "We believe that Jesus died and rose again, so we believe that God will bring with Jesus, those who have died believing in Him." *(1 Thessalonians 4:14)*

The Church teaches us that at death, the soul is separated from the body but in the Resurrection on the last day, God will give incorruptible life to our mortal body, transformed by reunion with our soul. We believe in the Resurrection of the body that we now possess and which at death will go into decay (except of course for some saints like St. Bernadette, whose body is still intact, and can actually be seen in Nevers, France).

"We sow a corruptible body in the tomb, but He raises up an incorruptible body, a spiritual body." We suffer 'bodily' death as a consequence of original sin, from which man would have been immune had he not sinned. Only our Blessed Mother, the Immaculate Virgin, had the privilege of being immune, as she never came under the influence of Original Sin. This is the meaning of the dogma of the Immaculate Conception, that Our Lady was conceived without Original Sin. And so she was assumed into Heaven, there to reign with her Beloved Son as Queen of the Angels and Saints and Queen of Heaven and Earth. She was foretold and promised by God from the moment of the fall of our first parents.

By His Death, Jesus has conquered death and so opened the possibility of salvation to all men. Left to ourselves, we would not have access to the Father's House; to God's life; or to happiness in Heaven. Jesus talks about it in John 14:2. However, we know that Christ, through His Death and Resurrection, opened the access for us and that through our Baptism we, His members, can have confidence that we too shall go where our Head and Source Jesus has preceded us *(Preface of Ascension)*. "He ascended into Heaven and is seated at the right hand of God the Father Almighty."

The Desert Fathers saw death not as something morbid but as an unlimited space filled with light. They liked to think of it, also, as a door about to be opened, as when you are waiting for a person dear to you to let them in, and as soon as the person comes your day is transformed. Such was their image of Christian death. As St. Francis of Assisi put it: "A door wide open, when 'Our Sister Death' arrives." I like to think of it as a child going home to a loving Father, to a beautiful 'Home', so wonderful that words cannot describe it.

I have been with many people dying, especially our dear old sisters. If there were no home to go to, death would be very sad indeed. But we know for sure there's a Heaven and that all our labours will be rewarded when we die, and that our names are already written in the Book of Life *(Philippians 4:3)*. so when we turn up, let's hope we're on the list and expected! It's a great blessing to witness the end of a life well lived in love with Jesus.

Leonard Lyons sees death like the sailing away of a ship:

> *"I am standing on the seashore. A ship at my side spreads her white sails to the morning breeze and starts for the blue ocean. She is an object of beauty and strength, and I stand and watch her till at length she is only a ribbon of white cloud just where the sea and sky come to mingle with each other. Then someone at my side says, "There! she is gone!"*
> *Gone? Gone where?*
> *Gone from my sight, that is all. She is just as long in mast and hull and spar as she was when she left my side, and just as able to bear her load of living freight to the place of destination. Her diminished size is in me, not in her, and just at the moment when someone at my side says, "There! She is gone!", there are other voices ready to take up the glad shout,*
> ***"There! She comes!" – and that is Dying."***

Recently I had the privilege of being very close to a dear friend who died of terminal cancer. He had fought it bravely for two years but now it was about to overtake him. I had a few little conversations with him about his illness, about Heaven, and about suffering and how to cope with it. Death was fast approaching so I said to him, "Norman, I think Jesus is coming to take you home." Immediately he responded, "You mean the end of one life and the beginning of another." "Yes," I said "I think so and there will be no more dreadful suffering and pain, and you'll see Jesus. I wonder what He will look like; and you'll see your parents, and our dear friends like Don, David... and please pray for me when you get there."

He simply held my hand in silence but I could feel his struggle to accept that this might be the end, for he had great plans to do so much more for the Lord. These were in fact his last words. His pain intensified, his worn out body reminded me of the crucified Saviour on the Cross, as he cried out in his last agony to the heavenly Father, "It is finished, the work is done." The next day, in the afternoon, Norman gave a cry in pain to His Father, opened his eyes for a second as his dear wife held his hand, and there peacefully breathed his last in the presence of his daughter and his wife, and he slipped away into the great unknown, but into the arms of his Maker. Such a beautiful life and what a homecoming he must have received with all the Angels and Saints surrounding him.

"Think not of them in sorrow; for they rest
Like weary travellers when the day is done,
Their task fulfilled, life's sweet reward is won
And they stand at God's throne among the blest.

O think of them as pilgrims that had prayed
That they might see the dawn light up the skies
And ever turned to God with hopeful eyes
Till for their steadfast faith they were repaid.

Think of rough paths that they shall tread no more,
Think of dark hours now buried in the past,
Think of their labour long through all the years
And then think of the peace of Heaven's shore
Where all things by God's glory overcast,
Speak of deep joy dimmed by no rising tears."

Terence McSwiney (1879 -1920)

Ray and his wife, Marion, have been close friends of mine for many years. They have been an amazing example of gospel living, accepting Ray's serious illness at a 'young' age, with such serenity. While he was unconscious in the Luton and Dunstable Hospital, Ray had an 'out of body' experience.

After his recovery he writes:
"I find it difficult to articulate but found myself one day, although seemingly asleep, moving smoothly through space. Although I was without my body, I felt in no way deprived or frightened. My thoughts at the time were very lucid and only loss of memory makes it difficult to share with others. I was moving smoothly and lightly and was aware of activity around me but unable to associate myself with it. I remember continually praising God. I don't recall being afraid or presenting any sort of resistance. I can remember coming to a place which remains fairly clear in my memory. I was confronted with what appeared to be a railway tunnel. As though on some sort of track, I had

the choice of going into the tunnel or to veer off in another direction. The tunnel was a part of a larger construction and seemed to be built of stone; brown, yellow, and grey in colour, it looked old and was overgrown with foliage. In fact it looked like a large bridge crossing my path but after all this time that part of the picture is becoming obscure.

I instinctively knew that the journey through the tunnel would take me to God and I was content to go on. Before I had the chance to move further though, I seemed to have switched to another track and at the time had the impression that it was Marion who had redirected me by changing the points! I am unable to recall my journey back again but know that I eventually found myself back in the hospital ward.

My recovery has been slow and is still incomplete. I found that in those days I could remember about ten minutes of my life at a time and although over the months it has improved it has brought great anguish in its wake. Losing my job and my modest skills at the same time made me very angry. I wondered how God treated His enemies if this was how He treated His friends. I must admit that my spirituality was as low as it could be and I seemed to have lost my faith completely.

It's only in retrospect that I see God's love for me and know that He wants to mould me to His Will. Anything as precious as God's attentive love is bound to be gained painfully because our animal nature will settle for less. Although my mental and physical abilities are very limited I can see that God gives me the choice in every situation to get closer to Him or to become increasingly embittered.

Over the last two or three years my faith has grown and although I tend to intellectualise too much I do at least know what I have to do to grow spiritually stronger.
I must be attentive to God and give myself to Him completely. I can only do this through deep and constant prayer.

Something else I would like to share with you is that, up until my illness, I had a deep and unremitting fear of death. It would manifest itself at any time, particularly at night, and would completely overwhelm me. The knowledge that one day I would die was almost too much to bear and the claustrophobic feelings that would ensue would make me sit up in bed shaking and in a total state of fear.

My experience of 'dying' has altered that and although I would not choose to die at any given moment, it is a great comfort to me that I have lost those neurotic feelings that undermined my faith and caused me such mental pain."

There are always many signs shown us with which God comforts us in our sad loss of those we love. Recently a dear couple near us had a serious car accident and their two beautiful sons were taken to Heaven in the prime of life, one six and one eight. God's mystery!

> "And with the morn, those angel- faces smile
> Which we have loved long since, and lost awhile."
> *(from 'Lead kindly light', Cardinal Newman)*

"Nothing can fill the gap when we are away from those we love, and it would be wrong to try and find anything. We must simply hold out and win through. That sounds very hard at first, but at the same time it is a great consolation, since leaving the gap unfilled preserves the bonds between us.

It is nonsense to say that God fills the gap: He does not fill it, but keeps it empty, so that our communion with another may be kept alive, even at the cost of pain."
(Dietrich Bonhoeffer)

How encouraging are the following words from Jane O'Shaughnessy, who died in March 1993 of leukaemia, aged eighteen.
This diary extract was written in the weeks leading up to her death.

"… I am told that I am dying … I'm not angry or bitter. I am in surprisingly good spirits. I joke, I laugh. It has not affected me in the sense that I'm depressed. I've been told off for not being depressed.
… I do have my days of sadness – but not depressant sad – a sort of pleasant peculiar sadness more filled with a warm sort of love and tenderness, like a soft rain. How marvellous!

My spirit, you see, is very strong at the moment. I can't be bothered to be ill. I am determined. My resilience is like the iron hand in the velvet glove … Like a running gushing brook flowing within me. Elusive, magical, enchanting. I will go to God. Whatever time I die I will go to God … I love people. I care for them … But I am me. I am mortal. I am only eighteen years old. Such a faith, such a love! It is something that I shall be able to treasure and uphold all my life long – no one can ever take it from me. I have it forever. For as long as I live and then until eternity. It will only be in death that I will truly live.

I see visions of darkness, winding pathways to a bright effervescent light. I see meadows, lush, green, mellow. I see these pictures as others would see their own memories... How can I see all this and be depressed, upset, alone? Why should I be miserable when I need not be? At least I am happy. I would do anything for my friends ...

I have no fear. It is not anything I have done. It is Love that gave me illness. Love. A special gift has been given. I must be special to cope with it. My life has been blessed, enchanting, hanging in the balance of yesterday, today, and forever ...

I am the luckiest woman in the world... I am not at all brave. I am terrified. And then I think of God and His warmth glows within me like a lukewarm sponge of peace and love.

Some people search all their lives. And now my time has come to reach high into the skies. And finally – a star shines on me. And finally – I can touch eternity. "

Heaven is home, and home is happiness and loved ones waiting for us inside the door! The Trinity, the angels and saints will be there to welcome us. We shall see our loved ones again, and love goes on and on into Eternity. We cannot imagine Heaven, but I know it must be wonderful. "Eye hath not seen nor ear heard what things God has prepared for those who love Him" *(1 Corinthians 2:9-10)*

St. Paul was taken up into the third Heaven but he couldn't find words to describe it. I believe Heaven will be everything we could wish for and more. Many saints have gone before us and none have come back to tell us what it is like. I suppose it would be impossible to describe it in our language, and even if someone tried we would not understand. Could anyone describe love or a very beautiful scene or garden? I think not. Some things in life cannot really be expressed in words. Heaven must be the same. Unimaginable, indescribable!

"Death surrenders us completely to God; it makes us pass into God. In return we have to surrender ourselves to it, in love and in the abandon of love, since when death comes to us, there is nothing further for us to do, but let ourselves be entirely dominated and led onwards by God."
('Hymn of the Universe', Teilhard de Chardin, p 136)

We shall see God face to face, and in our flesh shall we see God. Scripture tells us "No man can see God and live." To see God face to face is possible only for those who have passed beyond Death. Heaven is for us a mystery beyond our comprehension. It is a blest communion with the Trinity, the angels and saints. Scripture speaks of Heaven as light, life, peace, wedding feast, wine of the Kingdom, the Father's house, the heavenly Jerusalem, Paradise – the Father's home.

I am sure my Mom is in heaven, because every time I go away on holidays or have a week-end Retreat we put her in charge of the weather and she comes up trumps! Our loved ones are actually more powerful dead than alive! Dad must be there,too, enjoying his birds! Remember the Holy Souls. Because of God's transcendence, He cannot be seen as He is, unless He opens His mystery to man's immediate contemplation, and God does this sometimes for the great saints. The Church calls this contemplation of God, 'The Beatific Vision'.

St. Catherine of Siena and several others have had 'mystical experiences' of God and once her community thought Catherine was dead (and they almost buried her!) only to find that she had been taken up into such wonderful secret things of God that she did not want to stay in this life. Her confessor realised what was happening. As she opened her eyes, aware of what was going on around her she exclaimed, "Oh, I am so unhappy!" St. Ignatius, too, wanted to continue in this life if it helped bring the Kingdom of God to earth more quickly.

There is also the astonishing story of Catherine and the exchange of hearts with Christ, of how one day He took her heart from her and some days later gave her His heart instead; so that from that time onward she prayed: "My Lord, I offer you your heart." She wanted to be one with His will. This is surely true happiness on earth. "Your will be done on earth as it is in Heaven."

We all know many saints on this earth, not canonised but totally given to God. We all know at times a little of 'heaven on earth' as we experience moments of God's immense love and the kindness and compassion brought to us by different people. Most of us know the joy of friendship and the gift of another's love. The smallest thing we do to alleviate another's suffering is surely a way of bringing Heaven to earth. It could be something as small as a card, a phone call, a touch, a kiss, a meal shared, a cup of coffee together, a few pounds where needed, a prayer for, or with, a tear shed together.

Strangely enough, the more we die to ourselves, the more of Heaven we experience. The more we burn out of our hearts what is not of God, the more we will experience the freedom of spirit, and the detachment from earthly things that leaves the soul free to long for God and our homeland in Heaven. If we see everything He gives us in this life as gift: husband and wife, children, home, money, work, friends, health, then we will not be possessive of them and we will love with a love that is not ours but with the heart of Christ. We will live happily and in thanksgiving, and our way will grow brighter.

Sometimes you hear people saying, "Having my own space is Heaven", so to give someone space, respect, and reverence them as individuals would surely be creating for them 'a little heaven'.

The happiest moment in our lives is fleeting, and never satisfying enough! I cannot imagine life without Him or without the thought of another 'home' in Heaven, away from this Vale of Tears. We are so very helpless in the face of suffering that there must be more and better things elsewhere. Our comfort of each other, no matter how great, is still incomplete and imperfect.

Jesus tells us in the book of Revelation, that we have much to look forward to in Heaven; that there will be a new heaven and a new earth, for the first heaven and the first earth will pass away, and there will be a new Jerusalem, and no longer any sea. *(cf. Revelation 21:1-2).*
"I will give water from the well of life free to anyone who is thirsty, it is the rightful inheritance of the one who proves victorious. I will be his God, and he a son to Me." *(Revelation 21:6-7)*

"He will wipe away every tear and there will be no more death or mourning or sadness. The world, as we know it will be over. He, the Alpha and Omega, the Beginning and the End." (Revelation 21:4-6)

"They will see the Lord face to face, and His name will be written on their foreheads. It will never be night again and they will not need lamplight or sunlight because the Lord will be shining on them. They will reign for ever and ever." (Revelation 22:4-5)

And so to believe that we too will one day be gathered up into this new world, gives us hope indeed, to make the best of this home on earth in preparation for a better home in heaven. Let us try to keep our eyes fixed on Jesus, on eternal things.

"And a cloud came, covering them in shadow; and there came a voice from the cloud, 'This is My Son, the Beloved. Listen to Him!' Then suddenly, when they looked around, they saw no one with them any more *but only Jesus.*" (Mark 9:7-8)

The Lamb upon the throne, the King of all the Nations, the Messiah, Jesus the Lord, the Christ, will reign forever. His Kingdom will have no end. All authority is His, for He has won the Victory over all Evil through His death upon the Cross.

"You are worthy to take the scroll, and break the seals of it, because you were sacrificed and with your Blood you bought men for God, of every race, language, people and nation, and made them a line of Kings and priests to serve

our God and to rule the World.
In my vision, I heard the sound of an immense
number of angels gathered round the throne
and the animals and elders: There were ten
thousand times ten thousand of them,
thousands upon thousands shouting: 'The
Lamb that was sacrificed is worthy to be given
power, riches, wisdom, strength, honour, glory,
and blessing!'
Then I heard all the living things in creation,
everything that lives in the air, and on the
ground, and under the ground, and in the sea,
crying 'To the One who is sitting on the throne
and to the Lamb, be all praise, honour, glory
and power, for ever and ever!' And the four
animals said, 'Amen'; and the elders prostrated
themselves to worship." (Revelation 5:9-14)

We, too, can add our 'Amen' to their praise as we wait in
joyful hope for the coming of our Lord and Saviour, Jesus
Christ.

"How I love Your palace, Lord!
How my soul yearns and pines for Your courts!

My heart and my flesh sing for joy
to the living God.

Happy those who live in Your house,
And can praise You all day long;
And happy the pilgrims inspired by You
With courage to make the Ascents!"

(Psalm 84:1-2,4)

I often think of Eternity as I look at the sea. Who can fathom it's height, it's breadth, it's depth, it's wonder-only God! Imagine you are sitting by the sea shore. Listen as the water laps the edge of the sand. Hear the crying of the gulls. See a ship on the horizon as the sun casts its ruddy glow across the pathway of the sea. Be aware!

St. Thérèse and her sister Pauline were one day sitting by the sea, when Thérèse became engrossed in the golden path of light the sun was making across the sea. She thought of the golden track as a symbol of grace, guiding the little white sailed ship towards its destination. As she meditated , she decided she'd stay very close to God, till He would lead her with His golden light into Eternity, her true destination.

When my mother was dying, I came across a wonderful few verses in Psalm 107:28-32, which brought me so much comfort.
So have these words with you in case they also speak to your heart:–

"Then, they called to the Lord in their trouble
And He rescued them from their sufferings
Reducing the storm to a whisper,
until the waves grew quiet.
Bringing them glad at the calm,
Safe to the port they were bound for.

Let these thank the Lord for His love
for His marvels on behalf of men
Let them extol Him at the Great Assembly
And praise Him in the Council of Elders...

If you are wise study these things
And realise how the Lord shows His love."

This lovely poem, based on the Book of Revelation,
encourages us to keep our gaze heavenwards:

I saw the holy city, Jerusalem,
coming down from God out of heaven.
It had all the radiant glory of God
and shone like a precious stone.

I could see no temple in the city,
since the Lord God and the Lamb
were themselves the temple;
nor did it need the sun or moon for light,
since it was lit by God's glory
and the Lamb was a lighted torch.

By its light shall the nations live
and the kings of the earth will bring it their treasures.
Its gates will never be shut by day,
and in that city there shall be no night.

The throne of God and of the Lamb will be in its place,
and His servants will worship Him.
They will see Him face to face,
and His name will be written on their foreheads.

It will never be night again.
They will need neither lamplight nor sun,
for the Lord God will be shining on them,
and they will reign for ever and ever!

The Spirit and the Bride say: 'Come!'
Let all who listen, answer: 'Come!'
Indeed, I am coming soon.
Amen. Come, Lord Jesus! *(cf. Revelation 21 & 22)*

There is another favourite hymn which gives comfort to the bereaved and hope to the living:-

"When Christ shall come with shouts of acclamation,
And take me home, what joy shall fill my heart,
Then I shall bow in humble adoration
And then proclaim 'my God how great Thou art'."
(Karl Boberg (1859-1940)

A home is not fully a home without a mother. How blessed are we to have Mary, the Mother of Jesus, given to us as our Mother when Jesus hung on the cross dying. Jesus said to His Mother, "Woman, this is your son." (St. John representing all of us!)

Then to the disciple He said, "This is your Mother", and from that moment the disciple made a place for her in his 'home'." *(John 19:26-27)*

And so we ask Our Mother to intercede for us at the hour of our death:

"Holy Mary, Mother of God,
Pray for us sinners, now,
And at the hour of our death.
Amen."

"May the Angels lead you into Paradise,
the Martyrs welcome you as you draw near
and lead you into Jerusalem, the heavenly city.

May the choir of Angels welcome you
and where Lazarus is poor no longer,
there may you have eternal rest."

*(Hymn 'In Paradisum' -
the final commendation of the Requiem Mass)*

"See life with My eyes, and your whole life will be enlightened. Study My Word and let it dwell within you. Ponder in the silence of your heart the wonders of My Creation, and then your life will become so simple that nothing will disturb it. Blessed are those who see with the inner eye of goodness and truth. They shall see God"

A CALL TO UNDYING FRIENDSHIP

God is always offering us His friendship.

There was a time when man and woman lived on this earth in a wonderful friendship and harmony with God, we are told in the book of Genesis (the first book of the Bible).

We are also told of a breach in this friendship by our first parents' disobedience, and of God's amazing way of dealing with this first sin, redeeming the friendship by sending His very own and only Beloved Son, Jesus Christ, to patch things up. We know, too, that only through His Son, Jesus, could Adam and Eve and their descendants ever be restored to full friendship with God.

The poem overleaf was written especially for me by our very dear old Sister Madeleine, D.H.S. on Christmas Eve, 1975. She loved me dearly. It captures her vivid and fertile imagination and her delightful play with words.

Madeleine loved greatly, life, people, music, art, etc. and her amazing spirituality rings out clearly through her well chosen words.

The Spirit of the Father broods over a waiting world.

Freezing dusk is closing
   Like a slow trap of steel
On trees and roads
   And all that can no longer feel ...
But the pike is in its depth,
   Like a planet in its heaven;
And the badger in its bedding,
   Like a loaf in the oven,
And the butterfly in its mummy,
   Like a viol in its case;
And the owl in its feathers, -
   Like a doll in its lace.
While the Spirit of the Father broods over the waiting world.

Freezing dusk has tightened,
   Like a nut screwed tight
In the starry aeroplane
   Of the hurtling night.
But the eel moves in its hole
   Like the giggle of a sleeper:
And the hare lopes down the laneway
   Like an elfin Nessie monster.
The snail is dry in the outhouse,
   Like a seed in a sunflower;
The owl is pale on the gatepost,
   Like a clock on its tower.
And over a waiting world the Spirit of the Father broods.

Moonlight freezes the shaggy world
   Into a mammoth of ice;

Past and future
   Are the jaws of a steel vice.
But the trout lies in the tide-rip
   Like a key in a purse;
The deer are on the bare-blown hill,
   Like smiles on a nurse.
Flies sleep behind the plaster,
   Like currants in a bun;
Sparrows in the ivy-clump
   Dream of a midsummer sun.
While the Spirit of the Father broods over a waiting world.

Such a frost!
The freezing moon floats silently
In incandescent space …
A star falls …

On the hillside
   A wakeful shepherd stirs . . .
Soon, down the silvery slopes
   A single, soft cry drifts.
A Lamb is born …
While the Spirit of the Father breathes over a waiting world.

     As
          A new Star
               Is born!

"When peaceful silence lay over all,
and night had run the half of her swift course,
down from the heavens, from the royal throne,

leapt Your all-powerful Word;
Into the heart of a doomed land the stern warrior leapt.
Carrying Your unambiguous command like a sharp sword,
He stood, and filled the universe with death;
He touched the sky, yet trod the earth.
(Wisdom 18:14-16)

So, the Saviour was born. "And the Word was made flesh and dwelt amongst us." *(John, Prologue v14)* God and man were reconciled. Through Jesus' death man's friendship with God was restored.

Jesus Himself tells us in St. John's Gospel:
"A man has no greater love than to lay down his life for his friends." *(John 15:13)*. This is the epitome of love. It is exactly what Jesus did, freely, to show His friendship for us and restore our friendship with God. He also sent His Holy Spirit to be our friend and advocate, once He Himself returned to Heaven from whence He came. It is this Holy Spirit friend that Jesus appointed to give us the power to tell the world about Himself, and about the life He will give to those who believe in His Name. "He will be My witness, and you, too, will be My witnesses." *(John 15:27)*

Friendship was so important to Jesus, that He spent His public life on earth making friends, gathering round Himself twelve very special friends, as well as befriending even publicans and sinners. The choice of His friendship was free, as is all friendship. "You did not choose Me, no, I chose you." *(John 15:16)* We know that not everyone took up the special offer of His friendship. "You do not belong to the world," He told His friends, "because My choice withdrew you from the world. If the world hates you remember it hated Me before you." *(John 15:19-18)* Jesus' standard and way of life was diametrically opposed to the world's standard and way of life. To those who did accept His friendship, Jesus said, "You are My friends if you do what I command of you." *(John 15:14)*

What is the Church's track record in passing on the command of Jesus concerning friendship? "What I command you is that you should love one another." *(John 15:17)* The Church is supposed to be a community of friends.

But don't you remember the days when you went to Church but never spoke to a soul? You thought you saved your soul on your own and went to Heaven on your own! Thank God Vatican II has told us otherwise. How does the Church encourage us to be friends and 'belong' and have a sense of 'community'?

Before I tell you the answer I must first tell you the story of the frog.

Once upon a time there was a frog. But He wasn't really a frog. He was a Prince who looked and felt like a frog. A wicked witch had cast a spell on him. Only the kiss of a beautiful young maiden could save him. But since when do cute chicks kiss frogs?

So there He sat – an unkissed Prince in frog form.

But miracles happen. One day a beautiful maiden grabbed him and gave him a big smacking kiss.

Crash - boom - zap! There He was - a handsome prince. And you know the rest. They lived happily ever after.

Have you ever had the 'frog feeling'? Not all frogs are princes, of course. Normally, frogs are ugly, feel slow, low, puffy, drooped, pooped.

The frog feeling comes when you want to be bright, but feel dull.   You want to share, but are selfish.   You want to be thankful, but feel resentment.   You want to be big, but are small.   You want to care, but are indifferent.
Yes, at one time or another each of us has found himself on a lily pad floating down the great river of life, frightened and disgusted, but too froggish to budge.

So what is the task of the Church
in forming a community of friends?
To kiss frogs, of course!

But, seriously, a friend is someone who wants to share with you his life, his ideas, his dreams, his hopes, his pains, his sorrows, in a word, his love.
"I call you friends," Jesus said, "because I have made known to you everything I have learnt from My Father." *(John*

15:15) Good friends are proud to tell others of their friends' goodness and faithfulness. This can come about only as a result of each other's experience together. It is the same with our friendship with Jesus. We know Him best through our own personal experience of Him. "Now we no longer believe because of what you told us; we have heard Him for ourselves and we know that He really is the Saviour of the World." *(John 4:42).*

Again we read in the psalms: "I have learnt for myself that the Lord is great." *(Psalm 135:4)*

Nothing replaces personal experience of friendship.

Even Job after all his troubles could say: "I knew You then only by hearsay, but now having seen You with my own eyes, I retract all I have said and in dust and ashes I repent." *(Job 42:6)*

Friends love to share their successes and failures. Jesus, on the face of it, was more of a failure than a success, and it was only Jesus' friendship with His Heavenly Father that sustained Him at the blackest times. For us, too, when dark clouds appear, only His intoxicating Love can sustain us and carry us through.

In times of trial and difficulty, we certainly know who our friends are. One of our teachers, a guitarist, had an incredible experience one day as he walked along by the embankment. A young man had thrown his girlfriend into the river, but she couldn't swim and so was drowning. Our teacher passed by at the right time. He immediately jumped into the river, rescued the girl. They became good friends, and she's his wife today. A good recipe for a successful marriage is to try to be always best friends.

Let's share, now, a few thoughts with Jesus our best friend.

In Time of Trial.
When humiliated, and you would like to shake off everything unjust, ugly, distasteful; all that you consider to be a dead weight, all the circumstances that are wrong, hurtful, even violent; everything that militates against respect, reverence, goodness, truth, beauty, and peace, don't forget that 'the weight' may be the 'easy' yoke of Christ's Cross - His arms around your shoulders. Stay close to Him.

If you find yourself in a situation you cannot change yet, learn to stand beside the Cross. Yield everything to Jesus, your first Love. Yield to Him who loved you first, who called you by your name. Yield to Him who loves you without ceasing, unconditionally and unquestioningly. Yield to Him who never condemns you, but patiently waits for you to understand how much He loves you. Yield to Jesus, the Son of God, who became obedient unto death for you that you might have life.

I only know of one Victory Ground, one place of Glory, that is the Cross of Jesus Christ. Learn to run there whenever you need peace. There, you will see Him, suffering for you. There you will meet His lovely eyes, full of hope and compassion. Look up at Him. Yield to Him all your humiliations and upsets. See His dear Mother and ours, look at you with love and tenderness. Leave there your hopes, dreams, joys, sorrows, fears, anxieties, hurts and pains. Jesus your Saviour, your best friend awaits you. See His arms outstretched to embrace you. Hear His heart beat for you.

See Mary's sorrow, and remember how Simeon prophesied that a sword would pierce her heart. Rest there a little. Close your eyes and absorb the understanding between you. The weakness of the Cross is *power*. Absorb it. See everything in its perspective. Wait a moment. Listen to what Jesus has to say to you.

What's happening to you? Are you allowing life to steal your peace? Is life out of balance? Has the pendulum swung so far that the balance has gone and all you see is the humiliation and pain, the frustration and woe, the fatigue and the overwork, the 'no-way out' situation.

Allow me to pray with you
Like a gentle breeze, you breathe on us Holy Spirit of God. Melt our frozen hearts with the fire of your love. Cause our "waste places" to rejoice and bloom as they bring forth flowers like the jonquil. Let the water of your love gush forth in our deserts, as our parched land yields to springs of living water. Let our sorrow be turned into joy, as You strengthen our weary hands. Steady our trembling knees and speak words of courage to our faint hearts. Do not be afraid. I am with you (Isaiah 35)

○

When Clouds overwhelm you.

"The gloom of the world is but a shadow. Behind it, yet within our reach, is joy. There is radiance and glory in the darkness, could we but see. We only have to look. I beseech you to look.

Life is so generous a giver, but we, judging its gifts by their covering, cast them away as ugly or heavy or hard. Remove the covering and you will find beneath it a living splendour, woven of love, by wisdom, with power. Welcome it, grasp it and you touch the angel's hand that brings it to you. Everything we call a trial, a sorrow, or a duty, believe me, that angel's hand is there; the gift is there and the wonder of an overshadowing Presence. Our joys too; be not content with them as joys, they too conceal diviner gifts.

Life is so full of meaning and of purpose, so full of beauty - beneath its covering - that you will find that earth but cloaks your heaven. Courage then to claim it; that is all! But courage you have; and the knowledge that we are Pilgrims together, wending through unknown country, Home."   *(Extract from a letter of Fra Giovanni c.1513)*

Praise Him for the good and bad times. See His hand at work in every circumstance as the shadows give way to light. Our worst happening, or greatest loss or pain can often end up being (in some sense) the best thing that has ever happened to us. Being overlooked and rejected, can be a source of great personal freedom, as you grow in awareness of God's love for you, rising above people's opinion of you and living in the knowledge of His personal love. "Give me the wisdom that sits by Your throne." *(Wisdom 9:4)*

Close your eyes and be aware of the 'dark threads'. Be aware of the times the threads were knotted together and needed unravelling. Perhaps you have been overwhelmed at the death of a loved one, a failure, a fear, a heartache... Return to the scene – relive the event, seek the presence of Jesus in it. Dwell with it... Be aware of His healing presence. Speak to Him. Ask Him the meaning of what was happening to you. Listen to His reply. Do this frequently. When you are no longer upset by negative feelings coming from the event, then I believe you have 'let go' and become healed and at peace.

Allow me to pray with you
I pray that the Holy Spirit will reveal something of the divine pattern in God's plan for you. I pray that nothing may ever be wasted or lost. I pray you will be patient with yourself, and with God, and that you will allow things to happen for you in His time. I pray that all shall be well for you. Amen.

○

In time of Doubt
When the fetters of Rebellion make you despair to the point of almost forsaking Jesus, who called you once and for all; when the pain of frustration and abandonment overtakes you; when all seems wasted and lost, the way forward difficult, bleak, even frightening; return to that inner source of solitude and silence. Let the spring of life well up from within you, as

you hear Him whisper in the depth of your heart:–

"I am here, I never left you
I am with you forever
I am here to console you
Courage, Fear not, my child
I am always with you
Even when you sleep.
I am Jesus, your friend, your brother, your saviour,
your lover.
My love for you is everlasting
I do not change, I am.
Stay with me
Come close to me."

"Whoever comes to Me and believes in Me, from his breast will flow fountains of living water. Whoever comes to Me, I will not cast off." *(John 7:38)*

As you ponder with Him you will see that God's Radiance shines through our woundedness, our vulnerability. When we see no solution, all we can do is to abandon ourselves to God, in body and spirit and then we will find that the Kingdom of God is within us....

Jesus, You call us to be the light for You when you said:
"You are the light of the world. A city built on a hill-top cannot be hidden. No one lights a lamp to put it under a tub; they put it on the lamp-stand, where it shines for everyone in the house. In the same way your light must shine in the sight of men, so that, seeing your good works, they may give the praise to your Father in Heaven" *(Matthew 5:14-16)*

"It is better to light one candle than to curse the darkness."
(Chinese proverb)

Allow me to pray with you

Lord Jesus Christ, I come to you just as I am, in my despair and darkness. I come because You are the light that draws me to yourself, so that I might absorb your light, become your light and reflect your light. Set me ablaze for you. Let my light shine in the darkness so that others seeing it, may give You glory. Spare me from hiding your light or extinguishing your light, Spirit of God fill me, fall afresh on me. Risen Jesus, in Your light, let me see light. Amen.

○

At times of overwhelming joy

Sit still...   Close your eyes...   Be Aware

See Him in Everything. In:–
The Wonder of His Love .... Encapsulating
The Simplicity of a Primrose .... Endearing
The Richness of a Sparkling Crocus .... Awakening
The Surprise of the Blossom .... Enchanting
The Song of the Bird .... Uplifting

Pause: Enter in! . . . and adore.

The Majesty of the Mountains .... Breathtaking
The Cascading Streams and Waterfalls .... Energizing

The Music of the Rivers .... Calming
The Depths of the Sea .... Searching
The Beauty of the Firmament .... Inspiring
The Glory of the Stars .... Empowering
The Breath of His abiding presence .... Comforting
The Awesomeness of Stillness .... Deepening

Pause: Enter in! . . . and adore.

The Laughter of Children............................ Delighting
The Dawn of a New Day .... Life-Giving
The Cry of the Poor .... Challenging
The Kindness to the Elderly...................... Hope-Giving
The Courage of the Sick .... Amazing
The "Going Home" of a Friend .... Releasing
The Thoughts of the Prisoners .... Interceding
The Efforts for Peace .... Edifying

Pause: Enter in! . . . and adore.

The Forgiveness of a Friend .... Restoring
The Empathy of Another ....Renewing
The Sensitivity to Pain ....Strengthening
The Hope of Love .... Encouraging
The Knowledge of Eternity .... Sustaining
The Power of Healing Love .... All Embracing
The Mystery of the Mass......................... All consuming

Pause: Enter in! . . . and adore.

The Wonder of the Trinity....................... Overwhelming
The Glory of His Name .... Abiding
Forever and Ever Praising .... Amen. Amen

Allow me to pray with you

Everything was made for you Lord, in You, through You and with You. We offer You in praise and thanksgiving all that You give to us, all that we are and have, so that Your Joy may be in us and our joy in You may be complete. To You be glory and honour and wisdom and thanksgiving and power and strength forever. Amen.

○

In Time of Sharing

> *"I call you to witness for Me and to share with others the 'New' life which I am giving you constantly. Know that when you speak on My behalf, I am always with you. Many lives will be touched through your testimony. Do not be afraid to speak out and do not waste the opportunities I offer you."*

We hope we will become better friends with Jesus through our time spent together in prayer. We will want to take His message wherever we go. It won't matter whether we plod along at a snail's pace or whether we go at a scurrying rabbit's pace, all that matters is that we plod along for Him, and tell the World about Him.

The World is hungry for Evangelisation, for the message of Jesus, for the Good News of God's Love and Mercy. Pope Paul VI said, "To-day's Church needs witnesses more than teachers, witnesses who have experienced a new life, through Jesus Christ". What witnesses bring is a living Jesus, as they convey the Good News that they themselves have personally experienced, sometimes amid the shadows of life. His special friends (the apostles) were greatly persecuted, even imprisoned, for being His friends and for even using His Name.

When the angel of the Lord opened the prison gates at night to let the apostles free, as he led them out he told them: "Go, and stand in the Temple and tell the people all about this new life." *(Acts 5:20)*

○

The stories which follow show how people have coped with overpowering difficulty, or who have had extraordinary conversions themselves thus giving powerful testimonies to the power of God working in their lives. We thank them for sharing their lives with us. They will be rewarded enough by the knowledge that their journeys will help you in yours.

○

"THE KEYS OF THE KINGDOM"
(A testimony from ex-Guardsman John)

John is a dear friend whom I met many years ago at a Scripture week-end in Damascus House. He is now a deeply healed, faithful friend of Jesus. He is a bright shining light both in AA and beyond. Such joy when he telephones or writes with yet another Alleluia!

I am a recovering chronic alcoholic, who is sober today by the grace of God. Let me tell you how the Lord used Alcoholics Anonymous. My drinking led me into a locked ward, under Section 4 of the Mental Health Act, a vegetable on the floor but dangerous to myself and others and seriously anti-social. I was then very violent.

During my drinking I experienced delirium, tremors, blackouts (alcoholic amnesia) fits, shakes, withdrawal symptoms, hyperventilation and resuscitation when my heart stopped. I lost my dignity, became a liar, thief and cheat, lost my family, two jobs, (including being a policeman and soldier) my wife, five children. All went to 'alcohol', the 'rapacious creditor'! The remorse, horror and hopelessness of the next mornings were unforgettable. No words can tell the loneliness and despair I felt. I had met my match. Alcohol was my Master!

It was from the locked ward I was directed to AA. I came to believe that no human power could relieve my alcoholism; a physical, mental, spiritual illness, but God could and would if He were sought. Praise His Holy Name.

Alcoholics Anonymous - a twelve step Healing Programme - consists of admission of defeat, a trust in God, a clean house (clean your act up!) and helping others. It is a simple programme for complicated people which offers a new way of living. When alcoholics draw near to God He discloses Himself to them. That is my experience, and after that we do it all, 'one day at a time'.

After some time sober in AA I was to experience a sanctification of sorts when I decided about ten years ago to know Christ more. I was on an AA retreat when I first decided to make a serious full surrender to Christ and shortly afterwards I was to attend a Frances Hogan seminar. She is a Spirit-filled teacher of Jesus.

I asked a deeply committed Roman Catholic nun to witness my Third step Prayer of AA, which I prayed on my knees in front of the tabernacle. The prayer is as follows:- "God, I offer myself to Thee, to build with me and to do with me as Thou wilt. Relieve me of the bondage of self, that I may better do Thy will. Take away my difficulties, that victory over them may bear witness to those that I would help of Thy Power, Thy Love and Thy Way of Life. May I do Thy will always." As a result, I found a loving God, and I have been eighteen years sober, thank God. Hallelujah!

The Catholic sister placed her dear hands on my head and began to speak tenderly in a strange language. It sounded spiritually like a sort of Hebrew. I cried, there on my knees, tears of repentance. "That day in exchange for a bottle I had been given the "Keys of the Kingdom". I haven't looked back since. There are no hopeless cases in AA!

In sobriety I have been baptised and confirmed, I go daily to AA meetings, keep sober by love and service. Alcoholics Anonymous is a fellowship of many men and women throughout the world who stop drinking and stay stopped. AA works, if you work it! God bless all alcoholics. AA can be contacted by telephoning 0171-352-3001. Pick up the phone and not the drink. The first drink does the damage!

"A DAUGHTER RESTORED"

Prayer works! God restores!
(A Testimony from Margaret Duncan)

Margaret is the sweetest most wonderful woman whom I met for the first time in Gorleston years ago, with her dear husband, Warren, (now deceased) who was a tower of strength and whose hugs were unbelievable! What courage Margaret shows to-day, as she steps out into the great unknown future, her hand held tightly in God's hand.

By the time I reached Alcoholics Anonymous at the age of twenty-nine, I was well and truly beaten; mentally, physically and spiritually. Drink was destroying me but I was powerless to stop, no matter how hard I tried. I had asked God to help me many times before but He didn't seem to listen and I was convinced that He had no time for the likes of me. I know now that I had not been ready before and that He knew the exact time and place to step in and set me free.

I went to Mass every week and mumbled a few prayers most days I suppose as a kind of 'insurance policy'. Although I had always believed in God, I had picked up the idea that He was only interested in the 'good guys' and I certainly was not one of them! However, His plans and His timing are perfect and by that January of 1976, I knew that if I did not stop drinking I would die. My mind was quite made up that I would commit suicide. My family has a history of alcoholism and suicides and in fact my mother had walked into the sea and drowned herself on a cold January day just two years prior to this. By a strange 'coincidence' one day my husband's usual newspaper was 'on strike', so he bought a different paper. In it was an article about Alcoholics Anonymous which struck a cord in me, so I decided to give AA a try before I ended my life. I read somewhere recently that a 'coincidence' is just God being anonymous!

I believe that God had already gone ahead of me in AA because the first person I ever spoke to in AA was Father John, a Catholic priest. This kind and loving man had nearly been destroyed by alcohol. He understood exactly how I was feeling and supported me as I began to attend meetings while struggling to stop drinking. It was not easy and there were days when I came within an inch of drinking again but with the help of Father John and other new friends in AA, I managed to stay sober.

Many things happened in the next eighteen years. My first husband died leaving me to bring up two children. I got married again to Warren, a lovely man, I met in AA. I had two more children with him. In fact I had a lot to be thankful for, but there was still a very important gap in my life which caused me great sadness, despite my lovely family.

In 1964 further back in my past when I was not long out of school, I had a baby girl whom I had to give up for adoption. This caused me such grief. Bitterness and unforgiveness set in at that time causing me many problems in the years following. In November 1993 Sr. Josephine Walsh came up to Aberdeen to give a weekend on 'Healing and Wholeness in Jesus Christ'. That very weekend my daughter would be celebrating her 29th birthday and as usual at that time I was very distressed, wondering where she was and if she was even still alive. Sr. Josephine prayed with me a very simple prayer; she said something like 'Come on Jesus, you know where Margaret's daughter is and how she's longed all these years to see her again. Please bring her daughter back to her'.

I must confess I did not believe for one minute that the prayer would be answered. I thought the situation was completely hopeless, Although the natural mother is generally not allowed any information about her child the latter has access to that information by the age of eighteen. Therefore I felt sure that if my child was going to try to trace me she would have done so by now. However I thought it was very kind of Sr. Josephine to pray for me but I kept my doubts to myself about our prayer ever being heard.

Once again God's perfect timing was at work and exactly one month later my daughter, Helen, contacted me. She told me she had finally decided to try to find me on the very day that Sr. Josephine had prayed for me. I was walking on air. Words cannot describe the joy I felt at receiving the best Christmas present that I could ever have hoped for; especially when I realised God's abundant love for me and it was He giving me back my 'lost' child. My daughter bears a striking resemblance to me and we have so much in common that it is almost as though she has never been away. The whole family took her to their hearts and my husband Warren was delighted for me. I thought that I could never be unhappy again but my life was soon to change in a drastic and heartbreaking way.

Warren and I had just spent a wonderful weekend with my 'new found' daughter Helen and her husband. Three days later on the 27th April Warren was scheduled to play golf with his boss and a team from his office. I had spent a happy day with friends and returned home in good spirits only to receive a phone call telling me that Warren had suffered a massive heart attack whilst playing golf and had died on the spot. He was just 41 years old. I was devastated, the pain was overwhelming and I thought I would die of grief. On top of that I was scheduled for major surgery in two weeks time; how could I ever cope?

Three years on, I can look back and say that the Lord must have carried us through that valley of the shadow of death because humanly speaking we could not have survived. Friends rallied round, including Sr. Josephine who had become close to the whole family. God's immense love surrounded us like a cocoon and He took care of all our needs, supplying a strength and peace which were not human. Above all, He had returned my long lost child to me just before He called my husband home; surely another example of His love and mercy!

Today I am walking a new path. I still miss my lovely husband terribly but I know he would want me to make the best of my life and, apart from looking after our boys, I have now completed and passed my first year at University with an MA degree course. I do not know what the future holds for me but I do know that God loves me dearly, not because of anything I have done but just because He is my Father and I can safely leave my future in His loving hands.

"HOPE IN SICKNESS"

(Sister Helen Ward, D.H.S.)

Sister Helen is a very valued member of our Community. She has just celebrated her Ruby Jubilee, and has served God in Teaching for most of her Religious life. Now new areas of mission have opened up for her, including hospital chaplaincy work and teaching English to foreign students. She was privileged to spend five weeks in a Romanian orphanage, and visits and supports the refugees in Bosnia. If Sr. Helen can do a service for anyone she is there ever ready!

"If anyone would come after me, he must deny himself, take up his cross daily and follow me" *(Luke 9:23)*

These are inspiring words to read and reflect upon when things are going well, but quite a different story when unexpected suffering crosses your path like a bolt from the blue!

Life for me did not bring too many heavy crosses, apart from the tragic death of parents, redundancy etc. Such are the crosses of life for many people and time is the great healer. I was sailing along quite nicely when I developed a black mark between my toes and the diagnosis was a malignant melanoma. What was a 'melanoma'? I asked. I was soon to learn that it was a form of skin cancer. On hearing these words my world just collapsed. I felt my knees knocking. I could not stop shaking.

The news was devastating and I remember thinking "that God did not spare His own Son" so why should I be exempt from pain? I think if it had not been cancer the shock might not have been so great. I felt I could have died from the shock alone!

Many sleepless nights followed and life seemed to come to a standstill ... All sorts of things came flooding into my mind. Had the cancer spread into my system? Would I lose some toes? This was my biggest worry. Would my life-style change? How would I ever walk properly again? Would I be able to drive the car? etc.

Now where was my trust in God? I had given Him my whole life. I had so often 'preached' to others about handing over all our problems to the Lord, letting them go to Him, leaving them at the foot of the Cross etc. Yes, I knew all the theory, but what about the practice in my own life, not somebody else's?
Where was my Faith in a God of Love?

In the days awaiting a hospital appointment I certainly believed in God's words "Ask and you shall receive ..." I have never prayed so much in my whole life, so good came out of it! In spite of all the prayer, *I was at times overcome by fear.* "Do not be afraid", "Fear not" were just words to me. My main fear was the loss of some of my toes, and a few people assured me that this was inevitable!! But my toes were mine and I wanted them intact.

Eventually I was admitted to Stoke Mandeville Hospital where the cancer had to be cut out followed by a skin graft taken from above the knee and this new skin was grafted onto my two precious toes. This double operation was performed at the same time.

The night before the operation, the Hospital Chaplain came along to pray with me and to administer the Sacrament of the Sick and give me Holy Communion. A most moving experience where I felt the presence of the Lord in a real way and an incredible peace entered my life, 'a peace that surpasses all understanding'. My eyes were opened and I felt free to commit my life to the Lord afresh. 'I am with you always'.

The morning after the operation a doctor came specially to my bed bearing life-giving news – that the operation went well and I still had my five toes; he even counted up to five on his fingers but my response was to dissolve into tears and he went off in silence! Yes, his message was heard but the pain was still too powerful for words. A compassionate nurse nearby said to me "Did you hear what he said? " In spite of her business she found time to give me a big hug and just quietly said "what wonderful news!" "A real miracle, Lord", I said ...

During my four days in hospital I was not allowed out of bed; being so dependent on others for my basic needs caused much suffering on my part. Before leaving hospital I was given a special wheelchair with a raised up piece of wood for my right foot. When a porter arrived at my bed with the wheelchair, I said "Who is this for? It can't be me!!" My mode of transport had certainly changed!

I was sent to a superb rest-home where I received every care and attention, but my greatest pain here was, again, dependence on others. This lack of independence was a new experience for me and I found it so difficult to accept. The pains both from the toes and from the skin-graft were quite difficult to bear at times, especially in movement.

However the great day came when the plaster was removed and also the first dressing from my toes. Removing the toe dressing was beyond the competence of the nurse concerned. She did not realise I had some sutures and she just pulled gently while I yelled! She eventually called another nurse who tried to ease my pain, but in actual fact she made it worse and by this time I thought my toe had been pulled off! I have never known such pain. I could not see what was being done because of the blinding tears. Soon one nurse left the scene (thank the Lord) and the other one suggested asking the surgeon's help!!

How glad I was to see the surgeon coming with the proper equipment. He had performed the operation, so he knew exactly what he was doing and he restored my confidence. Thank the Lord for his skill, otherwise my toes might have been damaged for life! They were then washed in disinfectant. Oh the pain! I felt my right foot and leg did not belong to me! The muscle power had gone even after only two weeks of being wheelchair bound.

The thoughts came to me again "Will I ever walk properly? Will I ever wear proper shoes? etc. ... but the nurse reassured me that in time all would be well ..." but I honestly did not believe her. My faith again wavered ...

The sheer effort of trying to walk with a zimmer frame with wheels proved extremely difficult, as I could not balance the weight. So at first I just nervously hopped, the sore foot was too painful to put to the ground. I persevered with the help of my wonderful nurse; many tears were shed as I tried desperately to take a step forward.

With increased confidence progress in walking followed but one of my carers was constantly saying "Please don't limp!! Otherwise you'll go on limping, it will become a habit!" If this dear lady only knew the effort and pain involved in trying to walk!

Life's activities came to a standstill and many commitments were cancelled, but God did not need any of these activities. Quite a hard lesson to learn!

"To God be the glory ..." healing continued and each day brought added strength. Now nearly twelve months later I witness to the power of prayer and a first class Miracle in my life. My family and friends soaked me in daily prayer and the Lord certainly heals today.

> "I am the Lord who heals you". *(Exodus 15:26)*
> "Everyone who asks, receives". *(Luke 11:10)*

"LUCKY TO BE SITTING DOWN"
(Sister Marie Ragil, D.H.S.)

(Sister M. Ragil is French and was a teacher when, at the age of about 34 years, she contracted polio, which has left her paralysed from the neck down. When I met her in France about twenty five years ago, she was confined to bed all the time. About fifteen of us stood round her bed, admiring the painting she was just about to sign with her mouth. I was over-joyed when she gave me the picture, which has since given hope to many people. Now, thank God, and thanks to modern technology, it is possible for her to be put in a wheel chair during the day, and so her quality of life is much improved. Her article was first published in "Être Ensemble" (November 1993) and translated here by Sister Anne-Marie Davies, D.H.S., of the English Province.)

I have been in a rest house since November 1956. I have known the temptation of thinking that, when one is overtaken by illness or physical disability, life comes to a halt like a grandfather clock that can no longer be made to go.

One forgets that life can take other forms, forms which include illness and disability. My situation has given me the time to sit and evaluate things. Every moment, I live my mission as a Daughter of the Holy Spirit. Today, I'll share with you what it is that enables me to live.

WAYS TO FREEDOM

First of all, the acquisition of a certain autonomy: the possibility of writing and painting with my mouth. Thanks to that, I have had the joy of producing a few pictures and of dealing with my correspondence. I also manage to eat unaided, to switch the transistor and tape-recorder on and off, to turn the pages of a book, to use a typewriter. Having to live with my disability, to 'take it on board' calls for constant adaptation on my part.

So as not to be a burden on life around me and in order to facilitate the work of those who care for me, I have organised my life in such a way as to make it easier for them to give me the indispensable nursing care that I require. Total dependence on others, which I used to feel as an infringement on my liberty, has, little by little, become a way to freedom.

In practical terms this means, for example, accepting the service of whichever member of staff may be on duty; each one has her own particular way of working; it means leaving the initiative with others, accepting that the chair be placed here rather than there, that the towel be folded one way rather than another; that the books be arranged like this rather than like that.

The patience I practise with regard to my instruments is also a way of freedom: I don't always manage to get hold of them at the first go, and this is a constant reminder of my disability. This patience with myself, this acceptance of being 'on one's way one's whole life through' has to be worked at every day. Being immobile means that there are things which I experience more keenly than before, and for me the possibilities of 'escape' are very limited ... Yet, thanks to this (new-found) freedom, I feel 'at home with myself'.

'The Tree', painted by mouth by Sr. Marie Ragil, D.H.S.

I appreciate all the support derived from my community-life and my involvement in it, all the sisterly mutual help that is given. For my part, surrounded as I am by Sisters most of whom are elderly, I try to be of as much help to them as I can: writing an address, supplying an item of information, repeating a communication, sharing news, doing a reading or asking for a service.

I devote a portion of my time to listening. I share in animating prayer, reflection groups and in animating the Liturgy. "Our involvement in Mission is often expressed through simple human gestures, apparently without significance".

Our Rule, radio, tapes, relationships, visits, exchanges, keep me in touch with the outside world. The window of my room looks on the vegetable garden and a road that is much used by the farmers with their agricultural equipment. I have learned a lot and am eager to learn more about it. I rejoice in all the technical progress which is improving life for the disabled and facilitating work in all its forms. I dream of having a computer. Now that the house has bought a Fiorino my getting about has been made easier. By means of sloping rails I am able to get into the car without leaving my wheelchair. Once I am inside the car, the chair is secured by chains.

What helps me to live is the teaching of St. Francis de Sales.

> 'Do not fear
> what may happen tomorrow.
> The same loving Father

who cares for you today
will care for you tomorrow
and everyday.
Either He will shield you
from suffering,
or He will give you
unfailing strength to bear it.
Be at peace, then,
and put aside all anxious
thoughts and imaginings.'

From it I have drawn, especially, the spirit of freedom of the children of God. My life has become tranquil. When meditating on a text from the Rule of Life, I readily prolong my meditation with the writings of this Saint. I had the good fortune to meet, some twenty years ago, a priest of the Society of St. Francis de Sales who helped me to re-read my life in the light of the Gospel.

Since 1967 I have been a member of the F.C.P.M.H. (the Catholic Fellowship of Paralysed/Handicapped Invalids). I work with its team based at Auray, of which I am the secretary. It is my task to send out notices and write reports. For twelve years I belonged to the diocesan team. All this means that I have to keep informed, to read ... I have learned to be attentive to the life of these people, to change my ways of seeing things. My life as a member of this Fellowship and my life in community are complementary; the spirit of fraternal Gospel love I find in the Fellowship I must also bring to my community life.

To signify my solidarity with the sick and disabled I belong to the A.P.F. (the Association of the Paralysed, France). I try to take part in the working days organised by the Association.

Lastly, I see to it that there is time in my life for relaxation: to go round the grounds of Ker-Anna, to admire the trees, the flowers, to listen to the song of the birds. I like playing scrabble but my preference is for crosswords. These help me to keep my memory alert. I have invested in a new dictionary.

It is my firm conviction that "whatever be our situation, whether we are engaged in active work, retired, sick or suffering, and even in the experience of failure, we can always live the mission which is ours as Daughters of the Holy Spirit". *(Art. 11.)*

Mindful of those whose lives are full of ups and downs, those who don't have time to sit down. Yes, I think I can say that I am lucky to be sitting down!

O

"THE MIRACLE HUG"

(The Good Samaritan)

(This is the story of Roberto – now two decades sober. Hallelujah)

"A stranger came into the Alcoholics Anonymous Group. He was in a mess, a real mess, terribly upset. He muttered, sneered, scowled, and occasionally grunted. He even put a cigarette out on the back of his hand.

Everybody stared and his presence was alarming. He looked like a devil. The woman who had been giving her testimony, abruptly fell silent. One could hear a pin drop. The empty pause stretched on for ever. There was at least one person dying to fix the awkwardness with 'magic words'.

Then the old Jewish lady got up; put her cup of coffee on the table and walked over to the man spontaneously. She looked at him, smiled and hugged him. "Welcome", she said. She held him, touched him, and felt his great pain and soul-sickness.
Suddenly he buried his head into her loving shoulders and audibly wept. He poured his pain into her, crying like a baby. She held him like a mother.

Many in that room in the north of London that night silently cried. Others prayed for strength. Courage came to both: the courage of this little woman and the courage of the man to bring himself to the support group.

After this communion the old lady returned to her seat (almost as though nothing had happened out of the ordinary) picked her coffee up again, sat down ready to listen to the man seeking help. Then he began to talk. His name was Roberto. He was a recovering chronic alcoholic. He was very depressed. He was lonely. He was suicidal. He was afraid, in sheer terror. That night he needed to be held, touched and hugged. He didn't need 'magic words'. His clothes were a mask that covered his pain, loneliness, fear, terror, bewilderment and despair.

The hug was the miracle. The old Jewish woman risked rejection and ridicule. She loved unconditionally.
God is found in a prophet, a poet, a song and a hug. Yippee!"

○

Later I received the following letter from Roberto:

17th January 1998

Dear Sister Josephine,

This morning early I praised God for knowing you. You set me on a path to seek God (not joy) and found that by submerging myself in God, not so much for happiness, but for usefulness. Yippee! The Christian mystics are *working* mystics. Surrendered lives, saved to serve.

Jesus stops the flow of my misdirected forces and gives me His force to flow within me unopposed. Glory to His Name. After all those years of living the wrong way round, today I am eager to tell you that "He is able". The cleansing blood reached me, causing a transformation from the guttermost to the uttermost. God never takes anything away without putting something better in its place. For example, I thought I found fun in the stimulation of alcohol but real fun has come to me in the exaltation of spiritual living.

All love, my precious friend,

Roberto.

○

"BLESSED ARE THEY WHO MOURN"

(Margaret Clifford of Limerick shares how, in the depths of her mourning for her child, God consoled her.)

February 18th, 1989 started as usual at 7.30 with the noise of the blind going up in Shane's bedroom. My human alarm clock I called him. I remember wondering that morning if I would ever be free to sleep late again. As usual, within a few minutes, our two boys, Shane four, and Gareth six, were in our bedroom.

As the day progressed, I could not help feeling calm even though my husband Gerry was unemployed at the time. It had been a long time since I had felt this way. Later in the afternoon I took the boys down to visit my parents. At 5.30 p.m. the peace and calm I felt earlier was cruelly shattered. Shane, was killed by a car while playing outside my parents' home.

I will never forget the events that followed, finding him on the road, the look on Gareth's face when he looked at me and said, "Mammy, I am sorry! I could not help it." He had always been so responsible with his small brother and loved to act the older brother. The feeling of utter disbelief will stay with me forever. I will never forget my mother screaming, my father and sister leaning over Shane, my father searching in vain for some life, the ambulance arriving and going away with no siren on. That there was no siren told me there was no life.
In the midst of all this confusion all I could do was pray. I remember being taken into the house, the children were all lined up on the couch crying. My mother was still screaming. All I did was ask them all to stop and I continued to pray and continued to do so on the way to the hospital.

To bury him was the hardest thing I ever had to do. Yet, in another way, it was the nicest thing I ever did, because I believe God took me step by step and guided me along. I got the grace to attend Mass and receive Communion over the days of the funeral.

The morning after the accident, I went to Mass on my own to hear the pastoral letter from the bishop about Guardian Angels. The more I listened to the letter the more I realised that Shane was taken to confirm that letter because everybody told me I had an angel in Heaven. I knelt before the altar that morning and said "You loved him more than me. Thy will be done".

Our house seemed to be full of people that day. Among the people who came to sympathise with me was my friend, Rose, who had long been a member of a Charismatic prayer group. As tears rolled down her face she blessed me with holy oil and prayed to the Lord and Our Lady to strengthen me.

On the day of the removal, I went to the funeral parlour to spend some time with him. I was so frightened. I had never touched a corpse before. I felt so ashamed being afraid of my own flesh and blood. I value that time I spent with him because I said goodbye to him in my own way. I sang his favourite nursery rhyme, "Baa, Baa, Black Sheep" and the theme music to "Home and Away" which was his favourite programme. That night my husband and I just held hands over him and said goodbye to him in our way by saying his night prayer which we said with him so many times before: Good-night, Holy God, Good-night. And now I must go to sleep. And as I go I give to you , my little soul to keep.

On arriving at the Church the place was packed to the doors. I carried his little coffin into the Church with Gerry that night. I had brought him into the Church so many times before and this was to be the last. He used to say, "Mammy, bring me to God's house." When Mass was over he would ask for money to light lamps to Our Lady. Often, having given him only 10p, he would have about six lamps lit before I knew where I was.
God's healing is not conditional!

GOD HEALS WHEREVER YOU ARE!

(Letter from Sharon)

(I met Sharon at Dalmally while giving a Retreat to young people. She received much healing through reading John Woolley's book 'I Am With You'.)

Dear Sr. Josephine,

I have been blessed. God healed me in my own home of an old wound I never thought to have healed at Dalmally. I was never truly aware of the power of the Holy Spirit and the power of prayer in myself. I had thought that healing could only take place when people prayed over you. Not so!

> The tears welled up inside me
> Came from such a depth
> I could hardly catch my breath
> High into the sky.
> As they reached Heaven,
> With each giant sob
> They turned to the laughter
> Of pure release.

It was a miraculous miracle. Then my book arrived "I Am With You", and now I know *He really is*.

Love to you. God bless,
Sharon

JACOB AND ETHAN'S STORY
(by Richard and Angela Davison-Frances)

We heard of a very serious accident near to our Convent and Sr. Helen went to console the broken-hearted couple. Months afterwards, I asked them if they would share their testimony with us. Amidst many tears and at a great cost, they did. I thank them profusely. What an amazing couple!

Angela and I have always been close to Jesus, but it was always Angela who was close in a way that I never was. We both cared for our parents, helped charities and filled our hearts with love. God blessed us with two beautiful children, Jacob and Ethan. Our life together was very happy.

We were all driving home at 5.30pm, on a black night in November, when Angela saw a darkly dressed tramp walking in the road. We knew her as the bag lady. She had a mental problem. As her clothes were dark, we didn't see her till the last minute. Angela swerved sharply to avoid her, our car went out of control and straight into the path of an on coming car. We were almost off the road, when another car crashed into us. Ethan, aged six, who was behind me, got the main force.

When I carried Jacob, aged eight, out of the car he appeared unconscious but there was no sign of any cuts or bruises. His side of the car was undamaged. Ethan, I could see, had been winded like I had been. He had hurt his mouth but apart from that I thought he would be OK.

The following night, and the next day, were something that we pray no one else will ever have to endure. When we were told by the doctors that Ethan was near to death and that Jacob was virtually dead, both on life support machines, our world collapsed. We begged the doctors to keep the machines running. Soon it became obvious that even the machines could not keep the boys' bodies going for much longer. The comfort of seeing their chests moving up and down would soon be gone. The doctors did all they could to save our boys' lives.

We pushed the boys beds together to make one big bed and we all cuddled up together, as we always did at home. Then the machines were turned off! We saw a big smile appear on Jacob's face. We knew he was so happy finally to meet God. And I know I saw him wave Good-bye to me.

On arrival home, I prayed to God. I was crying so much. I just knelt down and said: "Daddy, you love me and I love you, so can I have my boys back, please, please, please..." My prayer was answered, and we have our boys back, in spirit anyway, and their spirits get upset when they see us cry. We often cry even though we know our boys are safe with the Lord. When we dream of our boys, we can even feel their kisses. Perhaps, because we focused on our love for our children, and our love for our Heavenly Father, rather than hate anyone, Our Lord and Saviour allows the spirits of our boys to come to us frequently.

We planned the funeral as a labour of love for our boys. A specially made double coffin with the boys cuddling each other (as they used to do in bed) was placed in a glass hearse pulled by two black horses. We filled the coffin with their favourite toys, and some of their birthday and Christmas presents. We both had the feeling that Ethan, a prankster, would make them drop the coffin or make the horses bolt! We told the boys not to do anything in church, as it was God's house, and if they wanted to do anything to do it at home. It had been raining solidly for days before the funeral but on the day itself, the sun shone, the grass and the grave were miraculously dry, as if God had organised the weather as a gift to us. The undertakers dropped the coffin in our hall way. We weren't surprised or upset, because we expected it to happen. There was a hold up outside the church and while the horses were waiting on our quiet country lane, a lorry, a JCB, and a bus all went past within inches of the horses, but they didn't bolt, despite our boys best efforts! They were always so full of fun!

Angela and I have often been asked if we hate the tramp, or the driver who hit us, or even God. We always reply, that the way the crash happened and the way our children died, without physical scars, was the work of God and we could never hate God. We have many signs of their presence still with us to day. Love lasts forever! The Spirit of the Lord has filled us with His peace and understanding. Even so, the pain of our grief is still unbearable, but we know that with the grace of God and the fellowship of the Holy Spirit and the support of our many wonderful friends, we can bear it...

○

"THE LORD WORKS IN MYSTERIOUS WAYS"

(by Lindsay Talary)

Lindsay is a man of great faith. He could not accept the evil of divorce, and wanted at all costs to expose it to the world. He decided to do away with himself, but two evils never make a right. Much prayer, including his own, rescued him. Now he is about to set up a project for the elderly.

He still prays his marriage will be restored.

In July last year, my wife, Marguerite, was granted her Decree Absolute. After twenty-nine years our marriage was over, and I felt that, for me, there was no reason to live any longer. Furtively, I immediately began to plan my suicide. Because I am such a lousy swimmer, I opted for death by drowning in a sluice at Willen Lake. It simply could not fail.

I took legal advice because I had heard of the legal problems a sudden death causes when someone dies intestate. Making my first and last will suddenly became a priority along with signed and dated declaration of intent to commit suicide and wording to the effect that it was my sole decision with no one else involved.

I also wrote a farewell letter to my wife and children. I was also advised to name the next of kin whom I would wish to be called upon by the police, to identify my remains, bearing in mind that he or she, would have to live with the memory of that experience for life. I also drew a rough map of the sluice on the lake, and shaded in the Willen Hospice Building on the extreme right.

In mid August of last year, the day and the moment had finally arrived. There I stood... naked, but for my red swimming trunks... the recollection of my son and daughter's angry words flashed back to mind, and I realised that these (their last spoken words to me alive) would haunt them for the rest of their lives. You see, we had a bit of an argument, as I was leaving home for the last time. I had dared shout out to them last minute instructions for feeding the dog at 5pm. and giving her medication for her fits, because I would not be back in time. In so doing I had disturbed a new computer game they had just bought and in which they were deeply immersed. I left with them yelling angry words at me.

Jesus had other plans for me. I was able to retrace my steps to my pile of clothes. I got dressed, took a late bus back, and slipped home, unnoticed by the family. My feelings that night were the most weird, I have ever experienced. I felt like I was a ghost, come back to eavesdrop on my wife and children. I felt I did not belong and the noises downstairs sounded ever so strange. It was a long long time before I was overcome by sleep.

You see, thirteen years ago I lost my job in a French bank in London. It came as a result of injustice in the work place. I was made to discredit myself with my own hands, and I was unfairly dismissed. I suffered a massive breakdown in the process. My directors were involved in B.T. share issue fraud on a large scale and I was the fall guy. My children were ages eleven, seven, and four years old, at the time. My wife was thirty five and I was forty two. I never regained permanent work, and only worked in two part time jobs, for a total of eleven months in all of the last thirteen years. Needless to say, chronic depression had set in, and I could only see the world and each day, in grey, black, and negativity. That's what depression is all about, but every cloud has a silver lining.

After the divorce, four months later the house was sold, and my wife and I went our separate ways. She took the children and the family dog with her to her mother's little flat. An awful lot of our treasured possessions were given away or simply skipped or dumped. I was in no fit state to even choose a room of my own to rent. So the Health Authority provided me with what is called 'Protected Lodgings'. One hot evening meal is provided and included with the rent.

For the next two months my days merged with my nights. I spent most of my time in bed, with my favourite prayer book 'I Am With You'. I feel I know this book from cover to cover. I prayed unceasingly. I was not eating properly but I began to go to many Retreats, seminars, and counselling courses. The divorce petition forced me to look at myself from inside out, and I did not like what I saw. I had become a man, who was, so he thought, unable to forgive, carrying a grudge which he had allowed to fester. My mind had become very analytical and powerful, and it ruled my life.

For thirteen years I had been unable to forgive and to forget. Suddenly with the help of my book, I was able to launch into forgiveness, and into trust once again. I so desperately wanted to change my life. I kept being chucked out of lodgings and was often on the move. Each move was more painful and humiliating than the previous one. I held to the belief that I had to sort myself out from within.

This had become my only priority in life. Often in my dark days the post man would bring a card, hand made, from my friend, Sister Josephine.

I never went back to Willen to finish the task of drowning myself. One day I had been evicted from a room in Heelands and had landed at my brother's house in London. I was baby sitting for my mother and father who were old and both were in a nursing home five miles away, from my brother's house. I helped to spoon feed my mother in the evenings. She had had a stroke two years ago and as a result is now completely paralysed. My brother was having a well-earned break from the caring role which he has held for many years now.

Whilst there, one morning, the phone rang and it was Sister Josephine inviting me to accompany her group to Medjugorje. When I mentioned this to my eldest daughter Chantal, who is a non practising Catholic, that I was going to Medjugorje for one week's pilgrimage, she burst out: "Oh, you're going to come back very blessed and you're going to come back transformed. That's what happens to most people who go there." Then she continued. "That's what my friend who has been there says too". I did not want to hurt Chantal's feelings; she's my daughter!

I found it hard to believe that I could find favour with God again. So intense were my prayers and so long, that it seemed as though He had gone dead on me. I had reached a stage of almost not expecting! Now, everything Chantal mentioned came true for me, and more much more! I came back completely cured from chronic depression. I came back at least forty years younger. I am a new man, totally, totally transformed! I am on a perpetual high, with Jesus and His Holy Spirit. If you have never experienced it, well... it is difficult for me to describe it to you. I can see beauty in nature... explain beauty in people... I can now see beauty everywhere... I actually am on a different planet.

Today, I am working as a volunteer at Willen Hospice, which overlooks the sluice and the waters which almost claimed my life. I work in the kitchens, fund raising, or in the day centre, and soon I shall work everywhere in the laundry, garden, shops and lottery. I find it hard to believe that I have found my idea of Heaven, at the very place where I had chosen to die a year ago. It is impossible for me to describe the joy, and peace that engulfs me when I am working at Willen Hospice.

The Lake is incredibly beautiful as I look at it now from a different angle! Now my days are very simple days and every day for me is an adventure. I live through one day at a time. I do hope that one day, you will all be able to experience Jesus and the Holy Spirit like I do now, if you have not done so already! I have at long last realised the miracle that takes place in giving of self to others. That's when we receive the most in return!

○

DON'T LOSE FAITH !

(What a treat to meet a Christian girl at the check out in Asda! "I love living," she said. This led immediately to a wonderful conversation about the Lord. You can evangelise anywhere! I asked Lisa to write her story for us.)

I lost faith, or I lost my faith, when I was at first school. We had gone on a field trip to London. In the afternoon we had a picnic and my best friend started to have breathing difficulties. So our teacher called for an ambulance. The ambulance lights were still flashing as she was lifted in, which was the sign that she was still alive. Then all of a sudden the lights went out, which means she did not make it. I stood there in dismay, and suddenly shouted at the top of my voice, "Oh, God, she is the same age as me. Let her live, please." A tear rolled down my cheek as I pleaded with God. And, yes, to my surprise the lights came back on, and the ambulance pulled away. She did pull through. Miracles do happen. There is a God.

Later I lost faith again, but now when I need some help I get my help and encouragement through God. I am a new born Christian through the fact that I did not know who to turn to in my hour of need, and someone gave me an old looking book with no cover and told me to let the book fall open of its own happening.

I did, and I found the person I needed through the Bible, because the sentence that seemed to jump out at me from that Great Book was, *"Come unto me all who are heavy laden and I will give you rest.*" I read that sentence and, yes, from that day forward I am a reformed Christian.

There are three words I would like to pass on to all: "I love living." You try them. Say them to people and watch their faces. Watch them smile.

God's not dead, He is alive.
Feel Him all over and within me and you,
Feel Him with your hands, feet and heart.
He will always be there
for you and anyone who wants
to let Him into their lives.

I leave you, now, with my prayer, now I am a reformed believer. Pray with me!

"Jesus, we enthrone You,
we proclaim You our King.
Standing here in the midst of us,
we raise You up with our praise.
And as we worship, build a throne,
And as we praise You, build a throne,
And as we worship, build a throne.
Come, Lord Jesus, and take your place.
Amen."

If you ask, you will always receive. He will always listen to you. His is always there; He will stay with you forever if you only ask Him in. Yes, ask Him in to your life, and feel the difference He can make for you.

Lisa Murray

"THE VALUE OF TIME-OUT"

(Letter from Philip)

Not having been to a week-end retreat of this kind before, I was a little apprehensive about going. There were several reasons for this. Firstly, I felt I might be out of my depth, because all the people in our Prayer Group were much better than me. Secondly, I was not sure that I could handle a long weekend of prayer etc. Thirdly, it was difficult not to be able to pay my share, being unemployed at the time.

The Retreat as such, was unforgettable for many reasons. Never before, had I had the privilege of meeting so many beautiful Christians people, whose commitment was so convincingly intense, and yet, who were so unpretentious. The brotherhood and love experienced there defies description.

As a purely spiritual experience, it also leaves me speechless to try to describe it adequately. Suffice it to say, that something strange and beautiful happened to me which left me with a yearning to love God in the Trinity. Through this, I learned to pray better and more often.

I have been fortunate, because of being unemployed, to have been able to attend Mass and receive Holy Communion every day but since returning from there my overall summation of the Buckden experience is expressed in one word: love. For that, I thank God and pray that I shall never weaken or fail Him. Recent experience has left me with the feeling that for many years, I have had with me a bag, full of gifts, which had never been opened; until, after Buckden, it has been unzipped, little by little, and all these magnificent gifts have been revealed, ready for use. *(Retreat at Buckden Towers)*

Friends make the world go round.

What would you do without friends? They help us to become ourselves, to know, to love, and to accept ourselves. Jesus' friendship helps us to know our truest selves. Worth spending time just now with Him, to find out a little more about who you really are to Him, as you dwell on the following thoughts.

No one can replace me because what I offer to the world is the gift that I am, an original, special design, unique in every way, both in genetic make-up and natural tendencies. There is no other like me. How wonderful! The mould was discarded after I came to be! My eyes were His choice, colour, shape, size. My hairs are numbered and counted, not even one lost without my Father knowing it. My shape, size, height were His choice too!

"It was You who created my inmost being and put me together in my mother's womb. For all these mysteries I thank You. For the wonder of myself, for the wonder

*of Your works. My days are listed and determined even
before the first of them occurred.
You know me through and through from having watched
my bones take shape when I was formed in secret in my
mother's womb."* (Psalm 139:13-15)

It was He that chose my parents. Had He wanted different
parents for me, it would have been no trouble to Him.
I was planned before time began. I thank Him for choosing
me and allowing me to be born. He could have made me
different but He wants me for His purpose just as I am.

"Does a woman forget her baby at the breast
or fail to cherish the child of her womb?
Yet even if these forget I will never forget you.
See I have branded you on the palm of my hands,
your ramparts are always under my eye." *(Isaiah 49:15-16)*

You have a duty to love yourself.
"Love your neighbour as yourself" Jesus said.
Pause and consider how you love yourself. Perhaps you
should start today! Be aware of God's goodness in you.
"To be nobody but yourself in a world which is doing its
best, night and day, to make you everybody else - means
to fight the hardest battle, which any human being can
fight and never stop fighting". *(E. Cummings)*

The use of finger prints shows us that no two thumbs are
alike. Are we unique only in physical ways? In the same
family we find family members so different.

What do you think of 'Personality' by Carl Sandburg?
"You have led a hundred secret lives, but you mark only

one thumb. You go round the world and fight in a thousand wars and win all the world's honours, but when you come home, the print of the one thumb your mother gave you, is the same print of thumb you had in the old home, when your mother kissed you and said good-bye.

From the whirling womb of time, come millions of men and their feet crowd the earth and they cut one another's throats for room to stand and among them all, are not two thumbs alike.

Somewhere there is a Great God of Thumbs. Who can tell the inside story of this?"

(Taken from the musings of a Police Reporter in the Identification Bureau)

The consequence of being unique is that no one else can do your job - the work allocated to you by God in His Great Master Plan for your life.

The great Cardinal Newman puts it beautifully:

> *"God has created me to do Him some definite service. He has committed some work to me which He has not committed to another. I have my mission - I may never know it in this life, but I shall be told in the next.*
>
> *I am a link in a chain, a bond of connections between persons. He has not created me for naught. I shall do good.*
>
> *I shall do His work - I shall be an angel of peace, a preacher of truth in my own place, while not intending it, if I but keep His commandments.*

Therefore I will trust Him. Whatever, wherever I am, I can never be thrown away. If I am in sickness; my sickness may serve Him; in perplexity; my perplexity may serve Him. He does nothing in vain. He knows what He is about. He may take away my friends, He may throw me among strangers, He may make me feel desolate, make my spirits sink, hide my future from me - still He knows what He is about".

Try to think of your qualities and good points, maybe even write them down. It's often other people who make us value ourselves, as they see in us good things about us that we ourselves do not see.

Thank God for who you are, for each of your talents, even if you think you have only a few. These can make the world a better place if used well. The man in the parable who had five talents made five more, and so he was much blest. The man who had one talent even denied it and had it taken away from him. The lesson must be to use the little you have, and it will grow and produce fruit. Are you using all your talents? If not, why not? Ask God to put you where you can use them to His Glory, for your sanctification and for the sanctification of others.

Sometimes God makes great demands on our talents and other times He may 'even seem to forget' we have them! Perhaps you need to ask Him to lead you to a group where you can develop your gifts and grow to full stature. Perhaps the most important thing to develop at this stage is a better self-image and awareness of who you are, so you can grow in confidence, and so continue to live to the praise of His Glory.

Good friends keep us on our toes!

They help us to see life in perspective, and to be grateful for all that we have received. They encourage us to be positive in our outlook and help us to give praise where praise is due. When it comes to praising our friend Jesus, we are lost for words. However, He accepts our poor efforts for Him. We can learn from the psalmists to do our best, and it is in that sense that we can use praise psalms.

During the quiet time alone at a weekend away at "The Briars" Residential Centre, Crich, Derbyshire, each person was asked to write their own psalm of praise.
Norman Baatz wrote this lovely poem:-

What beautiful sights God chose to create,
That artists, poets, sculptors are drawn to imitate.
What joys are given in so many marvellous ways,
To enhance, enlighten and appreciatively fill our days.

Blessed is the Lord in all and every nation,
Mighty in His awe-inspiring, wondrous creation.
His trees, sometimes with a myriad autumn shades,
Like jubilant, hosanna flags in many sunny glades.

The wonder that a trickling brook inspires,
Brings more knowledge of God in our deep desires;
Green meadows flanked by rambling hedgerows,
Birds singing and flying - where? He always knows.

Fleecy clouds, 'gainst pale blue, gracefully float by;
Dark green waves, topped white, over which seagulls fly.
Yielding sand, crispy shingle of the shining sea shore,
Where tides froth quietly and oft times roar.

What kind of God makes all of these delights?
That we can gaze and marvel at the sights?
A loving, gentle, forgiving, gracious kind of King;
A Saviour, counsellor, friend, 'daddy' ... in fact, everything.

Norman Baatz (22.11.94)

Have you tried Praise when you are in trouble?

Praise reaches the very heart of God.
The devil flees from praise. If I had to choose a form of prayer that has made me aware of God's presence everywhere, it would, I think, be the prayer of praise. I find it keeps my heart and mind lifted towards God and it gives me a sense of joy and well-being as I walk through each day.

I love to identify with different creatures to praise Him. I think of their colour, shape, size, differences and join my voice to the Chorus of Creation in a symphony of praise that delights Him.

When someone says something that hurts me, I've learnt to run to the foot of the Cross and praise God for it - yielding the hurt to Him - and drinking in His Peace. Praise transforms our sorrow into joy. Praise can work miracles.

The three young men – Shadrach, Meshach and Abednego – from the furnace of death teach us how praise works:

"May You be blessed, Lord God of our ancestors,
be praised and exalted forever.

Blessed be your glorious and holy Name,
praised and extolled forever.

May You be blessed in the temple of Your sacred glory
Exalted and glorified above all forever.

Blessed on the throne of Your kingdom
Praised and exalted above all else forever.

Blessed, You fathomer of the great depths
Enthroned on the cherubs
Praised and glorified above all else forever;

All things the Lord has made, bless the Lord:
  Give glory and eternal praise to Him.
Angels of the Lord! all bless the Lord:
  Give glory and eternal praise to Him.
Heavens! bless the Lord:
  Give glory and eternal praise to Him.
Sun and moon! bless the Lord:
  Give glory and eternal praise to Him
Stars of heaven! bless the Lord:
  Give glory and eternal praise to Him
Showers and dews! bless the Lord:
  Give glory and eternal praise to Him
Winds! bless the Lord:
  Give glory and eternal praise to Him.
Fire and heat! bless the Lord
  Give glory and eternal praise to Him
Cold and heat! bless the Lord
  Give glory and eternal praise to Him
Frost and snow! bless the Lord
  Give glory and eternal praise to Him
Dews and sleet! bless the Lord
  Give glory and eternal praise to Him
Ice and snow! bless the Lord
  Give glory and eternal praise to Him.
Nights and days! bless the Lord
  Give glory and eternal praise to Him

Light and darkness! bless the Lord
Give glory and eternal praise to Him
Lightning and clouds! bless the Lord
Give glory and eternal praise to Him
Let the Earth bless the Lord
Give glory and eternal praise to Him.
Let everything that grows on the earth! bless the Lord
Give glory and eternal praise to Him
Springs of water! bless the Lord
Give glory and eternal praise to Him
Seas and rivers! bless the Lord
Give glory and eternal praise to Him
Sea beasts and everything that lives in water! bless the
Lord
Give glory and eternal praise to Him
Birds of heaven! animals wild and tame! bless the Lord
Give glory and eternal praise to Him
Sons of men! bless the Lord
Give glory and eternal praise to Him
Priests of the Lord! bless the Lord
Give glory and eternal praise to Him
Spirits and souls of the just! bless the Lord
Give glory and eternal praise to Him
Devout and humble-hearted! bless the Lord
Give glory and eternal praise to Him
All who worship Him! bless the Lord
Give glory and eternal praise to Him
All who worship Him, bless the God of gods,

**Praise Him and give Him thanks,
for his love is everlasting."**

(cf Daniel 3.52-90)

All married couples! bless the Lord
Give glory and eternal praise to Him
All single people bless the Lord
Give glory and eternal praise to Him
All children and seekers of the Lord! bless the Lord
Give glory and eternal praise to Him
All the souls of the faithful departed! bless the Lord
Give glory and eternal praise to Him
All members of our families! bless the Lord
Give glory and eternal praise to Him
forever and ever. Amen. Amen.

I praise Him most, I love Him best,
all praise and love is His;
While Him I love, in Him I live,
and cannot live amiss.
Love's sweetest mark, laud's highest theme,
Man's most desired light,
To love Him life, to leave Him death,
to live in Him delight.
He mine by gift, I His by debt,
thus each to other due,
First Friend He was, best Friend He is,
all times will find Him true;
His knowledge rules, His strength defends,
His love doth cherish all;
His birth our joy, His life our light,
His death our end of thrall.
(St. Robert Southwell, S.J. b. 1561, d. Tyburn 1595)

Let everything that lives and has breath
Praise the Lord
Praise Him in His temple on earth
Praise Him in His temple in heaven
Praise Him for His mighty achievements
Praise Him for His transcendent greatness!
Praise Him with the blast of trumpets
Praise Him with lyre and harp
Praise Him with drums and dancing
Praise Him with strings and reeds
Praise Him with clashing cymbals
Praise Him with clanging cymbals!
Let everything that breathes, praise Him.
Alleluia!   *(Psalm 150)*

All the Psalms form the most wonderful prayers for us, suited to any and every occasion. If you're happy there's a Psalm; if you're fed up and think everyone is against you there's a Psalm; if you want to kill your enemies there's a Psalm, or if you want to take revenge there's a Psalm; if you feel sinful and need mercy there's a Psalm, or if you want to thank and praise God all day there's a Psalm. Why not make a habit of praying the Psalms as Jesus and Mary did? Your life will change!

"God is the shield that protects me"   *(Psalm 7:10)*

"I bless the Lord, who is my counsellor, and who in the night in my inmost self, instructs me; I keep Him before me always, for with Him at my right hand nothing can shake me."   *(Psalm 16:7-8)*

"My God lights up my darkness."   *(Psalm 18:28)*
"He put a new song into my mouth, a song of praise to our God."   *(Psalm 40:3)*

"Let me stay in your tent forever, taking refuge in the shelter of your wings."   *(Psalm 61:4)*

"Your love is better than life itself."   *(Psalm 63:3)*

"I will celebrate your love forever."   (Psalm 89:1)

"Before the mountains were born, before the Earth or the World came to birth, You were God from all Eternity and forever."   *(Psalm 90:2)*

○

My Father lived a life of praise and thanksgiving to God being especially close to God in nature. He wrote many poems of gratitude as a young man in his little hut by the Shannon river, Limerick. 'Plassey Falls' and 'Eventide' are two of my favourites.

PLASSEY FALLS

Loud roar the rushing waters
As they tumble o'er the fall
Where the wild duck love to linger
The curlew love to call

Where the swan in all his splendour
Soaring from the skies above
Has come to pay a visit
And to sing his song of love.

It is there beneath the green trees
That the fishermen delight
To cast a fly upon the stream
From morning until night
And listen to the murmurs
Of the ripples one and all
On the camp-clad hills of Plassey
Dear old Plassey Fall

As I gaze upon your waters
I watch the ebb and flow;
Clustered o'er the earthen banks
Dark green ivies grow
How my heart did break to leave you
As I sat and dreamt away
Those happy hours I spent with you
Beneath your banks of clay

The Monarch of the morning
Casts his rays upon your bed
Everything seems peaceful
Save those dark clouds overhead
The solemness was broken
As I heard the blackbird call
It wafted o'er the waters
Of dear old Plassey Fall

Loud roar the dreadful thunder
As I sat and watched the spray
The clouds rolled in so quickly
Like the rushing tides away.

All was hushed save here or there
The whisper of the trees
Set forth a wondrous melody
Upon the evening breeze.

There is music in your murmur
And gladness in the glen,
Something in your beauty
No bard can ever pen
But though I'm far away, dear place,
Those scenes I oft recall
Of your waters flowing ever
Over dear old Plassey Falls.

(J.C.Walsh)

EVENTIDE

Beneath the tall green beech trees
Stands our bungalow of green
By the riverside at Clareville
Just beside the bubbling stream
There we spent our summer evenings
Where the trout do sport and hide
Fishing on that rocky river
   At the close of eventide

In the evening when the sunset
Cast about its ruddy glow
See the tall trees all ablazing
Just around our bungalow
Hear the calling of the curlew
And the murmur of the tide
Coming o'er the waters gently
   Telling us 'tis eventide

And at night when we are sleeping
When the sunset is no more

There is One who watches o'er us
On that lonely Clareville shore
Sure our hearts are ever longing
For our summer sunnyside
When from winter's dream awaken
    All our hopes at Eventide.

(J.C.Walsh)

We don't mind spending time with friends.

"It's the time you've wasted for your rose that makes your rose so important," said the fox to the little Prince. "It's the time I have wasted for my rose –," said the little Prince, so that he would be sure to remember.

"Men have forgotten this truth," said the fox, "but you must not forget it. You become responsible, forever, for what you have tamed. You are responsible for your rose…"

"I am responsible for my rose," the little Prince repeated, so that he would be sure to remember." *('The Little Prince', Antoine de Saint Exupéry.)*

God never minds spending time on us. He never quits. He holds His responsibility for us till the end. "His Love is Eternal." *(Psalm 106:1)* "His Love is high as Heaven, His faithfulness as the clouds." *(Psalm 108:4)*

We may quit and run off but He will always follow us uphill or down dale, until we return to Him and accept His undying friendship.

"They failed to appreciate His great Love. They forgot

the God who saved them. They would not listen to His voice." *(Psalm 106:7,21,25)*

Friendship must be a two way process to succeed. We don't mind wasting time with our friends, so why not learn better how to waste time with our friend, Jesus, as we listen to His call to give Him time each day?

○

"I call you to pray; for prayer pleases My heart. Prayer will bring Peace to your mind and heart, as you learn to orientate your days towards Me. As you pray, you will experience My abiding Presence with you."

MORNING PRAYER

God of my life, I welcome this new day.
It is your gift to me,
the first day of the rest of my life.
I thank you for the gift of being alive this morning.
I thank you for the sleep which has refreshed me.
I thank you for the chance to begin life all over again.
Lord, this day is full of promise and of opportunity:
Help me to waste none of it.
This day is full of mystery and of the unknown.
Help me to face it without anxiety.

During this day, may I become
a more thoughtful person,
a more prayerful person,
a more generous and kindly person.
Lord, bless this day for me and for us all.
Fill it with your Holy Spirit. Amen.
(Dick Tobin, C.S.S.R.)

PRAYER ON AWAKENING

O Lord, now that I am awake,
and a new day has begun.
Waken me to your Presence.
Waken me to your indwelling.
Waken me to inward sight of you
and speech with you and
strength from you,
that all my earthly walk
may waken into song
and my spirit leap up to you all day, always.
Join my song to Creation's song in praising you.
Put a new song in my heart today.
Increase my faith,
Let the eyes of my mind be opened to see you in all
things.
Let my heart burn with love.
Let my will be so in tune with yours
that this day I will but please You.
Fill me with hope and joy and new life,
that I may serve you faithfully
rejoicing in your Word.   Amen.

NIGHT PRAYER

Lord, forgive me for all the wrong I have done this day.
Forgive me if I have been bad tempered or hard to live
with.
Forgive me if I have hurt those I love.
Forgive me for any word of comfort of praise or thanks
which I might have spoken but did not speak.
Forgive me for any help which I might have given
to someone in need but did not give.

Lord, I pray tonight for all mankind.
I pray for all my ancestors and family.
I pray for the good and the bad,
for the believer and the non-believer,
for those who are trying to lose you
and those who are trying to find you.

Give us all the restful sleep and peace of heart,
that comes from knowing that our sins are forgiven
and that we are always in the hands of a loving Father.
Father, into your hands I commend my spirit. Amen.

Thank you for today, for everyone I met on my pilgrimage
of life.
Tonight, I pray for the faithful departed,
especially my family members
and those who have no one to pray for them.

I pray for those who will die on the roads or from violence.
I pray for the lonely and depressed, the abused and the
persecuted.

I pray for the loveless and those who have never known
love.
I pray for the abandoned and the arrogant,
for those who don't recognise their need for you
and those who run it alone without you.
Save us all, Lord. Amen
(Irish Priest, C.S.S.R. 1992)

PRAYER FOR THE FUTURE

My Lord God
     I have no idea where I am going
I do not see the road ahead of me,
I cannot know for certain where it will end.

Nor do I really know myself,
     and the fact that I think that I am following
     Your will does not mean
     that I am actually doing so.

But I believe that my desire to please You
     does in fact please You.
     And I hope that I have that desire
     in all that I am doing.
     I hope that I will never do anything
     apart from that desire.

And I know that if I do this
     You will lead me by the right road
     though I may know nothing about it.

Therefore I will trust You always
    though I may seem to be lost
    and in the shadow of death.
I will not fear
    for You are ever with me,
    and You will never leave me
    to face my perils alone.

In this prayer Thomas Merton captures as well our contemporary fear of facing a dark future and our reaching out to God in trust. Frenchman by birth (1915) he migrated with his family to America. To complete his education he spent six years in England. He led a dissipated life and dabbled in various philosophies till he found Christ in 1938 and became a Catholic. After years of silence in a Trappist community he emerged as a poet and passionate writer, dealing with such topics as present-day spirituality, war, social injustice, and Christian dialogue with Eastern religions. He died in 1968 in Bangkok on his way to attend a Buddhist convention.

PRAYER OVER THE PAST

Late have I loved you,
    O beauty ever ancient, ever new!
Late have I loved you
    and see, you were within,
    and I outside, and outside I sought you.
Misguided as I was
    I had only eyes for the appearances of beauty
    which you made.

You were with me.
> but I was not with you.
> Those things held me back from you
> things whose only being was to be in you.

You called: you cried:
> and you broke through my deafness.

You flashed: you shone:
> and chased away my blindness.

You became fragrant;
> I inhaled and sighed for you.

I tasted,
> and now hunger and thirst for you.

You touched me,
> and I burn for your embrace.

(St. Augustine)

This prayer of St. Augustine expresses something of the struggle he went through in his search for the meaning of life. Born in the year 354 in Thagaste in what is now Algeria, he sought truth and happiness in different pursuits, all of which left him unsatisfied. At the age of 33 he became a Christian. He dedicated the rest of his life to the ministry, dying as a bishop in North Africa in the year 430.

PRAYER FOR PROTECTION

I bind this day to me forever,
By pow'r of faith, Christ's incarnation;
His baptism in the Jordan river;
His death on the Cross for my salvation;
His bursting from the spiced tomb
His riding up the heav'nly way;
His coming at the day of doom;
I bind unto myself today!

I bind unto myself to-day
The power of God to hold, and lead,
His eye to watch, His might to stay,
His ear to hearken to my need.
The wisdom of my God to teach,
His hand to guide, His shield to ward;
The Word of God to give me speech,
His heavenly host to be my guard.

Against the demon snares of sin,
The vice that gives temptation force,
The natural lusts that war within,
The hostile men that mar my course;
Or few or many, far or nigh,
In every place, and in all hours,
Against their fierce hostility,
I bind to me these holy powers.

Against all Satan's spells and wiles,
Against false words of heresy,
Against the Knowledge that defiles,
Against the heart's idolatry,

Against the wizard's evil craft,
Against the death-wound and the burning,
The choking wave, the poisoned shaft,
Protect me, Christ, till Thy returning.

Christ be with me, Christ within me,
Christ behind me, Christ before me,
Christ beside me, Christ to win me,
Christ to comfort and restore me.
Christ beneath me, Christ above me,
Christ in quiet, Christ in danger,
Christ in hearts of all that love me,
Christ in mouth of friend and stranger.

I bind unto myself the Name,
The strong Name of the Trinity;
By invocation of the same,
The Three in One, and One in Three.
Of Whom all nature hath creation;
Eternal Father, Spirit, Word:
Praise to the Lord of my salvation,
Salvation is of Christ the Lord.

(St. Patrick's Breastplate)

I put on the armour of God,
the helmet of Salvation, the breastplate of righteousness,
the belt of integrity, shoes to spread the Gospel of peace.
I put in my right hand the shield of faith.
I put in my left hand the sword of the Spirit to
cut the burning arrows of the evil one *(Ephesians 6:14-17)*
And I cover myself with the protection of the Precious
Blood of Jesus.

PRAYER AGAINST EVIL

In the name of Jesus Christ, I break any curse upon me or my family.
I bind away all evil from me and my family.
I bind all evil effects of the air, the atmosphere, the wind, the sun, the rain.
I come against the evil effects of pollution in any shape or form upon my health and that of my family.
I bind the evil of stress, of injustice, of poverty, of overwork, of divorce, of accidents, away from myself and my family.
I bind the evil of hereditary tendencies to illness of any kind away from myself and my family.

I pray the cleansing, healing Blood of Jesus upon us all.
I pray the healing of the Holy Spirit, upon every cell of my body, begging Him to infiltrate to the marrow of my bones.
I pray the healing power of Jesus upon my mind, my memory, my imagination, my will, my body.
I repent of all the sins of my ancestors especially any unrepented or unacknowledged sin.

In the name of Jesus
I cut all links between me and anyone not of God, and between any member of my family and any other person not of God. I pray the love of Jesus to be between us all.
I pray His forgiveness on us and on all those whom we have hurt or who have hurt us.   May only Your love surround us, Lord.   Amen.

PRAYER TO ST. MICHAEL ARCHANGEL

Holy Michael, Archangel, defend us in the day of battle; be our safeguard against the wickedness and snares of the devil. May God rebuke him, we humbly pray. And do you, prince of the heavenly host, by the power of God thrust down to hell satan and all wicked spirits who wander through the world for the ruin of souls. Amen.

PRAYERS TO THE GUARDIAN ANGELS

O Angel of God, my guardian dear,
to whom God's love commits me here.
Ever this day (night) be at my side,
to light to guard, to rule to guide. Amen.

Visit we beseech you, O Lord, this house and family. Drive far from it all the snares of the enemy. Let your holy angels dwell therein to keep us in peace. May your blessings be always upon us, through Christ our Lord. Amen.

EVENING PRAYER

"May He support us all the day long till the shades lengthen and the evening comes and the fever of life is over and the busy world is hushed and our work is done. Then in his mercy may He grant us a perfect night and rest and peace at the last. Amen." *(Cardinal Newman)*

Reverently

Come Holy Spir-it I need You — Come sweet Spir-it I pray — Come with Your Strength and Your pow-er — Come in Your own special way—

Come like a spring in the desert
Come to the withered of soul
Come with Your sweet healing power
Come now and make me whole.

Come like a spring in the desert

Slowly

A - noint-ing fall on me A - noint-ing fall on me, And let the power of the Holy Spirit fall upon me. A - noint-ing fall on me.

ONLY LOVE LASTS

Love is the skeleton on which the flesh and blood of friendship is built. We are called to love. Faith and Hope will pass away, but Love will go on forever, into eternity. Lord, teach us to love.

Love is His sign, love is His word, so His call is to love, to be friends, to make friends, to stay friends, to make the world a place of friendship.

"Love has many voices,
Love sends its greeting in the smile of a friend,
the contented sighs of a baby, the whisperings of the Spirit.
Love explodes in the laughter of children at play.
It longs for response in the stammerings of a lonely old man.
Love speaks in many places.
Love has many moods.
Love comes in all seasons.   Listen to love"

('Listen to Love', Geoffrey Chapman, 1970)

"Love flies, runs, leaps for joy; it is free and unrestrained. Love gives to all, resting in One who is highest above all things, from whom all good flows and proceeds. Love does not regard the gifts, but turns to the Giver of all good gifts. Love knows no limits, but ardently transcends all bounds. Love feels no burden, takes no account of toil, attempts things beyond its strength; love sees nothing as impossible, for it feels able to achieve all things. Love, therefore, does great things… "

LOVE IN ACTION

I listened to love
and love said to me:
Stretch out to my poor
And then you shall see
The life that I give
The joy from my heart.
The peace in your soul
That never will part

The wonder of life
This gift that is Mine.
The healing life's hurts
Treasured moments in time.
My Family so small
Take it into your heart.
It's My gift to your soul
Graces rich I impart

If dull and depressed
Think of others, I pray,
And then all your sorrow
Will be taken away.
Learn to love, learn to give,
For that is my will,
And then you will know Me
Forever. Amen.

(I wrote this poem on the plane on the way to help the refugees in Capljina - Bosnia, 7th February 1998)

LOVE FINDS A TIME FOR EVERYTHING

"For everything there is a season
and a time for every matter under heaven:
A time to be born, and a time to die;
a time to plant,
and a time to pluck up what is planted;
A time to kill, and a time to heal;
a time to break down and a time to build up;
A time to weep, and a time to laugh;
a time to mourn, and a time to dance;
A time to cast away stones,
and a time to gather stones together.
A time for embracing,
a time to refrain from embracing.

A time for searching,
a time for losing;
A time for keeping
a time for throwing away.
A time for tearing
a time for sewing.
A time for keeping silent
a time for speaking.
A time for loving
a time for hating
A time for war
a time for peace."

(Ecclesiastes 3:1-8)

LOVE

Love bade me welcome, yet my soul drew back,
Guiltie of dust and sinne,
But quick-eyed love, observing me grow slack
From my first entrance in
Drew nearer to me, sweetly, questioning
If I lacked anything.

A guest, I answered, worthy to be here,
Love said, You shall be,
I the unkinde, ungrateful; Ah! my deare,
I cannot look on thee.
Love took my hand, and, smiling, did reply
Who made the lips but I?

Truth Lord, but I have marred them, let my shame
Go where it doth deserve,
And know you not, sayes love who bore the blame?
My deare, then I will serve,
You must sit downe, sayes love and taste my meat,
So I did sit and eat.

('The Temple', George Herbert (metaphysical poet, 1633)

Love is the greatest - better than any other gift:
"Love is patient, kind, generous.
Love is never jealous, boastful or conceited
Love takes no pleasure in other people's sins, but
delights in the truth.
Love is always ready to excuse, to trust, to hope, to
endure what ever comes
Love does not come to an end" (1 Corinthians 13:4-5)

"Do you see My Love as the only thing which matters?
My Love streaming from the realms of the Spirit?
My Love infiltrating the dark places of earth ...
Love on earth ...
Lifting the commonplace into Heaven!"

('I Am With You', John Woolley, p 183)

Jesus commands us to love always and this should be our aim, since we are all brothers and sisters in Him. He calls us to Family Unity:

"You have only one Father, and He is in Heaven; You have only one Teacher, the Christ." (Matthew 23:9-10)

"For I have given them the teaching You gave to Me, and they have truly accepted this, that I came from You and have believed that it was You who sent Me." (John 17: 8)

"Lord, to whom shall we go? You have the message of eternal life and we believe; we know that You are the Holy One of God." (John 6:67-69)

Come, Lord Jesus, come!
(Revelation 22:20)

Allow me to pray with you:

"Deepen Your Love in me, O Lord, that I may learn in my inmost heart how sweet it is to love, be dissolved, and to plunge myself into Your Love. Let your Love possess me and raise me above myself, with a fervour and wonder beyond imagination.
Let me follow You, my Beloved..."

('The Imitation of Christ' - Thomas à Kempis, 1380-1471)

A CONVERSATON: HE AND I

"BE BRAVE *in Me, find comfort true,*
No matter what your pain.
Come 'home' to Me, drink deep My love,
And fear cannot remain.
Peace will descend as memories heal,
Forgiveness fill your soul.
Remember that I died for you,
Make My life now your goal."

"I'LL JOURNEY on with faith, hope, love,
My cross I'll learn to carry.
And if I fall, please pick me up
Holy Spirit let me not tarry.
Close to Christ's heart draw me each day
And on the morrow bless me
I'll try my best, I'll fight the fight
I'll pray Your love possess me."

THE POTTER   knows the shape of things
Weak vessels overflow
With pain or joy, with tears or song
In a world that's full of woe.
A star shines bright in every sky
A new door opens wide.

"TAKE UP *the challenge of new life*
My love in you abide.
Healed by Myself, you'll know My peace
Your neighbour you'll love better
And if let down, you'll journey on
And say, 'It doesn't matter!'
You'll know you're weak, My strength in you
My gifts are freely given.

I'm Jesus, Your undying Friend.
I'll lead you on towards Heaven!"

And so, I come to the end of the thoughts, prayers, testimonies and Scriptures given for this book.
I hope you will pray for me that the words written here will become a reality in my life, too, as we both journey onwards together towards our Homeland.

We are both pilgrims who know that the only Way Ahead is with our Undying Friend, Jesus Christ, our Lord and Saviour. In Him we can find everything, including all the love we need to help us and each other on our Way.

THE END

A few years ago, "God's Whistle" was conceived one afternoon, as I read the Scriptures, while recovering from a broken ankle. The text which inspired the book intrigued me. *"I will whistle for them to gather them together, for I have redeemed them and they will be as numerous as they were before".* *(Zechariah 10:8)*
The idea of God whistling for us, evoked wonderful scenes of the Shepherd's many calls to the sheep. All the chapters were given together as one thought, and nothing has been added or subtracted since that first inspiration. So, I began to write.

On recovery, while having a little walking holiday and hoping to work on my book, the car was broken into on the moors and the manuscript was stolen from the boot. I said to God: "That's a fine how-do-you-do ! If You want this book written, You had better give it back, since You know I have no other copy."

The miracle happened when the Devonshire police, about five weeks later, returned the manuscript by post, damp and smudged but complete. They had fine-combed the countryside, knowing how precious the manuscript was to me, and they found it scattered all over a field. I was overjoyed and very grateful.

Then just before the book went to print, the computer on which it was receiving its finishing touches, was struck by lightning and it blew up in my friend's face ! When he rang me to tell me the sad news, I could only think of the book. "How's the book?" I asked anxiously. He was none too pleased when I hadn't enquired about his safety first! Many people had been praying daily for the protection of this book. So, we know who was trying hard to get rid of "God's Whistle", but, of course as always, God won, since it is His book.

Copyright and Acknowledgements

I have sought diligently to obtain copyright permission for all quotes used in this book. If there are any omissions or inadequacies I apologise and will correct matters in any further reprints.

My thanks to all those who kindly responded and helped by giving permission generously for copyright material:
Rev. John Woolley; Fr. John ó Riordáin; The Dominican Order; Kevin Mayhew for permission to use from 'Hymns Old and New' licence 894012 the hymn by Aniceto Nazareth; Gujarat Sahitya Prakash,India, publishers and booksellers, for extracts from Fr. Anthony de Mello; Dartman, Longman and Todd for use of extracts from 'In Search of the Beyond' by C. Carretto, published and copyright 1975; Harpur Collins Publishers Ltd. for their generous permission to reproduce 'Footprints' by M. Fishback Powers; Lawrence Pollinger Ltd, and estate of Martin Luther King for use of extract from 'Strength to love'; Editions du Seuil for use of extracts from 'Le Milieu Divin' and 'Hymne de l'univers' by Pierre Teilhard de Chardin; Jim Walsh, my brother, for use of two of his lovely Poems of Dedication; Scripture quotations are from The Jerusalem Bible. Permission sought for excerpt from 'Velveteen Rabbit' by Marjorie Williams, and for prayers from 'The One who Listens', Fr. M. Hollings and E. Gullick.

Art work copyright belongs to Mrs. Gunvor Edwards, friend and artist who sensitively prayed through and illustrated the themes throughout this book and for the cover design ably assisted by her artist husband, Peter, and son Per. The drawing by Norman Thelwell is reproduced with permission sought from 'Mastering Watercolour', A. Batsford.
My thanks to Mrs. Carol Danes for her help and generosity in allowing me to reproduce 'Good Friday, Daisy Nook' and 'A Beggar' by Lowry; to Judith Sandling of Salford Museum and Art Galleries for her enthusiasm and help in reproducing 'The Cripples' and 'St. Simon's Church'; to Mary McGwynne, my sister, and Julie McGwynne and Laura and Andrea Clinton, my nieces, for photographs; to Sr. Marie Ragil for 'The Tree', painted by mouth.

My very sincere thanks to Rev. John Woolley for his contributions and constant encouragement; to Br. Tom O'Boyle for his words on hope; to Dom Benedict Heron, O.S.B., to Sr. Helen and other sisters for their co-operation; to Bishop Mario Conti for his inspiring foreword and support in work for God's Kingdom; to Tessa and Michael McBrien for their generosity and efforts to complete the text; to Joan Johnson, who first offered to type the manuscript and without whose meticulous help the manuscript would never even have begun; to Toni Pomfret who helped type two chapters; to Helen and Jamus Smith for their amazing and contagious faith; to those fellow pilgrims who constantly ask for a book to help them on their journey; to those who have courageously shared their personal testimonies; to my most kind friends and benefactors, especially Miss Winnie Young, David Lloyd, Mary Allen, Noelle Evans, who have so generously enabled the printing of this book to go ahead, to God's Glory and for the spread of His Kingdom on Earth. God bless you all.

○

○

JOIN OUR PRAYER CIRCLE

I am always ready to receive a letter or telephone call from you, and to pray with you for any special needs you might have.

I would also like to invite you to join our Prayer Circle, which has a rapidly-growing number of members drawn from all Christian traditions, and extending to various parts of the world. There is great strength in knowing that you are not on your own as we all pray for and support each other.

There is no charge or subscription involved. If you would like to join, would you please supply the following details opposite or write separately.

Together with our Community
of the Daughters of the Holy Spirit,
I pray for all the Members of the Prayer Circle every day.

Sister Josephine Sings
SONGS and HEALING TAPES / CDs

Dear Sister Josephine,
Please will you send me the following

... **Songs of the Heart**   ☐ Tape or CD ☐
... **Circle of Love**   ☐ Tape or CD ☐
... **Beyond the Christmas Tree** ☐ Tape or CD ☐
... **Inner Healing & Healing of Memories** (Talk) ☐ Tape
☐ CD

Tapes (£5.99)   CD (£9.99)

Please send to my address opposite

To: Sister Josephine Walsh, D.H.S,
13, Aspreys, Olney, Bucks, MK46 5LN,
England.
Telephone: 00-44-(0)1234-712162 or
00-44-(0)7803-393693 (mobile): Fax: 00-44-(0)1234-241995

☐ Yes, I would like to join your Prayer Circle.

☐ I would like to invite you to come and lead a Day or Week-end of 'Healing' in my area.

☐ I would like to join one of your own Days or Weekends on Renewal and Inner Healing to be held in your Convent or elsewhere.

☐ I have been specially blessed and I enclose a Testimony of God's goodness to me.

☐ I would like to know more about a subject mentioned in the book: *(please specify)*

Surname .... Rev / Sr / Mr / Mrs / Miss / Ms

Christian Name ....

Address ....

....

Post Code .... Telephone ....

If you would like a reply please could you help me by enclosing a S.A.E.

ADDITIONAL COPIES
available from

Sister Josephine Walsh
13 Aspreys, Olney, Bucks, MK46 5LN
England
+44-(0)1234-712162
Fax: +44-(0)1234-241995

○

Gerard and Toni Pomfret
Good News Books
15 Barking Close, Luton. Beds, LU4 9HG, England
24 hrs Telephone: +44 - (0) 1582 - 571011
Fax: +44 - (0) 1582 - 571012
E-mail orders@goodnewsbooks.net

○

Evelyn Heaney
140 Tamlaght Road, Omagh, Co. Tyrone, BT78 5LW
Northern Ireland
+44-(0)2882-243973
E-mail: evelynheaney@hotmail.com

○

Children of Medjugorje
Barry and Marie Authers
39 Pilgrim's Way West
Otford, Sevenoaks
Kent, TN14 5JQ
Fax: +44-(0)1959-523619